12/16/13

To Bishop Flores,
con respeto y oración,

Christaur

Healing From Violence

Christauria Welland, PsyD, is a clinical psychologist of Canadian origin. She began working in Mexico City in 1976 in some of the poorest areas of the city as a social worker and educator with an international organization. Since moving to San Diego in 1989 and obtaining a BA in Spanish, Dr. Welland has volunteered with Mexican migrant workers and their families. Her doctoral dissertation explored culturally appropriate approaches for Latino men in treatment for intimate partner violence, an interest that grew out of her experience working with Latino men in domestic violence groups beginning in 1995. During this period she also cofacilitated groups for partner abusive men at the U.S. Navy with David Wexler, PhD.

In 2003, she published *Violencia Doméstica 2000* with David Wexler, PhD, piloting this culturally adapted program for four years with Latino men's groups, and fine-tuning the material with their feedback. This program was published in Mexico in 2007, with the title *Sin Golpes: Como transformar la respuesta violenta del hombre en la pareja y la familia,* along with a client workbook by the same name, for distribution in the Americas.

Dr. Welland teaches the graduate course on domestic violence at Alliant International University, San Diego, and frequently speaks at conferences and trainings at state institutions and universities in the U.S. and Latin America, especially in Mexico and Peru. She has conducted quantitative research on risk factors for Intimate Partner Violence in the U.S. Latino population, and is currently piloting an IPV prevention-parenting course for Latino couples in the San Diego elementary schools, teaching effective marriage and parenting skills. Dr. Welland maintains a private practice in Solana Beach, California, and a hospital practice as a rehabilitation psychologist in National City, CA.

Neil Ribner, PhD, is a clinical psychologist and director of the doctoral program in clinical psychology (PsyD) at the California School of Professional Psychology (CSPP) at Alliant International University (AIU) in San Diego. He is also professor of psychology at CSPP-AIU, where he teaches courses in psychotherapy and family therapy. Dr. Ribner's main professional interests are in child and family psychology, particularly in such areas as parenting, divorce, marital relationships, child custody, and stepfamilies. He supervises doctoral research in these areas and has published and presented numerous professional papers on family violence and cultural factors in psychological treatment. In addition to his academic endeavors, Dr. Ribner is actively involved in clinical practice, counseling children, adolescents, couples, and families. A large part of his practice involves performing custody evaluations for the Family Court in San Diego, and he trains interns and other psychologists in doing such evaluations. Dr. Ribner also consults with several San Diego agencies, including Social Advocates for Youth and the U.S. Navy Child and Adolescent Psychiatry Residency Program. He is the author of *First Session With Teenagers* and the editor of the *Handbook of Juvenile Forensic Psychology*.

Healing From Violence

*Latino Men's Journey to a
New Masculinity*

Christauria Welland, PsyD
Neil Ribner, PhD

SPRINGER PUBLISHING COMPANY
New York

To all the Latino men I have worked with over the years, in gratitude for what
they have taught me about the courage to change.

Christauria Welland

To my wife, Linda, who through her strength, compassion and love taught me
the true meaning of being a man.

Neil Ribner

Copyright © 2008 Springer Publishing Company, LLC

Springer Publishing Company, LLC
11 West 42nd Street
New York, NY 10036
www.springerpub.com

Acquisitions Editor: Philip Laughlin
Project Manager: Carol Cain
Cover design: Mimi Flow
Composition: Apex Publishing, LLC

08   09   10   11/   5   4   3   2   1

Library of Congress Cataloging-in-Publication Data

Welland, Christauria.
  Healing from violence : Latino men's journey to a new masculinity /
Christauria Welland, Neil Ribner.
      p. cm.
  Includes bibliographical references and index.
  ISBN-13: 978-0-8261-2477-7 (alk. paper)
  ISBN-10: 0-8261-2477-1 (alk. paper)
  1. Marital violence—United States. 2. Hispanic American men—Psychology.
  3. Abusive men—Behavior modification—United States.
  I. Ribner, Neil. II. Title.
  HV6626.2.W49 2008
  362.82'9208968073—dc22   2007029730

Printed in the United States of America by Bang Printing.

Contents

Contents   xiii

Foreword

As the local, state, and national demographics continue to change, the need to address diverse individuals within a culturally responsive framework also increases. The most recent United States Census Bureau (2007) data indicates that minorities are now in the majority in more than three hundred counties across the country, with Latinos being the largest and fastest-growing throughout the nation. It is clear that with the current demographic trends and lack of cultural understanding, there is a national crisis occurring for many racial/ethnic groups in this country.

In the United States difference has equaled pathology. As a result, Latinos, and many other ethnic groups, are socially placed and racially stratified in a deficit position with a silenced voice. This is further reinforced by the literature documenting that immigration status, voluntary vs. involuntary (Ogbu, 1998); family history, spiritual/religious beliefs, and acculturation status (Borrayo & Jenkins, 2003; Falicov, 1998; Flores, Tschann, Marin, & Pantoja, 2004) all play a role in the overall mental, spiritual and physical health of Latinos. The dominant Eurocentric perspective has not only misinformed and miseducated mainstream society, but it has also attempted to reeducate Latinos about our own culture. More specifically, many Latinos are situated in areas that are poverty-stricken, with poor educational systems, poor access to health care, and an internalized lived experience that potentially shifts from one of *orgullo* (pride), to one of feeling misunderstood and ostracized. Ultimately, many Latinos seek to be and become the "Latinos" mainstream society tells them they should be. The assumption is that it is acceptable for the mainstream to socially, culturally, and politically reconstruct Latino culture through their own misinterpretations of Latino values, beliefs, and *costumbres*. This is clearly evident in the way mainstream society has constructed images of Latino men and masculinity.

Images of the Latino men in the media quickly indicate that our social and intellectual potential are limited to gangs, the military, and blue-collar jobs. The socialization process for Latinos and for men in general informs men, and women, that to be anything more than aggressive, tough, and emotionally inept individuals is socially uncomfortable at best. What is comfortable is reinforcement for the strong provider and protector who lacks communication skills and expresses very little emotion. In essence, for men to display antisocial traits through their behaviors is socially acceptable. The socialization and reinforcement of men's behaviors, immigration stress, and the racial stratification of Latinos have often left Latino men battling one another and other loved ones with acts of violence and abuse. Furthermore, we have socialized Latino men to be seen, but not heard. As a result, both men and women have failed to listen to the inner voices of Latino men and therefore lack the necessary personal and professional skills to help them. *Healing From Violence: Latino Men's Journey to a New Masculinity* powerfully gives voice to Latino men through personal narratives about being men, immigrants, survivors of abuse, and perpetrators of violence.

Intimate Partner Violence (IPV) is a worldwide public health problem that cuts across culture, socioeconomic status, and geography (Mattson & Ruiz, 2005). Moreover, there is a paucity of literature addressing how IPV impacts different racial and ethnic groups in the United States. It is also not understood which outreach and intervention models are most effective for these different groups (Moracco, Hilton, Hodges, & Frasier, 2005). Literature addressing the specific needs of Latino men and masculinity has seldom attempted to deepen our understanding of what is needed to facilitate a transformation from the stereotypical *machista* male to the more prosocial Latino male, reflecting the variation in which machismo and masculinity manifest within the culture. *Healing From Violence: Latino Men's Journey to a New Masculinity* bridges this gap in the literature and offers suggestions on how therapists and educators can assist Latino men in recreating a masculine ideology that more accurately reflects their lived experiences as Latino immigrant men in the United States.

Machismo, a form of masculine ideology, is often a misunderstood cultural value of Latinos. Until more recently, the masculinity literature on Latino men primarily sustained a monolithic negative perspective (Quintero & Estrada, 1998). As a result, Caucasian Americans have redefined the term and reduced it to a one-sided negative stereotype. The positive elements of machismo have been neglected in the Western interpretation. Studies have shown that next to Latinos, Caucasian Americans are the second-highest ethnic group in their value of traditional masculinity. A noteworthy difference between the masculine construct valued by Caucasian Americans and the Latino *Machismo* is the social acceptance of these concepts by Caucasians over Latinos (Mirande, 1997). For example, when masculine ideologies such as toughness, competition, and assertiveness are associated with Caucasian males, the terms are more culturally and socially accepted than when applied to Latino males (Gallardo & Curry, in press).

For Latino men, male identity, or machismo, is multidimensional, consisting of both positive and negative elements. The positive dimensions include honor, respect, bravery, dignity, and family responsibility. These virtues are of tremendous importance and a source of great strength for the Latino community. Viewing machismo from the more dialectical perspective, of both positive and negative aspects, allows for more flexibility and utility within a therapeutic or counseling setting (Gallardo & Curry, in press). Most importantly, it highlights the importance of changing the stereotype of machismo to be more consistent with the variations in Latino male identity (Torres, Solberg, & Carlstrom, 2002). An expansion of the definition of machismo and a deeper appreciation for gender role adherence in Latino men provides insights into what is needed to be successful in counseling, outreach, education, and community interventions.

In examining the counseling and psychotherapy literature, it is evident that there are racial and ethnic health disparities throughout the country. This is particularly salient for mental health professionals and for the profession in general. As recently as 2002, the American Psychological Association voted to pass the Guidelines on Multicultural Education, Training, Research, Practice, and Organizational Change for Psychologists. Many would argue that the need for cultural "guidelines" that reflect the world views and specific cultural contexts of individuals who represent the racial and ethnic diversity in this country is long overdue.

The guidelines reflect the need to shift from the traditional Eurocentric mode of thinking to one that is more culturally responsive and reflective of individuals within their own social and cultural contexts. The dominant Western Eurocentric model of education and training have situated mental health professionals without the necessary skills to understand and address the needs of a multiculturally diverse nation. Traditional models of training have also placed the need to be clinically responsive before the need to be culturally responsive, leaving most "clinically responsive" therapists without the skills to intervene in a culturally conscientious manner. The end result of this limited Eurocentric perspective is well-intentioned therapists who make unintentional violations that simultaneously increase mental health disparities through high dropout rates, premature termination, and racial and ethnic individuals feeling misunderstood, misdiagnosed, and pathologized. Latinos are one of these racial/ethnic groups that are often misunderstood and misperceived.

Healing From Violence: Latino Men's Journey to a New Masculinity is a well-timed book that reflects the immediacy of addressing two national areas of deficiency that continue to be misunderstood and mistreated: (1) a Latino immigrant male understanding of intimate partner violence; and (2) treating Latinos in culturally responsive ways within a culturally consistent framework. Welland and Ribner provide an in-depth analysis of understanding Latino masculinity, as it is inextricably tied to immigration issues, masculine ideology, and male socialization. In order to treat Latino men and intimate partner violence in a culturally responsive way, it is imperative that we begin to change our stereotypes and expand our definitions of masculine ideology in Latino male culture. In deepening our understanding, we provide a foundation that is more congruent with the multiple ways in which Latino male identity is reflected within the culture, and we provide ways in which we can begin to affirm and expand Latino men's definitions of themselves. Most importantly, Welland and Ribner help us begin to respond to Latino men within a culturally specific framework.

Miguel E. Gallardo, PsyD

Assistant Professor—Pepperdine University
Graduate School of Psychology
President—California Psychological Association

REFERENCES

American Psychological Association. (2002). Guidelines on multicultural education, training, research, practice, and organizational change for psychologists. *American Psychologist, 58*(5), 377–402.

Borrayo, E. A., & Jenkins, S. R. (2003). Feeling frugal: Socioeconomic status, acculturation, and cultural health beliefs among women of Mexican descent. *Cultural Diversity and Ethnic Minority Psychology, 9*(2), 197–206.

Falicov, C. J. (1998). *Latino families in therapy: A guide to multicultural practice.* New York: Guilford.

Flores, E., Tschann, J. M., Marin, B. V., & Pantoja, P. (2004). Marital conflict and acculturation among Mexican American husbands and wives. *Cultural Diversity and Ethnic Minority Psychology, 10*(1), 39–52.

Gallardo, M. E., & Curry, S. (in press). Machismo. In *Encyclopedia of counseling psychology.* Thousand Oaks, CA: Sage Publications.

Mattson, S., & Ruiz, E. (2005). Intimate partner violence in the Latino community and its effect on children. *Health Care or Women International, 26,* 523–529.

Mirande, A. (1997). *Hombres y machos: Masculinity and Latino culture.* Boulder, CO: Westview Publishers.

Moracco, K. E., Milton, A., Hodges, K. G., & Frasier, P. Y. (2005). Knowledge and attitudes about intimate partner violence among immigrant Latinos in rural North Carolina. *Violence Against Women, 11*(3), 337–352.

Ogbu, J. U., & Simons, H. D. (1998). Voluntary and involuntary minorities: A cultural-ecological theory of school performance with some implications for education. *Anthropology and Education Quarterly, 29*(2), 155–188.

Quintero, G. A., & Estrada, A. L. (1998). Cultural models of masculinity and drug use: "Machismo," heroin and street survival on the U.S.-Mexican border. *Contemporary Drug Problems, 25*, 147–168.

Torres, J. B., Solberg, S. H., & Carlstrom, A. H. (2002). The myth of sameness among Latino men and their machismo. *American Journal of Orthopsychiatry, 72*(2), 163–181.

United States Census Bureau (2007, August). Population Press Release. Retrieved August 10, 2007, from the Census Bureau's Internet site, http://www.census.gov/Press-Release/www/releases/archives/population/Preface.

Preface

Healing From Violence: Latino Men's Journey to a New Masculinity was written for anyone with an interest, whether professional or personal, in the topic of intimate partner violence (IPV) in the Latino community. Because it is mainly the result of a qualitative study, an extensive literature review, and many years of clinical experience working with Latino partner abusive men, it provides a unique, phenomenological view "in their own words" of a pervasive problem that tears Latino families apart and brings grief not only to the victim and children but often to the perpetrator as well.

Researchers and clinicians in the fields of psychology, social work, marriage and family therapy, sociology, Latin American studies, Chicano studies, multicultural studies, and gender studies will benefit from the qualitative and quantitative research in this book. Clinicians, interns, and supervisors at agencies that conduct domestic violence treatment groups for Latino men will find in it a theoretical and research base for their Spanish-language treatment programs and an exploration of essential treatment issues in the words of men whose experiences are very similar to their clients'. There are ample quotations from men who have completed their court-ordered treatment and clinical tips from the authors and their colleagues, who have decades of combined expertise in treating Latino partner abusive men.

Intimate partner violence is one of the most common and disturbing social phenomena in the world today. After over 3 decades of research, prevention, and treatment interventions, the problem persists in epidemic proportions in virtually every country on earth, the United States included. Women are abused physically, sexually, and emotionally, and children, often victims of abuse themselves, witness and are traumatized by this out-of-control behavior in what should be the safe sanctuary of their home. The negative effects of IPV flow down the generations. In fact, the strongest risk factor for committing or being a victim of IPV is witnessing it in one's own family as a child.

In Latin America as in the United States, IPV affects millions of men, women, and children. In the United States, as the population of both first-generation Latino immigrants and American citizens of Latino descent continues to grow, the need for an appropriate response to IPV in this population grows with it. As is often the case with minority health problems, little research has been conducted on Latino men and IPV. More research has been conducted with Latina victims, but rarely have partner abusive men been the focus of intensive study. Recognizing this gap in the knowledge base, we decided to investigate the phenomenon of IPV from the standpoint of Latino immigrant men who had completed a year of court-ordered treatment in Southern California. First, we conducted a survey of over 150 Latino partner abusive men to establish their demographic and risk factor profile. Then we conducted 12 in-depth qualitative interviews with men selected from the survey members, men who were purposely chosen to be as different from each other as possible in every other way, except as regards partner violence.

We asked them about their childhood experiences of violence, their beliefs about being a man, about women, and about marriage. We wanted to know what it was like being an immigrant and how this affected their married life. We asked them about their violence to their partner and why they thought they had behaved this way. They told us what was helpful in their therapy group, what they wished they had learned in addition to the curriculum, and what kind of therapist traits had been most effective or ineffective for them. They talked about the process of change, what motivated them, and their spiritual and moral beliefs. When the analysis was complete, we had a compelling description of IPV among Latino immigrants. They also told us what topics they wanted to explore in therapy that would be specifically tailored to their cultural needs: parenting education; transformation of male gender roles; discussion of ethnic and gender discrimination; relationship stress related to immigration; sexual abuse in relationships; and the inclusion of their spirituality. We then put these findings to the test, creating a treatment program for Latino men and piloting it with an IPV treatment group in Spanish for 4 years, fine-tuning our material and taking into account the responses of our clients to the new model of therapy designed for them. We clarified phrases and changed vocabulary or examples based on their feedback. Since then we have conducted quantitative research to extend and clarify our findings empirically; these findings are incorporated into the text.

Healing From Violence: Latino Men's Journey to a New Masculinity gives Latino men who have been violent a voice; it tells their story from the inside out. They are quoted as they discuss some of the deepest and most difficult moments of their lives—violence that was perpetrated on them, violence they committed, what accompanied it, why they think it happened, and what was helpful to them in their quest to change. They speak of their journey toward recreating and maintaining a healthy relationship with their partner and their children. They speak of a process of transformation, of growth, of introspection and social awareness—of becoming a different kind of man.

A word to therapists and those directly involved in the process of helping men to become accountable for their actions and to change. The men who participated in our interviews were clearly the cream of the crop, those most motivated to share their experience of transformation. Not all the men we study or treat will be as amenable to change; not all will have the insights these men gained in the course of treatment. Nevertheless, they give us important information about what motivates Latino men in therapy. What worked for them may very well work for other men like them, who arrive for therapy angry and resistant but over time realize that this period of coerced treatment may just be what they needed to reexamine old beliefs and attitudes and alter behaviors that have led them to a relationship impasse or its total destruction.

Acknowledgments

This book is the fruit of many years of research and clinical work, and as such, there are numerous people to thank for their contributions. First of all, we are grateful to our editor, Philip Laughlin at Springer. It would be hard to imagine finding an editor more encouraging, helpful, and punctual with his comments and feedback. Nancy Johnson, PhD, and Oliva Espín, PhD, provided invaluable commentary when this book was in its earliest form. David Wexler, PhD, through all the years of cofacilitating and supervising IPV groups with the U.S. Navy in San Diego, was a mentor and example for Christauria. His theoretical and practical contributions to understanding and responding to the psychological needs of violent men is basic to the insights found in this work. The cofacilitators who worked with Christauria over the 4 years of the pilot program, Heather Rafferty, PhD, María Esther Ortiz, PhD, Scott Robinson, PhD, Chad Cox, PhD, and Michelle Kole, PhD, were essential to the development of the program and its refinement with our clients in real time. Thanks to Drs. Howard Nathan, Karen Hyland, and Elizabeth Allen in the administration at Professional Community Services, El Cajon, California, for their unfailing support for the pilot group and for our research.

Most of all, we thank the Latino men who have accompanied us on this journey of discovery. Their enthusiasm, cooperation, and passion for the dissemination of knowledge about preventing IPV was inspiring and filled us with hope for men all over Latin America as well as the United States. As one of the participants remarked, "I'm from Mexico too. I was like that, and I changed. If I can do it, so can they." We feel privileged to have been able to engage in qualitative research and clinical work that brought us so close to their experience. We were moved by their willingness to let down their masculine guard and reveal their vulnerabilities, their pain, their shame, and their hope to us. Their courage and openness in discussing their personal hero's journey through pain and darkness into light paves the way for other men like them to leave the past behind and create a new life for themselves and their families. As Leonardo said so simply, "I like that my therapist taught me another way to be a man."

CHAPTER 1

What Is Intimate Partner Violence?

The National Center for Injury Prevention and Control (NCIP) (http://www.cdc.gov/ncipc/factsheets/ipvoverview.htm) defines intimate partner violence (IPV) as "physical, sexual, or psychological harm by a current or former partner or spouse. Intimate partner violence can occur among heterosexual or same-sex couples and does not require sexual intimacy." Intimate partner violence varies along a continuum of severity and frequency that can range from one relatively minor blow to chronic, severe battering. There are four main types of IPV: physical violence, sexual violence, psychological/emotional violence, and stalking (Saltzman, Fanslow, McMahon, & Shelley, 2002, cited in NCIP IPV Web site overview, para. 3). Physical violence is "the intentional use of physical force with the potential for causing death, disability, injury, or harm. Physical violence includes, but is not limited to, scratching; pushing; shoving; throwing; grabbing; biting; choking; shaking; slapping; punching; burning; use of a weapon; and use of restraints or one's body, size, or strength against another person" (para 3). To illustrate the frequent chronicity of this form of violence, Tjaden and Thoennes (2000) found that two-thirds of women physically assaulted by their partner suffered multiple victimizations, averaging 6.9 assaults by the same partner, and lasting an average of 4.5 years. Research using data from the National Crime Victimization Survey (1992–1999) of physical and sexual IPV demonstrates that over a 6-month period, 25% of victims were assaulted at least twice by their partner (Rand & Saltzman, 2003). Sexual violence, which may include "use of physical force to compel a person to engage in a sexual act, whether or not the act is completed; attempted or completed sex acts involving a person who is unable to understand the nature or condition of the act, to decline participation, or to communicate unwillingness to engage in the sexual act, e.g., because of illness, disability, or the influence of alcohol or other drugs, or because of intimidation or pressure; and abusive sexual contact" (Saltzman, Fanslow, McMahon, & Shelley, 2002, cited in NCIP IPV Web site overview, para. 4). Disturbingly, Tjaden and Thoennes (2000) found that over half of women raped by their partner suffered an average of 4.5 rapes by the same partner, over an average of 3.8 years. Threats of physical or sexual violence are defined as the use of words, gestures, or weapons to communicate the intent to cause death, disability, injury, or physical harm. Psychological/emotional violence in-volves trauma to the victim caused by acts, threats of acts, or coercive tactics. Psychological/emotional abuse can include, but is not limited to, humiliating the victim, controlling what the victim can and cannot do, withholding information from the victim, deliberately doing something to make the victim feel diminished or embarrassed, isolating the victim from friends and family, and denying the victim access to money or other basic resources. Stalking is often included among the types of IPV. Stalk-ing generally refers to repeated behavior that causes victims to feel a high level of fear (Tjaden & Thoennes, 2000).

HOW SERIOUS IS THE PROBLEM OF INTIMATE PARTNER VIOLENCE?

Worldwide Intimate Partner Violence Statistics

In 48 population-based surveys from around the world, 10%–69% of women reported being physically assaulted by an intimate male partner at some point in their lives. In large national studies, the range is between 10% and 34% (World Health Organization [WHO], 2002). The results of the WHO Multi-country Study (2005), where identical methodology was used to collect data in 10 different countries, indicate that violence by a male intimate partner (also called "domestic violence") is widespread in all of the countries covered by the study. However, there was a great deal of variation from country to country, and from setting to setting within the same country. The wide variation in prevalence rates indicates that this violence is not inevitable, as is sometimes assumed. The percentage of ever-partnered women who had ever experienced physical or sexual violence, or both, by an intimate partner in their lifetime ranged from

15% to 71%, with most sites falling between 29% and 62%. Women in Japan were the least likely to have ever experienced physical or sexual violence, or both, by an intimate partner, while the greatest amount of violence was reported by women living in provincial (for the most part rural) settings in Bangladesh, Ethiopia, Peru, and the United Republic of Tanzania. Yet even in Japan, about 15% of ever-partnered women reported experiencing physical or sexual violence, or both, at some time. The WHO study reports one of the first transcultural studies of patterns of IPV; most of these women experienced physical violence only, or both physical and sexual violence. In a report published by the United Nations in October 2006, *Ending Violence Against Women: From Words to Action,* there is clear recognition of the threat that IPV poses to women's health and progress and the toll it takes on nations' development.

> State strategies to address violence should promote women's agency and be based on women's experiences and involvement, and on partnerships with NGOs and other civil society actors. Women's NGOs in many countries have engaged in innovative projects and programmes, sometimes in collaboration with the State. Generic aspects of good or promising practices can be extracted from a variety of experiences around the world. Common principles include: clear policies and laws; strong enforcement mechanisms; motivated and well-trained personnel; the involvement of multiple sectors; and close collaboration with local women's groups, civil society organizations, academics and professionals. (p. 3)

Intimate Partner Violence Statistics in the United States and Canada

Due to differences in methodology and definitions of IPV (with the exception of the Multi-country Study mentioned above), statistics regarding the prevalence and incidence of IPV can be somewhat confusing. Most large-scale surveys include only physical and sexual violence, while others may also take stalking and psychological or emotional abuse into account. Tjaden and Thoennes (2000) found that most IPV incidents in the United States are not reported to the police. About a quarter of physical assaults and a fifth of rapes were actually reported; thus the data we do have is likely to be a large underestimate of the true magnitude of the problem.

Nearly 5.3 million incidents of IPV occur each year in the United States among women ages 18 and older, and 3.2 million occur among men. Most assaults are "relatively minor" and consist of pushing, grabbing, shoving, slapping, and hitting (Tjaden & Thoennes, 2000). About 1.5 million women are raped or physically assaulted by an intimate partner per year. This translates into about 47 IPV assaults per 1,000 women (Tjaden & Thoennes, 2000). Although rates of female-to-male assault, both minor and severe, are very similar to those committed from male to female (Pan, Neidig, & O'Leary, 1994), Straus and Gelles (1990) emphasized that the meaning and consequences of this violence can easily be misinterpreted. Female-to-male violence is rarely injurious and is frequently a response to male-to-female violence, that is, self-defense or retaliation. This is not to say that there are no women who are the dominant and primary aggressor in relationships. However, the rate of injury for women who have been assaulted by their partner is 13 times greater than it is for men (American Psychological Association [APA], 1996; Cantos, Neidig, & O'Leary, 1994).

These findings suggest that IPV is a serious criminal justice and public health concern. Intimate partner violence results in nearly 2 million injuries and 1,300 deaths nationwide every year (Centers for Disease Control and Prevention [CDC], 2003). It is primarily a crime against women. In 2001, women accounted for 85% of the victims of IPV, 588,490 total, and men accounted for approximately 15% of the victims, 103,220 total (Bureau of Justice Statistics, 2003). In 2002, 76% of intimate partner homicide victims were female; 24% were male (Fox & Zawitz, 2004). One national study found that 29% of women and 22% of men had experienced physical, sexual, or psychological IPV during their lifetime (Coker et al., 2002).

According to the nationally representative Canadian Violence Against Women Survey (VAWS), 29% of ever-married women have been assaulted by their partners at least once (Canadian Centre for Justice Statistics, 2005). The 1999 General Social Survey (GSS) found that in the 5-year period prior to the survey, 37% of women who had been victims of spousal violence had reported an incident to police (Canadian Centre for Justice Statistics, 2005). While these data from the GSS were not nationally representative, they provide a valuable profile of the nature and characteristics of police-reported spousal violence incidents. Among all family violence victims, 62% were victims of violence at the hands of a spouse. Females were much more likely than their male counterparts to be victims of spousal violence (85% versus 15%). The most frequently reported spousal violence offense was common assault for both female and male victims (64% and 60%). While both females and males were more likely to be victimized by current spouses, approximately one-third of females and males experienced violence at the hands of an ex-spouse.

Pregnancy and Intimate Partner Violence

Between 4% and 8% of pregnant women are abused at least once during their pregnancy (Gazmararian et al., 2000). A Harvard School of Public

Health study (Silverman, Raj, Decker, & Reed, 2006) found that violence from male partners both in the year prior to and during a woman's pregnancy harms the woman's health during pregnancy and the health of newborn children and increases the risk of serious health complications. Abuse also increases a woman's risk of delivering prematurely and having a child who is born clinically underweight and in need of intensive care.

Latinos in the United States

In 2005, the U.S. Bureau of the Census reported that there were an estimated 42.7 million Hispanics in the United States, making people of Hispanic[1] origin the nation's largest and fastest-growing ethnic minority, comprising 14% of the nation's total population. This estimate does not include the 3.9 million residents of Puerto Rico (U.S. Bureau of the Census, 2006b). By 2050, the Hispanic population of the United States is estimated to rise to 102.6 million, or 24% of the nation's total population. Sixty-four percent of the Hispanic population, or 27 million Hispanics, are of Mexican background. Another approximately 10% are of Puerto Rican background, with about 3% of the population each of Cuban, Salvadoran, and Dominican origins. The remainder are of some other Central American, South American, or other Hispanic origin. The Hispanic population is younger on average than the general population, 27.2 years versus 36.2 years. Forty-nine percent of Hispanics live in California (12.4 million) or Texas (7.8 million). There are 13 states with at least half a million Hispanic residents: Arizona, California, Colorado, Florida, Georgia, Illinois, Nevada, New Jersey, New Mexico, New York, North Carolina, Texas, and Washington. One-tenth of U.S. households (31 million) have members over the age of 5 who speak Spanish. Of these, 50% also speak English very well. Fifty-three percent (18.3 million) of the foreign-born population of the United States is from Latin America, with 10 million being from Mexico. Other countries of birth that contribute large numbers of Hispanics are El Salvador (937,000), Cuba (925,000), the Dominican Republic (688,000), Guatemala (590,000), and Colombia (500,000). These statistics clearly establish the need for research and clinical work tailored for and directed to the growing Latino population.

The Latino Population and Intimate Partner Violence

Data from the National Institute of Justice's National Violence Against Women Survey (Tjaden & Thoennes, 2000) indicate that Latina women are equally as likely as non-Latina women to report physical assaults, either by an adult caregiver when they were children or by their partners, 53.2% for Latina women versus 51.8% for non-Latina women. In the same National Institute of Justice (NIJ) study, 628 women and 581 men identifying themselves as *Hispanic* were surveyed; this very broad category includes Puerto Rican, Cuban American, Mexican American, and Central or South American. The NIJ survey reported that Hispanic and non-Hispanic women were nearly equally likely to report physical assault or stalking victimization, which contradicts earlier findings that showed that rates of intimate partner physical violence among Latinos were higher than the general population (Sorenson & Telles, 1991; Straus & Smith, 1990). The National Family Violence Resurvey of 1985 reported that 17%, or almost 1 in 5 Latino men, assaulted their partners and that 7% of assaults were severe in nature, compared to 12% of assaultive men and 3% of severe assaults in the general population. Straus and Smith (1990) pointed out that three key structural factors increased the level of partner abuse for Latinos: urbanicity of residence, low income, and youthfulness of respondent. When these factors were held constant through logistic regression, the rate of partner violence decreased to match the national average. When the perpetrator was unemployed the incidence of male-to-female Latino partner abuse was also twice as high for both minor and severe violence, 33% and 16% respectively (Straus & Smith, 1990). However, Sorenson found a lower rate of IPV among Latinos (Sorenson, 1996). For this reason, the NIJ report states that the data is inconclusive and no firm statement regarding prevalence can be made.

Other researchers analyzing National Alcohol and Family Violence Survey data (Kaufman Kantor & Asdigian, 1997; Kaufman Kantor, Jasinski, & Aldarondo, 1994) have discovered considerable heterogeneity among ethnic subgroups in the Latino population, making any general statements about "Latinos" and IPV difficult to support.[2] There is considerable racial, cultural, religious, linguistic, and socioeconomic diversity in the Latino population, which makes generalizations subject to inaccuracy and increases the potential for stereotyping. As a result, therapists and researchers unfamiliar with the extensive diversity of this population should strive to increase their knowledge of the subgroups with whom they work.

Kaufman Kantor and her colleagues found the highest rates of Latino IPV among Puerto Ricans (20.4%), followed by Mexicans (10.5%), then Cubans (2.5%). Being born in the United States was an additional risk factor for Puerto Ricans and Mexican Americans (17.9%), who were the most likely to be violent to their partners. Puerto Ricans (18.8%) followed by Mexicans and Mexican Americans (7.7% and 5.4%) were more likely than Cubans to approve of a man slapping his partner. These researchers hypothesize that structural factors rather than cultural values contribute to abuse, such as unemployment, alienation, and cultural marginality. However, they also point out that unemployment, leading to loss of male dominance and thus status, as well as disrupted support from extended family may be factors in explaining increased abuse among second-generation men. Cuban American researchers observe that Cuban American families tend to be more bicultural, to be less male-dominated, and to have more political and economic power than other Latino subgroups. These variations may be due to the differences in their immigration history as educated political refugees versus economic migrants. Compared with other Latinos, Cuban Americans as a group are older and have more education and higher median household incomes (Pew Hispanic Center, 2006a). When risk factors for IPV are discussed in future chapters, some reasons for the lower rates of IPV among Cuban Americans will be hypothesized. More detailed data on other Latino subgroups and IPV are not currently available in the literature.

Other Ethnic Groups and IPV

The National Violence Against Women Survey (Tjaden & Thoennes, 2000) found no significant differences between the rates of lifetime prevalence of IPV among White, African American, and Hispanic women. Each of these groups demonstrated alarming rates of rape (17.7%, 18.8%, and 14.6% respectively), physical assault, including being the victim of child abuse (51.3%, 52.1%, and 53.2%), and stalking (8.2%, 6.5%, and 7.6%). The small sample of Asian Americans surveyed made significance testing for rape and stalking impossible. However, rates of rape, assault, and stalking stood at 6.8%, 49.6%, and 4.5%.

The ethnic group with significantly higher rates of rape, physical assault, and stalking was American Indian /Alaska Native, with percentages standing at 34.1%, 61.4%, and 17% in the three categories. The study points out that because members from different nations were analyzed as one group, significant differences in the level of violence in specific tribes may be masked. As is typically the case when seeking statistics for IPV in the United States or other countries, there are conflicting data sets. For example, the Bureau of Justice Statistics and the National Crime Victimization Survey report consistent data demonstrating that African Americans and Hispanics are at greater risk of violent victimization than other groups, although these studies did not publish information on other ethnic groups (cited in Tjaden & Thoennes, 2000).

Femicide is the leading cause of premature death among African American women between the ages of 15 and 44 (cited in Campbell, Sharps, Gary, Campbell, & Lopez, 2002). Sixteen percent of African American women had been physically abused by an intimate partner over a the 5-year period prior to the Commonwealth Fund survey (Schoen et al., 1997). Fifty-two percent of femicides in New York City from 1990 to 1994 were committed on African American women, although the city is only 25% African American. In Philadelphia, 60% of the violence-related injuries for African American women were cases of IPV (Family Violence Prevention Fund, 2007).

A focus group of Chinese immigrants in San Francisco estimated that 20%–30% of Chinese men are violent to their intimate partners, while a survey in Northern California found that 25% of Filipina women had been abused by their husbands in the Philippines or the United States, or both. Santa Clara County, California, is 17.5% Asian, but 33% of femicides committed by intimate partners were of Asian women (Ford Foundation elibrary, 2007). The Family Violence Prevention Fund of San Francisco's telephone survey, where 18% of the respondents were Asian, found that Asian women tended to be less likely to categorize various interactions as domestic violence than women of other ethnic groups.

In a study of South Asian women in Boston, 40.8% of the participants had been physically and/or sexually abused by their partners in their lifetime; 36.9% reported having been victimized in the past year. Similar statistics were found for Vietnamese Americans (Asian and Pacific Islander Institute on Domestic Violence, 2007). Clearly, as data accumulate for every ethnic group in the United States, IPV sadly emerges as epidemic among women in these groups as well.

Immigrant Women and IPV

Immigrant women often feel trapped in abusive relationships because of immigration laws, language barriers, social isolation, and lack of financial resources (Orloff & Little, 1999). Despite federal legislation (the Violence Against Women Act [VAWA], renewed in 2006) that has opened new and safe routes to immigration status for some immigrant women who are victims of IPV if their spouse has legal status, abuse is still a significant problem for immigrant women. Forty-eight percent of Latinas in one study reported that their partner's violence against them had increased since they immigrated to the United States (Dutton, Orloff, & Aguilar Hass, 2000). One-fifth of the immigrant women surveyed reported that their partners use threats of deportation and of not filing or withdrawing immigration papers as an abusive tactic in the relationship. One-fourth of the participants stated that it was their immigration status that prevented them from leaving the abusive relationship. The Immigrant Women's Task Force of the Northern California Coalition for Immigrant Rights found that 34% of Latinas experienced IPV either in their country of origin, in the United States, or both (Jang & Morello-Rosch, 1991). In another study Latina migrant farm workers surveyed reported a 25%–35% rate of IPV in the previous 12 months (Rodríguez, 1998). A survey in South Carolina found that 70% of 300 Hispanic women reported being victims of domestic violence and 43% suffered multiple assaults (http://findarticles.com/p/articles/mi_m0DXK/is_6_22/ai_n13795154, 2005).

Abusers often use their partners' immigration status as a tool for controlling them. That is, in such situations, it is common for a batterer to use his partner's immigration status to force her to remain in the relationship, unless she is aware of the VAWA legislation and it applies in her case.[3] Immigrant women often suffer higher rates of abuse than U.S. citizens because they may come from cultures that accept IPV or because they have less access to legal and social services than citizens. Additionally, immigrant batterers and victims may believe that the penalties and protections of the legal system do not apply to them. Frequently, due to their undocumented status, they are not eligible for all the services available to other women, especially economic and retraining assistance. These are the very services likely to motivate a woman to leave an abusive marriage, by creating favorable conditions for survival on her own. Abused immigrant women who attempt to flee may not have access to bilingual shelters, financial assistance, or food. It is also unlikely that they will have the assistance of a certified interpreter in court, when reporting complaints to the police or a 911 operator, or even in acquiring information about their rights and the legal system.

INTIMATE PARTNER VIOLENCE IN LATIN AMERICA

The National Survey on Violence Against Women conducted in Mexico in 2006 at health centers around the country (Instituto Nacional de Estadística, Geographía e Informática [INEGI], 2007, p. 3) found a prevalence of physical IPV of 20% and 9% sexual IPV among women 15 years of age or older. The violence had taken place in the women's most recent or current intimate relationship, making these statistics not entirely comparable to the U.S. lifetime prevalence rates cited. Forty-three percent of Mexican women surveyed reported some form of violence, including emotional (38%) and economic (23%) as well as physical and sexual abuse. There were differences among states, ranging from a rate of 26% physical abuse in one state to 13% in another. In another study, the National Survey on Relationship Issues in the Home (INEGI, 2005), researchers found that 55% of women suffered more than one type of abuse and that women who had been abused as children were more likely to be abused as adults (55% versus 34%), while 65% of those physically or sexually abused as adults had been abused as children. Sexual violence was more prevalent among older women (ages 40–49) than their younger counterparts. Seventy-four percent of women did not report the violence to any authority.

Like most clients,[4] Latino men in treatment feel the need to have their situation *normalized*, as much as is possible for men who are violent. It is never our goal to minimize their harmful behavior. Nevertheless, they are our clients, and we do need to reach them to be able to treat them. Knowing that men all over the world, including men in the United States, have a high rate of IPV is both of concern and of comfort to them. It is important in the therapy group to help men realize that they are part of an international effort to end IPV and that their treatment is not simply another way of pointing the finger at Latinos or singling them out for punishment. Many of the men in IPV treatment groups initially believe that Latino men are more *machista* and more violent to their partners than other men. Just reviewing the statistics with them seems to help establish rapport, help remove some of the stigma and shame they feel as violent Latino men, and open the door for treatment and change.

In 1995, the first national Public Opinion Survey on the Incidence of Family Violence was conducted in Mexico (Duarte, 1995). Funded by the Population Fund of the United Nations and conducted by experts in the field of IPV, it consisted of a survey of nine cities. The representative sample of 3,300 was stratified by region, socioeconomic and educational level, gender, and age. Twenty-one percent of the survey participants knew someone, usually a child or a woman, who had been physically or sexually abused within the previous 6 months. Other statistical studies conducted in Mexico have demonstrated lifetime prevalence[5] rates of physical domestic violence against women of anywhere from 28% to 60%, with 33% being the prevalence rate in Mexico City (Fawcett, Heise, Isita-Espejel, & Pick, 1999; Miranda, Halperin, Limón, & Tunón, 1998; Ramírez-Rodríguez & Patino-Guerra, 1997; Valdez & Juárez, 1998). One study in Mexico (Granados, 1996) found that over half the women who had been physically assaulted had also been sexually abused by their partners.

The Multi-country Study of IPV conducted by the World Health Organization (2005) found that the lifetime prevalence of physical IPV in Peru was 48% in the capital, Lima, and 61% in the Andean province of Cusco. Sexual violence perpetrated against women was 23% in Lima and 47% in Cusco. In the same study, corresponding statistics for Brazil were 27% physical IPV and 10% sexual IPV in an urban environment, versus 34% physical IPV and 14% sexual IPV in a rural setting. Worldwide, in fact, there was a tendency for rural settings to present higher rates of IPV than urban settings, although the urban rates were by no means low or of little concern.

Lifetime prevalence rates for IPV in other Latin American countries range from 10% in Uruguay, to 13% in Paraguay, 27% in Colombia, 28% in Nicaragua, and 30% in both Antigua and Barbados (WHO,

2002). These statistics were compiled from various national studies and as such are not directly comparable to each other, a methodological weakness that was overcome with the 2005 WHO study, although most Latin American countries were not included in the WHO research.

ABOUT THE MEN WHOSE VOICES
ARE HEARD IN THIS BOOK

The Interview Participants

When our anonymous demographic and risk factor survey of 159 Latino men in treatment for IPV in Spanish-language groups in San Diego County, California, was conducted (the results are presented and discussed in chapter 4), men were given an opportunity to participate in further in-depth interviews. Over 60 men expressed interest in being interviewed. The 12 men who were selected for the qualitative portion of the study were chosen through maximum variation sampling (Lincoln & Guba, 1985), based on the information they provided on the supplementary form that was offered to all survey participants. These 12 participants met the criterion for length of treatment of 40 weeks or more, up to a possible 52 weeks. They were purposefully selected based on widely different ages (22 to 52 years), different socioeconomic levels ($8,000 per annum to $48,000 per annum), different educational backgrounds (zero formal education to 14 years of formal education), rural versus urban backgrounds from many diverse regions of Mexico, different immigration status (permanent residents versus undocumented immigrants), positive or negative history of child abuse and witnessing domestic violence in the family of origin, and finally, being positive or negative for intoxication during the violent incident. All the participants were raised in homes where Spanish was the first language, due to a lack of indigenous participants in the study who met the criteria. Indigenous is the term used to refer to the peoples of Mexico whose native languages are other than Spanish.

Eight of the men were interviewed in their own homes, and 4 were interviewed at agencies. Two of the interviews were 90 minutes in length, whereas the other 10 interviews lasted for 2 hours each.

Meet the Participants

All names have been altered to protect the confidentiality of the participants, as have the names and identifying information of the therapists mentioned by them. The participants are listed by age, in ascending order.

Ramón

Ramón was the youngest participant (22), and the one who had been in the United States for the least time, only 6 years. Ramón is from a small *rancho* (rural agricultural community) in central Mexico, where he received a sixth-grade education. His responses demonstrated intelligence and insight. Ramón suffered a particularly abusive childhood. He was frequently beaten by his alcoholic father; the most severe trauma he experienced was witnessing his father's life-threatening abuse to his mother on several occasions. His grandmother brought her to the United States when Ramón was 13, to protect her from being murdered. He then lived with his aunt and uncle until he came to this country at the age of 16.

Ramón suffers from symptoms of posttraumatic stress disorder (PTSD), such as intrusive recollections and emotional reactivity. He is not an alcoholic.

He had always planned never to be violent to his partner or his children because of what he endured, but the single event of domestic violence for which he was arrested involved a sleight to his honor that he felt he had to avenge at the time, goaded on by his brothers. However, he felt he could only hit his partner if he became drunk, so he drank a great deal to facilitate his action. Ramón demonstrated fairly rigid gender roles, consistent with his rural upbringing. It is particularly challenging for him to be living with a Mexican American woman who has a different vision of female gender roles than he expects.

Blas

Blas is a 31-year-old from a small city in south-central Mexico. He completed eighth grade and is currently employed as a welder. Blas is separated from his wife and has informal custody of their three children. He was extremely dysphoric almost from the beginning of the interview, sobbing uncontrollably on several occasions. He wanted to continue, however, to be able to "tell his whole story to another person." Blas appeared to have symptoms of PTSD due to repeated emotional and physical trauma from the age of 6, when his mother died and he was sent to be raised by five abusive uncles and their abused wives. He lived with them until he was 16.

Blas was arrested once before for domestic violence, when he attended an English-language group for 40 weeks, with little change. He admitted that he had been violent to his wife on many occasions, pushing, threatening, and coercing her sexually. He realizes now that his jealous and violent behavior destroyed their relationship. Blas explained that he was so distraught when his wife threatened to take his children away, to go and live with her and her newfound lesbian lover in Tijuana, that he didn't care about the consequences of his actions. He could not stand the thought of being separated from his children. He picked up a knife and threatened to kill her, even though he insisted that he would never have actually hurt her.

Blas was able to compose himself halfway through the interview. He was deeply repentant and demonstrated that he had learned a great deal about equality, new gender roles, anger management, and communication from the Spanish program he had just completed. He continues to care for his children, since his wife has become a methamphetamine addict. Blas was given a referral to counseling for depression and trauma recovery, as well as a legal referral to clarify custody issues.

Ceferino

Ceferino is 32 years old and was raised in Tijuana, Mexico, across the border from San Diego, California. He came from a family of 16 and was one of the middle children. Ceferino also wept and sighed constantly as he recounted the emotional and physical abuse he suffered from an early age, from both his parents. The abuse and neglect that he endured was the most severe of any of the participants, and he described symptoms of PTSD and depression. Ceferino ran away from home at 13 and never lived at home again. He was able to complete ninth grade but became an alcoholic and a drug addict before the age of 14. He states that his current mental state is much improved due to substance abuse treatment and the IPV group.

Ceferino was never arrested for IPV. Rather, he was mandated by family court as part of the reunification plan with his children, who are now in their mother's custody, even though the children were taken away from her some time ago due to child abuse. However, he admitted to verbal abuse and forced intercourse in the relationship. The latter takes on added significance from the fact that his partner had been raped by her father at age 20 and has a daughter from him. Ceferino and his partner have been separated for 4 years. He now has a girlfriend and reports that his new relationship is very different, because he has learned to be respectful and to communicate, and he is no longer under the influence of drugs and alcohol. Ceferino also demonstrated remorse for his past abuse and spoke with enthusiasm about his new life free of violence and abuse toward women and children. A referral for counseling to deal with past trauma was given to Ceferino at the close of the session.

Rogelio

Rogelio is 34 years old, from a small *rancho* in southern Mexico. He has lived in the United States for 19 years, and as a restaurant manager he had the highest income of any of the participants, $48,000 per year. Rogelio was very enthusiastic about the interview and stated that he would like to continue being involved in helping his compatriots to change their ways.

Rogelio self-described as an alcoholic for 15 years, and he attributed much of his bad behavior to that, although he added machismo as a factor. Rogelio had been moderately violent to his wife, as well as to a previous partner, but the incident for which he was arrested was severe. He was very drunk and jealous, and he tried to choke her. He stopped when he heard the voice of his daughter, about 5 years old, screaming at him to leave her alone. Rogelio deeply regrets that he subjected his children to witnessing his traumatizing behavior. He was himself raised in an atmosphere of frequent, moderate violence, both to himself and to his mother, and he feels terrible that he repeated the cycle himself. He reported making great gains in the program, learning to be honest with himself and others. He acquired a new self-esteem from the experience of being able to control his impulses to drink and to be abusive, and he feels like a new man.

Raúl

Raúl is 34 and was raised in Mexico City, in one of the roughest neighborhoods of that metropolis. He was one of the few men who was not abused by his parents and did not witness abuse. However, he lived in a violent area, and he reported learning to fight at an early age to defend himself and his younger siblings. Raúl had the most education of all the interviewees, having completed high school and 2 years of accounting school. However, his status in the United States is undocumented, and he works as a cook for $12,000 per year.

Raúl gave up drinking when he married at 17 (a shotgun wedding), and he worked very hard to support his family both in Mexico and in this country. In the process, he distanced himself from his wife and lost her to another man. He was extremely verbally abusive and jealous with his first wife and was physically abusive and controlling with his second wife as well. Raúl reported becoming an alcoholic after the separation from his first wife because he was so disappointed in himself for not living up to his father's and his own expectations.

It was not clear until almost the end of his very articulate interview whether he had changed his views on gender roles, but at that time it became evident that he had given his lifestyle a great deal of thought and had decided to discard the attitudes and behaviors that were destroying him. He is now trying to be a good father to his four children and is not in a hurry to establish a new relationship.

Lucio

Lucio is 41 years old and also from Mexico City. He received a sixth-grade education. Lucio is undocumented, although he has lived in the United States for 21 years. His current salary is $12,000, and he was able to dedicate only 90 minutes to the interview because he works at two jobs.

Lucio experienced emotional neglect and some abuse from his father as a child, and he described the resentment he feels toward him. He also reported a long history of alcohol abuse, and some drug abuse many years ago. However, after a DUI (driving under the influence of alcohol) arrest in 1992, he was mandated to treatment and has been sober ever since.

Lucio gave many thoughtful replies to the interview questions, demonstrating that he has benefited from the group support and the teaching he has received during this past year. His violent behavior was a first for him, and it surprised and shocked him so much that he instructed his stepdaughter to call the police just moments after the incident. He has modified his views on gender roles and conflict resolution considerably during this year.

Leonardo

Leonardo, age 42, was born and raised in a small city in Baja California Sur, Mexico. He completed high school and currently earns $33,000 per year as a skilled laborer. He is a permanent resident. Leonardo reported a childhood without physical abuse from either parent, although they did use corporal punishment sparingly. Leonardo was hurt by his mother's verbal abuse, however, and by her partiality to his sisters. On one occasion, he witnessed his father throw his mother against the wall, and he eloquently described his feelings about this incident. Leonardo also witnessed a murder outside town when he was 8 years old, which made a deep impression on him.

Although he was drunk at the time of the incident, he does not consider himself an alcoholic, but a social drinker. However, he deeply appreciated the experience of being in Alcoholics Anonymous per court order, and has taken other men there, too. The relationship problem underlying the incident, which was the only violent incident in the relationship, was his wife's conversion to an Evangelical church 5 years before, which profoundly disturbed him. Leonardo now sees that he cannot control what she does.

He reported that even though his father was "not a *machista*," he learned to be one from the environment in which he grew up. From his therapy, Leonardo has learned how to be a different kind of husband and father, and he relishes his new role. "I like that she [the therapist] taught me another way to be a man."

Juan

Juan, age 43, was born in a small town in central Mexico and moved to a *rancho* in Baja California when he was about 5. He was the second of 17 children. Juan was able to finish sixth grade in the village but spent 6 years in first grade, due to an inability to absorb information. Juan attributes his school failure to a combination of traumatic situations. At 5, he witnessed the grisly death of his grandfather, who was dismembered by a bus. That same year, he was raped by a neighbor, which he kept a secret. From his early childhood he witnessed his alcoholic father beat his mother severely, and he also frequently received severe abuse from his father, including hard and frequent blows to the head. He also reported emotional abuse and neglect by both of his parents throughout his childhood.

Juan was married for 23 years and has four children. However, he reported that he did not know how to communicate with either his wife or his children, and he isolated himself in his room and drank. Juan has now been sober for 3 years, following a DUI arrest and treatment. His violence toward his wife was quite severe: two punches to the eye, in the presence of his children. He reports becoming enraged when he realized she had brought her young lover to live with her and the children. He is now divorced and lives with another woman, with whom he has a much more satisfying relationship. Now that he has completed the course for the second time, he realizes the mistakes that he made. The topic that he appreciated the most was gender equality. A referral was given to Juan for counseling to help him heal from trauma.

Ignacio

Ignacio is 43 and has lived in the United States since he was 15. He is a permanent resident. He was raised in a small village in central Mexico, and he moved to this country with his family. He completed the 11th grade in San Diego and was employed as a skilled laborer until he suffered a serious head injury on the job some time ago. The injury affected his memory and concentration; for this reason the interview was cut short after 90 minutes.

Ignacio was extremely ashamed of what he had done to his wife. He reported that there had been verbal abuse and the silent treatment between them in the past, but she crossed a line in his mind when she went out "clubbing" with female friends and was out all night. He was overcome with jealousy and became suspicious and angry. After arguing with her for hours, he finally pulled out his (unloaded) gun and threatened to kill her. He thought that was the end of it, but a few days later he came home from work and she was gone. A restraining order was issued. In spite of his humiliation over the incident, Ignacio appeared to harbor some resistance to taking responsibility for his behavior, even after 43 weeks of treatment. Although there was no violence in his family, he had always learned that the man is in charge, and he felt that his wife had wronged and humiliated him. However, Ignacio has not harassed his wife since the restraining order was issued, and he reported having modified his parenting style as a result of treatment.

José

José, age 45, completed sixth grade in his *rancho* in southern Mexico. He recounted a history of frequent, severe-to-moderate physical and emotional abuse by both his parents. Although he did not witness violence between his parents, he frequently saw male neighbors attacking their wives without consequence in the village, where such behavior was viewed as normal.

José reported having difficulty understanding fairly simple words and concepts that were used in the treatment group. He managed to complete 48 weeks of treatment with one of the most talented therapists in the region (based on the reports of José and other participants) without understanding the word "equality." This provided us important information regarding teaching style, which is discussed later.

José was so anxious to talk about his experience that even after the interview questions were completed, he asked if the researcher would listen to a longer version of his childhood abuse. He reported that it was very difficult to discuss such issues in depth during the group, not only out of shame, but also because of time constraints. He reported chronic symptoms of PTSD that he used to medicate with alcohol. Now that he is sober, he still finds that "nothing makes it better. The pain never goes away."

Gregorio

Gregorio is 47 and lives in a tiny house in rural San Diego. He was raised in central Mexico and only completed second grade. Gregorio was not arrested for hitting his wife, but for hitting his 16-year-old daughter. He was angry because she had gone out her bedroom window to be with her boyfriend. The next day his wife and daughter moved out, never to return. He thinks that part of his wife's reason for leaving him was that he has a serious kidney disease that necessitates dialysis twice a week and considerable care, which she was tired of providing.

However, he admitted that he used to be violent to her when they were in Mexico, when he was an alcoholic. He has been sober for about 8 years, after being arrested for DUI twice. Gregorio attributes his "new personality" to his involvement in AA, where he learned to be an "honest and respectful man." He is deeply grateful to the United States for all he has received here, not only better health, but a better way of living. He used to be *machista*, but now he realizes that men and women have equal rights. He was the only man who was not initially angry and resentful about being mandated to treatment for domestic violence, because he understood right away that he was wrong and that he had let anger get the better of him.

Hilario

Hilario was the oldest of the participants, age 53. He was born and raised in central Mexico, in a village where domestic violence was unacceptable to the whole community. However, his parents were emotionally and physically abusive to him, sometimes severely so. He vowed he would never hit his own four children, a promise he has kept. Hilario never went to school but reported that he knows how to read a little.

Although he was not arrested for it, Hilario did slap his partner across the mouth on one occasion, when she threatened to sleep with a younger man in his presence. He did not self-identify as *machista*, but he demonstrated the most rigid gender roles of any of the participants. He attributed many of the relationship problems of Mexican immigrant couples to the wife's becoming "liberal."

Hilario recounted the changes in his wife over the years of their marriage. If the story were true, it speaks volumes about his inability to look out for himself or to cope effectively in the face of injustice and cunning. However, he was motivated enough by his wife's insults to quit drinking, just to prove her wrong. Hilario was one of the men who was most affected by his prolonged separation from his children.

SUMMARY

Throughout the remainder of this book, readers will hear these men articulate their experiences, both of their own childhood and of the experience of being violent to their partners and their subsequent treatment. As we come to understand them and the unfolding of their lives, our understanding of IPV and how to help those who commit it will deepen.

In chapter 2, we will briefly review some of the relevant literature. Although there is little on Latino IPV per se, there is a wealth of research on IPV in general. In subsequent chapters we will explore the phenomenon of IPV among Latinos and learn from them how to treat the perpetrators most effectively. Chapter 3 focuses on the Latino population and general treatment issues. In chapter 4 we review the results of a demographic survey of 159 Latino men in treatment for IPV. In chapters 5 through 9 we will delve into the lived experience of these men, compare and contrast it to the literature, and include the findings of our quantitative research as well.

NOTES

1. In this book, the term *Latino* will be used, unless the literature cited uses the term *Hispanic*, as is the case with Bureau of the Census data.
2. In spite of this, for brevity's sake, we will refer to *Latino* men throughout this book, although at times we will focus only on Mexican men and clarify this in the text. Clinical tips may be equally as effective with other Latino men, but are subject to clinical research, as well as the experimentation and adaptation of the therapist experienced with different cultural groups.
3. VAWA stipulates that a victim of IPV may only qualify for immigration assistance if she is married to a U.S. citizen or a permanent resident.
4. Throughout this book, we will periodically insert text boxes with clinical tips based on the literature and/or our extensive experience working clinically with Latino men mandated to IPV treatment.
5. Lifetime prevalence refers to at least one incident of partner violence throughout the course of one's life. Studies have demonstrated, however, that most IPV consists of multiple assaults.

CHAPTER 2

Why Do Men Assault Their Partners?

THEORETICAL PERSPECTIVES ON THE ETIOLOGY OF PARTNER ABUSE

There is no one comprehensive theory of the etiology of partner violence, nor is there one factor that accounts for marital aggression in 100% of cases (APA, 1996; Feldman & Ridley, 1995; WHO, 2002). Several theoretical approaches are consistently cited in the literature, but no one approach can account for the multiple social and cultural contexts in which partner abuse occurs (APA, 1996). An ecological model that explores the relationship between individual and contextual factors and considers violence as the product of multiple levels of influence on behavior is currently favored by many researchers and clinicians, including the World Health Organization (Corsí, 1994; Heise, 1998; WHO, 2002).

Very few research designs on the etiology of IPV in the United States have included ethnicity, socioeconomic status, urban/rural residence, or immigrant status as variables of interest (APA, 1996). A review by Hage (2000) found only 15 published articles over the course of 20 years on ethnic minority perpetrators of IPV. Most research conducted on Latinos as regards IPV has been conducted with Latina female victims of domestic violence (e.g., Bauer, Rodriguez, Quiroga, & Flores-Ortiz, 2000; Coffin-Romig, 1997; Jasinski, 1998; Perilla, Bakeman, & Norris, 1994;

Sorensen & Telles, 1991; Vasquez, 1998; Wiist & McFarlane, 1998). A recent review of the literature, including recent doctoral dissertations, revealed only six studies on Latino partner abusive men since 1999. Three of these, including Christauria Welland's doctoral dissertation (Welland, 1999), were based on investigations of Latino male perpetrators, and none of these were studies of psychological characteristics of Latino perpetrators. There was also a complete absence of treatment outcome studies for Latino men who undergo court-mandated therapy as a result of their conviction for domestic violence. This deficiency in diversity studies makes the application of theories of etiology to diverse populations hypothetical at best. *Violence and the Family* (APA, 1996) states that "understanding the ways in which racial and ethnic differences affect a family member's attitude toward violence within the family and his or her attitude about seeking help outside the family is critical to any understanding of how to stop violence in the family." (p. 16)

An important issue in the discussion of etiology is the apparent study of two different populations of abusive men in the research. One field of research has been conducted using large, nonclinical populations and quantitative surveys. For example, Straus and Gelles (1990) and their colleagues studied large representative samples of the general population and documented a type of partner abuse that Johnson (1995, pp. 283–294) calls an "intermittent response to the occasional conflicts of everyday life, motivated by a need to control the specific situation." Johnson labeled this type of abuse "common couple violence"; it rarely escalates into serious or life-threatening forms of violence, and it occurs about six times per year on the average. It is also likely to be reciprocal, although women are much more frequently injured than men because of smaller size and strength (APA, 1996). Common couple violence appears to occur in a virtually nonoverlapping population of violent families, when compared to the "patriarchal terrorism" category of abusers, who have been researched in feminist studies. Research on this population of often severe abusers has been based on data obtained from battered women who have sought refuge at shelters, hospitals, and other institutions (Johnson, 1995), as well as in the work of Jacobson and Gottman (1998), who studied severely abusive men directly.

Patriarchal terrorism indicates a type of male-to-female-only violence that stems from a need to be in charge of the relationship and to control the woman by any means necessary, whether by threats, intimidation, emotional abuse, isolation, economic abuse, sexual abuse, and/or physical violence. This type of violence occurs with greater severity and frequency and is rooted in patriarchal ideas regarding male ownership of female partners. Johnson pointed out that the data strongly suggest that the two forms of violence have different psychological and interpersonal roots, requiring differential theory development, or synergizing theories (Johnson, 1995). Dutton (Dutton & Nicholas, 2005; Dutton, 2006) pointed out that Johnson failed to mention the high rates of female-initiated IPV that have been well documented in many national surveys. Although the aim of this book is to describe the experience of Latino men who have been violent to their partners, consistent data regarding women who are primary aggressors cannot be ignored, whether in research, theory development, clinical practice, or prevention programs (Ehrensaft et al., 2003).

Ecological Approach

Straus and Smith (1990), in their comments on policy implications, stated that

> the high rate of assault by women on their husbands and the finding that physical punishment is part of the etiology of both child abuse and spouse abuse suggests that family violence is not just a problem of "macho" males. It is built into the family system and the society as it is presently constituted. Consequently, programs to aid victims and treat aggressors, important as they are, will not be sufficient. (p. 365)

The fact that violence is "deeply embedded in the fabric of society" (Straus & Smith, 1990, p. 366) was demonstrated by Argentinean researcher Jorge Corsí, who proposed an ecological theoretical approach to family violence, following Bronfenbrenner's (1979) ecology of human development (Corsí, 1994). The World Health Organization also cited the ecological model as the most accurate and complete description of the etiology of IPV, stating that this type and other forms of violence result from a complex interaction of individual, relationship, social, cultural, and environmental factors (Heise, 1998; WHO, 2002). Corsí's theory stresses the need to take a broader view of family violence as a problem that crosses boundaries and permeates social and personal life. The theoretical model encompasses all levels of society, from macrosystem (societal) to exosystem (community) to microsystem (relationship) to minisystem (individual). Violence, or approval of violence, is found at every level.

Attempts to explicate male-to-female partner abuse with family systems theory, where the interactions of both partners would determine the outcome of family events, have been widely criticized as secondary victimization, or blaming the victim (Johnson, 1995). This may be the case when the system being examined is the microsystem, the family. However, the levels of survey-based mutual violence and female-initiated

IPV statistics are disturbing and are indicative that violence in intimate relationships is not restricted to men. Women can and do inflict harm independent of self-defense or mere retaliation (Dutton, 2006b). Not to mention systems theory in this chapter would be to neglect an important area of research that will ultimately benefit all members of the family. However, the focus of our study and of most efforts worldwide to reduce and eradicate IPV is male-to-female intimate violence.

In Corsí's ecological view, the macrosystem or societal level of violence is to be found in the forms of social organization, belief systems, and lifestyles that make up a culture or subculture. At this level are found attitudes toward the use of force in conflict resolution, the concept of roles, rights, and responsibilities in the family, beliefs regarding power and obedience, and cultural beliefs and values about men, women, children, and the family as a whole. The World Health Organization included attitudes in favor of suicide as personal choice rather than a preventable act of violence, norms that give priority to parental rights over child welfare, norms that support male dominance over women and children, the use of excessive force by police, and political conflict. Additional to these are the health, educational, economic, and social policies that maintain high levels of economic or social inequality between groups (WHO, 2002).

The exosystem is defined as the immediate community, which mediates between the broader culture and the individual. It includes the school, the church, communications media, the workplace, recreational institutions, and judicial and public safety organisms. In this area, Corsí identified institutional legitimization of violence, violent modeling in the media, the lack of adequate legislation in the area of family violence, the scarcity of resources for victims of violence, institutional blaming of the victim (Trujano Ruíz, 1991), and impunity for perpetrators. High levels of residential mobility, heterogeneity, and population density are all associated with violence, as are communities where drug trafficking, high unemployment, or social isolation are rampant. Rates of violence are greater in areas of poverty and deterioration, where there are few institutional supports (WHO, 2002).

In Latin America, depending on the country, the legal and judicial systems are still in the process of establishing prompt and effective responses to family violence, whether child abuse or partner abuse (González & Duarte, 1996; Pan American Health Organization, 2005). In the United States and Canada, in spite of all the advances made in the legislative and judicial fields, IPV is still a major public health epidemic, and violent modeling in the media and institutional violence are still of great concern. Change is slow and requires massive and concerted effort.

The microsystem is comprised of the personal relationships of the individual, with the family, as its basic structure, taking a privileged place.

At this level, Corsí related violence to personal history, such as abuse in the family of origin, the learning of violent conflict resolution behaviors, authoritarianism in family relations, low self-esteem, and isolation. Immediate social relationships with peers, intimate partners, and relatives can increase the risk for both victimization and perpetration of violence. Repeated violent encounters may result from frequent interaction and shared living arrangements (WHO, 2002).

At the level of the individual, which is sometimes called the mini-system, Corsí described other factors that form a subsystem of interdependent dimensions. The cognitive dimension consists of the cognitive structures and schemas that make up the cognitive paradigm of the individual. Specifically, the violent man has a rigidly defined view of the world. He perceives his wife as provocative, maximizing every stimulus that could be interpreted as a threat. On the other hand, he minimizes the effects of his own actions, and he finds it extraordinarily difficult to observe his own actions or emotions accurately. He confuses his jealous imaginings with reality, and he acts accordingly.

The behavioral dimension includes the entire repertory of actions through which a person relates to the world. The violent man adopts dissociative behaviors, acting like a well-adjusted person in public but unleashing a second set of violent, jealous, threatening behaviors in the privacy of his home.

The psychodynamic dimension refers to intrapsychic activity at various levels, such as conscious emotions, anxieties, and conflicts, as well as manifestations of the unconscious. The partner abusive man responds to unbearable challenges to his inner balance by striking out in violence, a method that ensures rapid resolution of the immediate threat. His external ego is overdeveloped in the area of doing and achieving, and his emotional world is repressed. In order to preserve his masculine identity and keep these two areas in balance, he must exercise constant self-control over such emotions as pain, sadness, pleasure, and fear. The personality of the violent man, as a result, has elements of lack of emotional expression, low self-esteem, poor verbal communications skills, especially of emotions, resistance to self-knowledge, and the projection of responsibility and blame.

The interactive dimension refers to rules and standards for interpersonal communication and relationships. As an example, Corsí (1994) described the interpersonal standards at work in a violent relationship in Argentina. Although such standards may not be identical in other Latin American countries, his description is still compelling for clinicians working with Latinos, as well as other cultural groups:

A strongly asymmetrical bond of dependency and possessiveness is formed.... The man tries to control the relationship, that is, the flow of information; the making of decisions; her behavior, even her ideas or ways of thinking....Once established, control must be maintained through methods that may include violence. A game of complementary roles is created, where the woman, socialized to be submissive and obedient, is the interlocking piece of the puzzle for the man socialized to be the breadwinner, to control situations and to take charge. (p. 60)

The ecosystemic theory of partner abuse renounces any attempt on the part of psychology or sociology to simplify the problem down to one causal factor. On the contrary, it opens the field to a wide array of interdependent variables that lie at the root of this vast social problem (Corsí, 1994). Understanding how such multidetermined risk factors are related to violence is a vital step in the public health approach to the prevention of violence (WHO, 2002).

Sociocultural Approach

Sociocultural theory is also sometimes called feminist psychological theory (APA, 1996). It is posited on a feminist analysis of the connection between societal patriarchy and the abuse of individual female partners.

> Men who assault their wives are actually living up to cultural prescriptions that are cherished in Western society—aggressiveness, male dominance, and female subordination—and they are using physical force as a means to enforce that dominance. (Dobash & Dobash, 1979, p. 24)

Thus, wife beating is simply one manifestation of the system of male domination of women that has existed historically and cross-culturally; it is buttressed by patriarchal norms that support male dominance in marriage. Therefore, feminist theorists contend that the male abuser is neither deviant nor pathological. He is, rather, a faithful adherent to the patriarchal culture. The basic premise of the sociocultural theoretical approach is that the male–female power differential in relationships is to be understood in the context of the entire patriarchal society where gender inequality is "structurally and normatively embedded," not just in the spousal relationship (Yllo & Straus, 1990, p. 392). Men batter because they expect to have the power in the relationship and to dominate their partner. Their male sex role identification prepares them for "male privilege." They are socialized to dominate, including through the use of violence. In support of this theory, in a quantitative state-by-state American study it was found that male-to-female IPV was highest in the states where economic, educational, political, and legal inequality was the greatest (Yllo & Straus, 1990). The rates of severe violence against wives ranged from 6% in the states with the highest level of acceptance of patriarchal norms to 3% in the more egalitarian states. Nationally, the mean of severe male-to-female partner abuse in the 1985 National Family Violence Resurvey was 3.4% (Straus & Gelles, 1990).

Although the above and other international studies demonstrate that patriarchal values do influence violence against female partners, researchers point out that 88% of male partners socialized in American patriarchal culture are not violent to their female partners in any given year, and that only 3%–4% of American men commit severe partner violence (Dutton, 1995). Dutton also stated that the large discrepancy in actual percentages of violent male partners socialized in this culture, coupled with the equally high or higher rates of partner abuse in gay and lesbian relationships (Coleman, 2003; Lie, Schilit, Bush, Montague, & Reyes, 1991; Renzetti, 1992), would indicate that the impact of sociocultural factors on male partner behavior varies widely. O'Leary (1993) suggested that a patriarchal society, although a critical factor, is not sufficient to explain the development of IPV.

Feminist analysis has made and is making a vital contribution that to the understanding, prevention, and treatment of partner violence, especially for victims, through educational measures aimed at entire societies. Feminists continue to have a major impact worldwide on the legal and societal changes necessary to initiate and ensure a safe and egalitarian environment for women (González & Duarte, 1996; United Nations Development Fund for Women [Unifem], 2007). Even so, the sociocultural approach appears not to account for a sufficient amount of the variance to satisfactorily explain the differences in behaviors occurring in intimate relationships (Dutton, 1995).

Social Learning Approach

Social learning theory was pioneered by Albert Bandura, whose research demonstrated that high-status adults (e.g., parents) are the most effective models for aggression, and dependent children are the most compliant learners (Bandura, 1979). Habitual actions such as violence are acquired through observation and maintained by rewards that reinforce the behavior. The reward may be the discovery that one gets one's way when violence is used against another.

Dutton (1995, 2006a), Saunders (1993), and Holtzworth-Monroe and Meehan (2004), among others, have demonstrated that men who witnessed their fathers assault their mothers when they were boys are significantly more likely to assault their own partners. Their fathers' behavior has become a model for their own actions. Five decades of psychological research on aggression within and outside the family support the conclusion that violence is a learned behavior, and that much of that learning takes place in the home (APA, 1996). Corporal punishment of children is practiced by over 90% of American parents, and over 50% of adolescents are physically punished by one or more parents (Straus & Yodanis, 1996). Families, providing the first and most intense experiences of learning for children in general, also have the potential for modeling violence, which may then affect children for the rest of their lives (cf. Eron & Slaby, 1994).

Cross-cultural research demonstrates that societies where wives are abused have condoned violence against women over many generations (Campbell, 1992). In a longitudinal, multimethod anthropological study conducted in rural Mexico, Fry (1993) compared the rates of aggression in two villages. The village where verbal approaches to parenting and discipline were favored over corporal punishment of children had a much lower rate of fights, assault, IPV, and homicide. Parents in this village expected their children to exercise self-control and to respond to reason. Fry suggests that verbal, nonviolent approaches to parenting have the power to break the intergenerational cycle of learned violence as a means of conflict resolution.

Dutton (1995) pointed out that the social learning approach to partner violence does account for individual variation in behavior and that it relates wife assault to a large body of research on aggression. However, social learning theory also posits that violence is triggered by an external event, and research demonstrates that partners of abusive men frequently report that their partner generates tension within himself, without the mediation of an external trigger. Some abusive men create the event that triggers their violence. Furthermore, social learning does not lead to violence in a linear fashion, for some men do everything to disidentify with their violent fathers, rather than identifying with the aggressor, and they succeed. Thus, although social learning theory does much to explain partner violence, it fails to account for the total psychological complexity of the event.

Cognitive-Behavioral Approach

Cognitive-behavioral theory holds that partners in a relationship are violent because of skills deficits. Violent men lack functional conflict resolution and communication skills. They are inexpert at recognizing or managing stress. They manufacture dysfunctional thoughts, distorted cognitions, and negative attributions toward their partners. Thus, when conflict arises in the relationship, or in their own dysfunctional thought processes, they fall into a pattern of problem solving that ultimately leads to violence (Holtzworth-Monroe & Hutchinson, 1993). Violent men consistently misinterpret their partner's actions as having hostile intent. Negative, hostile thoughts frequently lead to destructive, contemptuous criticism from either partner in a conflicted relationship. In 85% of troubled marriages studied by Gottman (1994), the man cuts himself off from the woman's criticism by stonewalling, a communication impasse that blocks all possibility of problem solving.

Partner abusive men appear to have a general template for thoughts that maintain distress, and a pessimistic outlook toward their intimate relationships (Seligman, 1991). This pessimistic view leaves these men very vulnerable to rumination on a list of grievances and to consequent righteous indignation, followed by overwhelming negative emotion. They become distressed, and they stay disturbed in a vicious cycle that practically ensures the continuance of negative partner interactions. Emotional flooding results, defined by Gottman (1994) as "susceptibility to frequent emotional distress" (p. 95). The flooded partner comes to think the worst of the spouse virtually all of the time, and problems appear severe and insoluble. Toxic self-talk, or cognitive distortion, leads to more and more emotional flooding. Men have been found to be physiologically more susceptible to flooding than women (Levenson, Cartensen, & Gottman, 1994). Even at lower levels of negativity they secrete more adrenaline and take longer to recover from autonomic arousal than women. This may explain the tendency to defend against flooding by stonewalling, so as not to be overwhelmed by negative emotion.

The research on partner abuse as it relates to cognitive-behavioral skills deficits is an important area in the theoretical understanding of marital conflict and subsequent violent behavior. This is evident from the fact that many treatment programs utilize a cognitive-behavioral treatment model for abusive partners (Dutton, 2006a; Saunders, 1991; Welland & Wexler, 2007; Wexler, 1999, 2006). Nevertheless, cognitive-behavioral theory does not explain the underlying psychological etiology of the cognitive dysfunction, but merely points out its existence. Theorists and researchers have attempted to deepen their grasp of the intrapsychic factors that affect an intimate partner's violent behavior.

Clinical Model/Psychopathology

There has been substantial debate over whether abusive men can be categorized as having any significant psychopathology (Feldman & Ridley, 1995). However, research conducted since the 1990s has given the field a much clearer picture of who the client is in actuality, rather than only theoretically or by report. The use of the Minnesota Multiphasic Personality Inventory (MMPI; Caesar, 1988) did not discriminate between partner abusive men and controls. However, with the administration of the Millon Clinical Multiaxial Inventory (MCMI), partner abusive men scored significantly higher than non–partner abusive men in borderline personality symptomatology, dependent/compulsive typology, passive-aggressive tendencies, and dysphoric symptoms (Hamberger & Hastings, 1986; Hastings & Hamberger, 1988; Dutton, Bodnarchuk, Kropp, Hart, & Ogloff, 1997a). Maiuro, Cahn, Vitaliano, Wagner, and Zegree (1988) reported a broad spectrum of diagnosable profiles among men in treatment for partner violence, including depression, impulse control disorder, learning disabilities, attention deficit disorder, cyclic mood disorder, adjustment reactions, and organic personality syndromes. In a review of studies conducted on partner abusive men, Bornstein (2006) found that trait dependency, but not dependent personality disorder, was significantly higher among partner abusive men than among controls. This emotional dependency leads to abuse when important relationships are perceived as under threat. Furthermore, advocates for battered women have been reluctant to accept the possibility that psychopathology may explain some of the etiology of partner abuse, for fear that this would in some way exonerate the partner abusive man from taking personal responsibility for his behavior (Jacobson, Gottman, & Wu Shortt, 1995; Walker, 1995). Most clinicians who treat IPV offenders are trained to take such pathology into account and to treat the client within the framework of group therapy, while still focusing on the need for accountability. Some partner abusive men clearly require ongoing individual therapy for resolution of trauma, attachment issues, and alcoholism, which will be discussed later.

Typologies of Partner Abusive Men

There is an extensive literature regarding the demographic and psychological characteristics of partner violent men in the general population of the United States. Four typologies have been discovered, which are commonly seen by both researchers and clinicians working with perpetrators (Dutton, 2006a; Holtzworth-Munroe, Meehan, Herron, Rehman, & Stuart, 2000). Briefly, these are Type I: Generally Violent-Antisocial or Instrumental-Undercontrolled; Type II: Family Only or Impulsive-Overcontrolled; Type III: Dysphoric-Borderline or Impulsive-Undercontrolled; and Type IV: Low-Level Antisocial. Holtzworth-Munroe, Meehan, Herron, Rehman, and Stuart (2003) found that these subtypes continue to differ among themselves over time. All groups of partner abusive men are more likely to demonstrate psychopathology than the general population (Geffner & Rosenbaum, 1990). Examination of individual differences has important treatment implications, as will be discussed later.

Type I: Generally Violent-Antisocial or Instrumental-Undercontrolled

Type I: Generally Violent-Antisocial or Instrumental-Undercontrolled partner abusive men are more emotionally abusive, more belligerent and contemptuous, more likely to report violence between their parents, more likely to be violent outside of the relationship, and more likely to be antisocial and drug dependent. These men are also more severely violent, including threatening to use or using a weapon against their partners and kicking, biting, and punching their partners. O'Leary (1993) found that the severity of violence by the perpetrator was positively correlated to the presence of a personality trait or disorder in the perpetrator that was associated with the violence. Jacobson et al. (1995) found two distinct populations of partner abusive men based on physiological reactivity, that is, whether the heart rate increases or decreases during the first 5 minutes of a marital interaction. Type I partner abusive men have lowered heart rates and are labeled "vagal reactors." This behavior was probably learned in childhood as a response to child abuse and serves to focus the attention of these men to maximize the impact of their verbal aggression and to achieve desired control over the partner. Their partners were also more likely to remain with them and to be more depressed and fearful than the partners of Type II partner abusive men. Saunders (1993) theorized that this group blocks painful childhood feelings with PTSD-type symptoms such as psychic numbing or dissociation.

Type II: Family Only or Impulsive-Overcontrolled

Type II: Family Only or Impulsive-Overcontrolled partner abusive men are more likely to slap their partners. Like Type I men, they have experienced very high levels of parental violence. These men are overwhelmed by emotional distress and respond with physical abuse when their anger escalates and their partner attempts to withdraw. This type was associated with less severe childhood victimization, more liberal gender role beliefs, and lower levels of anger. They reported less conflict and more satisfaction in their marriages. Type II partner abusive men had accelerated heart rate, a sign of defensive reaction as a response to stress. This subtype was more likely to suppress or overcontrol their emotions and to have a conformist personality. Alcohol was involved in one-third of this group's violent incidents, which Saunders (1993) suspected they use to help release painful emotions.

Type III: Dysphoric-Borderline or Impulsive-Undercontrolled

Type III: Dysphoric-Borderline or Impulsive-Undercontrolled men are characterized by extreme jealousy, anger, and depression, including suicidality. They were the least likely to have used alcohol during the violent incident. Although less likely to use severe physical violence, they engaged in frequent psychological abuse and reported their marriages to be the least satisfying. On the MCMI scales, this type's score was likely to be strongly correlated to passive-aggressive, avoidant, and borderline personality disorder. Saunders (1993) theorized that this emotionally volatile subtype may have suffered psychological and perhaps sexual abuse in childhood. Dutton (1995, 1998), in describing the abusive personality, theorized that more than rage is going on in the mind of the abusive man. The guiding force that focuses the rage must be something that has been learned about male–female relationships. His research on the Type III batterer focused on the cyclical or emotionally volatile abuser. This subtype has also been called "dysphoric borderline" (Holtzworth-Munroe & Stuart, 1994).

> Intimate violence is a complex action, filled with the rich symbolism of the woman as lover/savior/mother/betrayer. It is awash with obsessions and revulsions, tensions, jealousy, and rage. (Dutton, 2006a, p. 20)

Dutton found that those with cold, rejecting parents experienced more severe, extensive, and frequent PTSD-like symptoms of trauma. Those who had been regularly shamed as children had similar symptoms. The abusive men in his study were more affected by the trauma witnessed and/or received in childhood than strictly from the modeling of abusive behavior. Three factors must coexist for the abusive personality to develop: being shamed, especially by one's father; an insecure, angry-ambivalent attachment to one's mother; and the direct experience of abusiveness in the home. These men experience either abandonment or engulfment in their intimate relationships. They feel a need to shame and humiliate the other to obliterate their own shame and humiliation. Their partners describe them as having dual personalities. "I never know which one is coming in the door at night" and "He's living on an emotional roller coaster" are some of the statements hundreds of partners made in qualitative interviews. Their rage is displayed only to their partner, who is like a "lightning rod for all the emotional storms in their lives" (Dutton, 1995,).

Type IV: Low-Level Antisocial

Type IV: Low-Level Antisocial partner abusive men (Holtzworth-Munroe et al., 2000) commit less severe violence than the Type I perpetrator and yet are higher on the continuum of violence than the Type II batterer. Their psychological profile is also more similar to the Type I batterer than the other types. Holtzworth-Munroe and colleagues theorize that many of the men who attend IPV treatment who were formerly classified as Type II may in fact fit better into this fourth category, based on their histories and their personality characteristics.

In the area of typologies, no research other than a study by Welland, Robinson, Elliott, and Arellano (unpublished) is currently available in the literature that has been conducted specifically with the Latino population of partner abusive men. Welland and colleagues demonstrated in an empirical study of Latino partner abusive men that alcohol abuse, drug abuse, psychological abuse from the mother in childhood, physical abuse from the father, trauma symptoms, low self-esteem, and insecure/avoidant attachment styles were significantly more prevalent in Latino domestic violence perpetrators than in their nonviolent counterparts. We will expand on these results in later chapters.

Attachment Theory and Its Application to the Violent Man

Sonkin and Dutton (2003) stated that violent men who grew up in families where the attachment figure was not sufficiently present, attentive, or responsive expended much energy focusing on whether or not the attachment figure would meet their needs. According to attachment theory (Holtzworth-Munroe, Stuart, & Hutchinson, 1997), "individuals internalize their experience with caretakers, forming an internal representation or 'working model' of relationships" (p. 728). These same questions are evoked in their adult relationships, consciously or unconsciously. Adult attachment theory focuses on the bond between adult intimate partners and describes their conflict resolution and stress management strategies. The working models of relationships guide partner selection and predict affect regulation style (Gormley, 2005).

Securely attached individuals have more positive beliefs about relationships, longer-lasting romantic relationships, and less jealousy. Partner abusive men have been shown to have significantly higher levels of insecure or of fearful attachment. Insecure attachment is also known as anxious-ambivalent attachment and includes excessive anguish on separation, followed by anger, resistance, and difficulty being comforted. Excessive jealousy is also found in this style, produced by a deep-seated fear of abandonment (Holtzworth-Munroe et al., 1997). Anxious adults also engage in excessive help-seeking behaviors, are impulsive, have difficulty with affect regulation, are angry and resentful, have displaced aggression, and have lower levels of self-control (Lopez & Brennan, 2000). Fearful attachment is also called anxious-avoidant attachment in the literature. These men are afraid of becoming close to others so as not to be hurt and tend to have a dismissing style with their partners. They give the impression of avoiding dependency, but they too are fearful of being abandoned. Lopez and Brennan (2000) described these adults as having trouble with intimacy and closeness, having restricted, overcontrolled affect, having limited emotional intelligence, and being defensive, angry, and given to rages.

Partner abusive men who are insecurely attached can benefit from understanding why they have trouble regulating their anxiety and why they feel a need to control others to soothe their emotions. But beyond insight, one of the primary goals of therapy for these men is to develop new and effective ways to manage their attachment-related anxiety. The therapist must be the soothing voice he is so desperately seeking until the client learns to find that voice within himself. This will come about if therapy focuses on affect regulation, which is an integral part of most programs, but not necessarily explicitly connected to attachment issues.

Psychodynamic/Self Psychology Approach

Research has demonstrated that partner abusive men experience a sense of helplessness and powerlessness that leads them to seek to control their partner by any means (Babcock, Waltz, Jacobson, & Gottman, 1993). The psychodynamic theory of self psychology has been applied to the internal phenomena theorized to be at work in the intrapsychic and interpersonal space of the abuser (Wexler, 1999). Partner violence can be conceptualized as a desperate attempt to reestablish self-cohesion, or a sense of personal integration, when the assaultive man feels that his fragile sense of self is being threatened.

The self psychology approach proposes that some partner abusive men resort to violence as a means to regain power because of a sense of profound helplessness, dependency, and fragmentation. The outcome of their behavior may be very negative, but the intent is to protect the sense of self (Brown, 2004; Wexler, 1999). Violence becomes a functional response to a deeply felt psychological need, rather than merely a sociocultural response. This approach does not discard theories of cognitive misattributions, sociocultural scripts regarding masculine superiority, or social learning as important components of the phenomenon of partner violence. Rather, the self psychology approach attempts to enter the subjective world of the abusive man as well, to explore the narcissistic injury, or emotional vulnerability, that the man may experience prior to the violent episode.

Dutton and Holtzworth-Munroe (1997) pointed to a traumatic upbringing as the precursor to exaggerated anger, jealousy, anxiety, proneness to shame, and consequent blaming behavior; partner abusive men with histories of childhood violence and shaming tend to respond to perceived abandonment or rejection with outbursts of anger that mask all other unacceptable emotions. Through some lack of affective attunement on the part of early caregivers, a common experience for many abusive men raised in abusive and neglectful homes, the psychological development of the child is cut short, and he lacks the ability to self-soothe (Wexler, 1999). As a result, abusive men look to their partners to provide them with a selfobject experience, a relationship where they have an ally who makes them feel strong, nurtured, and integrated. A selfobject experience provides an "organizing function," which is defined as "any experience that helps the person feel more organized internally" (Shapiro, 1995, p. 46). Affective attunement, new insight, or companionship can be organizing functions. The woman's perceived failure to provide such a selfobject experience leaves the man feeling helpless, powerless, ashamed, defective, and enraged. As this constellation of familiar feelings washes over him, in what Dutton (1995) called "a red tide," he succumbs to violence as a learned behavior, in order to short-circuit the pain of his emotions and to shift them onto his partner, so that he will not have to feel the shame in which he is engulfed.

By taking theoretical approaches to partner abuse a step further into the psyche of the abusive man, self psychology does not exonerate the violent man from taking responsibility for his behavior. However, an empathic approach has the advantage of understanding the subjective rationale for the behavior, as terrible and harmful as it may be objectively. This opens the door to treatment.

THEORIES OF ETIOLOGY OF IPV AMONG LATINOS

No specific research has been conducted with the male Latino population regarding of the etiology of IPV (Perilla et al., 1994). Perilla (1999) stated that IPV is a human rights issue, connected as it is to "torture, inhuman or degrading treatment or punishment" cited in the United Nations' Universal Declaration of Human Rights (1948), although it is not treated as such in legal case interpretation. Some theorists have hypothesized that histories of social oppression could be explanatory factors, unlike theorists in the United States who tend to focus more on personal history when reviewing proposed causative factors. In *Family Violence and Men of Color* (Carrillo & Tello, 1998), the various authors of chapters on different ethnic groups posited that the etiology of much of the IPV among men of color springs from their histories of being targets of racism and discrimination, not only in their own lives, but in preceding generations as well. They did not address the equally staggering statistics of male-to-female IPV in their countries of origin, where it is doubtful that racism and discrimination played such a powerful role. Although there is little doubt that social oppression plays a part in violent behavior, such a macro and exosystemic explanation of IPV among ethnic groups in the United States would appear to minimize the importance of the demographic and psychological risk factors described in the following section. It also fails to explain why there is such a high incidence of IPV in the sending countries of each of these ethnic groups. When treatment for partner abusive men (or anyone who utilizes violence against another human being) is discussed, we will advert to the crucial importance of taking personal responsibility for violent behavior, as a necessary step to stopping it and replacing it with more adaptive behavior. Thus, in later chapters when we discuss the issue of discrimination with our Latino clients, we choose not to make these experiences a large part of treatment, because men must own their personal behavior if it is to change. This can be done without exonerating the larger culture of the role it plays in socialization and oppression.

In their study of abused Latina women, Perilla and colleagues found that ecosystemic variables such as high levels of stress and the female partner making a greater contribution to the family income were positively related to abuse. Although the measure that they used to test for significance of the female holding traditional gender roles did not account for any of the variance, the finding that a woman's financial independence makes her more vulnerable to abuse suggests that gender role expectations on the part of the male of being the sole provider may have been involved (Perilla et al., 1994). This finding suggests some support for the sociocultural approach, where attitudes of male superiority might be threatened by a woman's receiving a higher wage than her partner. The variable that did account for the most variance in Perilla et al.'s study was the construct of mutuality, defined by Genero, Miller, and Surrey (1992) as empathy, communication, understanding, and mutual respect, or "the bidirectional movement of feelings, thoughts and activity between persons in a relationship" (p. 40). Low levels of mutuality were associated with high levels of abuse. This finding suggests that the cognitive-behavioral model of domestic violence, positing skills deficits in self-management

It was precisely mutuality that was missing in the relationships of the men we interviewed, as it is often missing in the relationships of the men in IPV therapy groups. Once these men have learned the rationale, necessity, and importance of these skills and have some experience putting them into practice in their relationship, healing begins to take place in many cases. Their partners frequently report that this aspect of their marriage is dramatically improved. Mutuality is thus related to relationship skill building as well as to learning and experiencing gender equality, while letting go of machismo.

and communication, may apply to partner abusive men. Apart from skills deficits, the habits of machismo are diametrically opposed to the concept of mutuality, which presupposes a certain regard for the other's dignity and equality to oneself.

WHAT PUTS MEN AT RISK TO BE VIOLENT IN THE HOME? RISK FACTORS

The World Health Organization (2002) identified some of the risk factors for various types of violence: prevailing cultural norms, poverty, social isolation, alcohol and drug abuse, and access to firearms. Being rejected or neglected by parents increases children's risk for aggressive and antisocial behavior, both as children and as adults. Addressing risk factors at different levels of the ecological model may contribute to decreases in more than one type of violence.

Researchers have been able to identify some of the most important risk factors that are related to partner abuse in the United States (Hotaling & Sugarman, 1986; Kaufman-Kantor & Jasinski, 1998; Saunders, 1993). Although risk markers are correlated to the perpetration of IPV and not considered causative, they must be taken into account for understanding the phenomenon, as well as for treatment and prevention (APA, 1996). Risk factors vary depending on the typologies mentioned above; however, there are three prominent risk factors that are found consistently across the population of partner abusive men.

Childhood Violence

A consistent risk marker for abusive men is having witnessed parental violence or being physically assaulted oneself (Hotaling & Sugarman, 1986), with witnessing being the stronger predictor (Ehrensaft et al., 2003; Kolbo, Blakely, & Engleman, 1996). Straus, Gelles, and Steinmetz (1980) found that when abuse as well as witnessing was experienced, the additive effect led to a rate of adult partner abuse 5 times higher than for men with nonviolent childhoods. In support of this, Caetano, Schafer, Clark, Cunradi, and Raspberry (2000) found that childhood experience of violence increases the risk of IPV in Latino families. In their study, over one-third of Latino partner abusive men had observed threats or acts of violence between their parents, and 50% reported being a victim of child abuse. Latinos of the medium acculturation group were at greater risk for IPV from both genders than the high or low acculturation groups. Aldarondo, Kaufman Kantor, and Jasinski (2002) found that a higher percentage of Mexican partner abusive men had witnessed father-to-mother

IPV as children than other Latinos or Anglos in their study, and that significantly more Puerto Rican partner abusive men had witnessed mother-to-father IPV, while Mexican men were significantly less likely to have witnessed this form of violence.

Experiencing violence in the family of origin and high levels of relationship conflict were positively correlated to the risk of wife assault among Mexican men. The risk of spouse assault among Mexican American men was increased by conflict and by lack of economic resources. Even ordinary corporal punishment toward male children is associated with violence toward both partner and children in adulthood, as well as with higher levels of depression, overall approval of violence, and increased marital conflict (Straus & Yodanis, 1996). Klevens, Restrepo, and Roca (2000) found that young Colombian men who received competent and nurturing parenting from at least one caregiver were more resilient than other youths who had not received positive effects from family environment to buffer them from negative impacts.

Low Socioeconomic Status, Unemployment, and Low Educational Achievement

Although partner abuse occurs in all economic and ethnic groups, the rate of assault in the lowest income families was over 5 times the rate in the highest income families in the first National Family Violence Survey, 11% versus 2% (Straus et al., 1980). Bensley et al. (2000) also found that low income level was associated with increased risk for IPV, although 18% of female victims reported incomes over $50,000. In addition, low education was associated with increased risk for IPV. Blue-collar workers, the unemployed, and the underemployed had higher rates, as did African Americans and Latinos in the Straus et al. survey. The stress of unemployment, inner-city living, and low income affect minority groups at much higher rates than the general population. Along with earning low income, the abusive man is frequently also poorly educated. It is difficult to separate poverty from ethnicity as independent predictors of violence.

Using statistics from the U.S. Census Bureau's 2005 American Community Survey, the Pew Hispanic Center (2006b) calculated that the median income of Latino households in 2005 was $36,000, while Whites earned $50,000, Asians $59,000, and Blacks $30,000. Twenty-three percent of Latinos lived in poverty in 2005, versus 10% of Whites, 12% of Asians, and 25% of Blacks. A total of 64% of Hispanics in 2005 were Mexicans (40% foreign-born), 9% were Puerto Rican, and 3.5% were Cuban. All other nationalities of Hispanics in the United States were less than 3% each of the total. Hispanics had the lowest median age, at 27 years. Large numbers of Hispanics have moved into states where there was previously a small percentage. In some states, the increase is over 50% in the past 5 years. Over 75% of Hispanics who have arrived in this country since 1990 are unable to speak English well, highlighting the need for therapeutic services in Spanish. Fifty-two percent of foreign-born Hispanics received less than a high school education.

The variables of low socioeconomic status, unemployment, and low educational achievement have been identified as environmental stressors that heighten the likelihood of violent means of conflict resolution in Latino adolescents (Hill, Soriano, Chen, & LaFromboise, 1994). Similarly, the authors' survey of partner abusive Latino men (Welland & Ribner, 2001), detailed in a later chapter, found that poverty, unemployment, and low levels of academic achievement were very common among Latino perpetrators mandated to IPV treatment. A later demographic questionnaire administered to Latino perpetrators as part of a preliminary study of risk factors demonstrated very similar demographic findings (Welland et al., unpublished).

Alcohol Use and Abuse

"Strong links have been found between alcohol use and the occurrence of IPV in many countries. Evidence suggests that alcohol use increases the occurrence and severity of domestic violence" (WHO, 2006, p. 1). Tolman and Bennett (1990) have shown that alcohol is not a directly causative factor in partner abuse. Some men who drink frequently do not abuse their partners, but those who drink chronically are at greater risk. The authors hypothesize that the relationship between chronicity and violence may be due to family arguments over drinking, paranoia from cognitive deficits, or severe withdrawal symptoms, including irritability. Fals-Stewart (2003) has shown that the likelihood of engaging in any IPV among partner abusive men, even after controlling for relationship conflict and severity of alcohol abuse, is 8–11 times greater on days when men drank alcohol as compared to days of no drinking. Severe IPV was 11 times more likely on drinking days versus non–drinking days. Drinking, especially heavy drinking, by previously partner abusive men represents a very significant risk factor for recurrence of physical violence.[1]

Violence and the Family (APA, 1996) suggests that a history of family violence may be the single most influential risk factor for the abuse of alcohol and drugs. Victims may self-medicate to numb the emotional aftermath of abuse. Perpetrators of partner abuse frequently have a history of childhood victimization, and many may abuse substances to dull the memories and the symptoms of posttraumatic stress disorder (Saunders, 1995; Welland et al., unpublished). The excessive use of alcohol as well as the use of cocaine and methamphetamine are associated with more severe violence (APA, 1996), although some research suggests that severe intoxication reduces violence (Coleman & Straus, 1986; Neff, Holaman, & Schluter, 1995). Brecklin and Ullman (2002) found that alcohol use by physically and sexually abusive men is related to more severe assault outcomes, such as physical injuries and the need for medical attention, than is no alcohol use.

Tolman and Bennett (1990) calculated that, on average, 60% of partner abusive men across 13 studies were chronic alcohol abusers or alcoholics, a finding that is in accordance with what is clinically observed in IPV treatment groups. However, not all of the men who drank frequently and who committed violent acts were intoxicated at the time of the incident. Some men use alcohol abuse as an excuse to explain their violence (Kaufman Kantor & Straus, 1990); Gelles (1974) found that some men become intoxicated specifically to be able to engage more freely in the violence they are planning. Sugarman, Aldarondo, and Boney-McCoy (1996) demonstrated that alcoholic drinking on the part of the female partner is as much a risk marker for her being abused as is the male's drinking. The relationship is a complex one: The woman may use alcohol to escape from a violent reality, and/or her drinking may add to the marital conflict, which increases the risk of violence.

Some mention should be made of the proliferation of methamphetamine abuse in the United States, because the use of this illicit substance is often associated with uncontrolled, violent outbursts. Taylor and Chermack (1993) found that drugs with a depressive effect are associated with violence, while Fagan (1990) and others have demonstrated a link between IPV and the use of stimulants such as cocaine and methamphetamines. Clinical observation would also indicate that methamphetamine or "crystal" use is related to violence between partners, whether the perpetrator was actually arrested while under the influence or not. Countless incidents of partner abuse go unreported, especially when both parties are using illegal drugs and do not wish to involve law enforcement in their relationship.

In a study conducted by Lipsky, Caetano, Field, and Bazargan (2005) of Blacks and Latinos utilizing an urban emergency department, male respondents with a history of IPV perpetration were 2.5 times more likely to report heavy drinking than nonviolent men and 4 times more likely to report illicit drug use. The authors suggest routine screening for alcohol abuse and IPV in emergency rooms as a potential contribution to the prevention of future IPV. Field, Caetano, and Nelson (2004) found that approval of marital aggression and the expectation of male aggressivity were significantly higher among Blacks and Latinos than among Whites. Across ethnicities, approval of marital aggression, alcohol as an excuse for misbehavior, and impulsivity were more common among men than women.

Alcohol in Latino Populations

In general, Latin American culture, comprising the 21 countries from Mexico to Argentina, tolerates and promotes heavy drinking, according to a study by Negrete (cited in Tseng & MacDermott, 1981), although there are regional differences. Alcohol-related mortality figures (accidents, homicide, and violence) for Latin American countries are among the highest in the world, especially in Mexico, Argentina, and Chile, which have the largest urban centers. While the proportion of all deaths worldwide that can be attributed to alcohol use is 1.5%, that figure is 4.5% for the Latin American and Caribbean nations (Pyne, Claeson, & Correia, 2002).

Frequent festive occasions are accompanied by drinking, and drunkenness is common. The cultural pressure to drink, and "to hold one's liquor," is primarily directed at men. Heavy drinking is a sign of virility; there are 10 male problem drinkers to every 1 female. However, no significant difference was found in approval of heavy drinking for reasons of virility between Hispanics and Whites in a national survey (Caetano, Clark, & Tam, 1998). Neff, Prihoda, and Hoppe (1991) found that machismo was a factor in all groups where alcohol consumption was a problem, not just among Latinos.

Pyne and colleagues found that men in Latin America are more likely to drink excessively than are women, and men are also less likely to abstain from alcohol use. Alcohol plays an important role in instigating unsafe sexual practices and violence, especially toward family—women and children. Women have far fewer problems with alcoholism than men (in Mexico, 1% of women and 14% of men). Socioeconomic status also reveals important differences. In Argentina, for example, among men in wealthy areas, 0.6% were alcoholics and 7.5% were heavy drinkers. In poor areas, in contrast, the respective figures were 13% and 20%. Work supported by the World Bank, such as social capital research, the Global Burden of Disease and Voices of the Poor studies, and numerous consultations with civil society organizations and indigenous communities reveals that the poor in developing countries perceive alcohol use—particularly among men—as detrimental to their well-being and their efforts to build human and social capital (Pyne et al., 2002). Tolerance of alcoholism on the part of spouses has been high in the past, regardless of the drinker's neglect of the family and his violence. Nevertheless, in 2002, women in a Mexican village, fed up with their men stumbling home drunk or falling over in the corn fields, blockaded beer delivery trucks from access to selling alcohol in their community, having finally decided to take matters into their own hands. It is unclear for how long this approach was effective, but it demonstrates the growing frustration of women in Latin America with

alcohol abuse and a willingness to combat it (http://www.briansbelly.
com/news/archive1202.shtml, 2002).

Research with Latinos in the United States has shown that alcohol
abuse among high-risk segments of the Mexican American population
is a major social and health problem (Gilbert & Cervantes, 1986). Mexican Americans, especially males, are overrepresented in alcohol treatment
programs (Leal, 1990). Mexican Americans drink more, have more problems related to alcohol, and are more accepting of drinking than Cuban
Americans or Puerto Ricans (Caetano, 1988). Forty-four percent of a
randomized sample of Mexican Americans were frequent heavy drinkers,
and 22% of these met the criteria for problem drinking, while only 8%
of Puerto Ricans and 3% of Cuban Americans did. Mexican American
women also drank more than their other Latina counterparts, with 7%
reporting problems. Mexican Americans perceive drinking as a way of
being friendly and are more tolerant of drunkenness than other Latinos.
The Mexican American pattern of drinking is similar to the pattern studied in Mexico, except that Mexican Americans drink more often, perhaps
a reflection of acculturation and greater buying power. Caetano et al.
(1998) found that acculturative, socioeconomic, and minority stress all
contribute to higher levels of alcohol consumption among ethnic minorities in the United States. However, because of the heterogeneity within
the Latino ethnic group, broad generalizations are likely to be inaccurate
and invalid when Latinos are studied as a single group, rather than by
individual nationality.

In a study of Latina women whose partners were abusive, the men
who drank more frequently perpetrated higher levels of abuse (Perilla
et al., 1994). In contrast, Aldarondo et al. (2002) found no significant
difference in the male-reported levels of alcohol consumption among
Anglo and Latino partner abusive men. However, when Mexican American women reported their abusive male partner's alcohol consumption, it
was significantly higher than for other Latino and Anglo groups of partner abusive men. On the other hand, Olona (1993) found that there was
no significant relationship between alcohol abuse and IPV for the Latino
men living in Los Angeles in his study. He hypothesized that violent men
may be abusive regardless of whether they are drinking or not. Significantly, however, 88% of the Latino partner abusive men he studied met
the criteria for alcoholism using the Michigan Alcoholism Screening Test;
43% admitted that they had been drinking before their arrest. Fifty-four
percent of the men in the control group, who had not been mandated to
domestic violence treatment, although many endorsed items demonstrating partner abuse, met criteria for alcoholism. These findings corroborate
previous research showing that alcohol abuse and dependence is a serious
problem in some sectors of the population (Leal, 1990).

OTHER RISK FACTORS IN PARTNER ABUSE

Behavioral Deficits

Several studies report that violent male partners lack assertiveness skills, especially in initiating assertive communication (Maiuro et al., 1988; Rosenbaum & O'Leary, 1981). Interestingly, this low assertiveness was found in the men who felt the most need for power. Dutton and Strachan (1987) hypothesized that the need for power in such men produces greater anger and anxiety, which then explodes into violence when they are unable to muster the necessary skills to manage their affect.

Insecure or Avoidant Attachment

Holtzworth-Munroe, Stuart, and Hutchinson (1997) found that men violent to their partners were significantly more likely to have an insecure or avoidant attachment style with their partner than nonviolent men. Attachment theory as it relates to IPV has already been discussed above. The findings of Holtzworth-Munroe et al. were replicated by Welland et al. (unpublished) in a population of partner abusive Mexican immigrant men. Such attachment styles make it more likely that men will struggle with jealousy and misperceptions of their partners' intentions, prompting them to lash out when they feel threatened with abandonment, and that they will have difficulty establishing a healthy, secure relationship.

Psychopathology

This risk factor was discussed more fully under theories of etiology. Broad definitions of psychopathology, for example, Axis II disorders, could probably be applied to most abusers (Saunders, 1995). Most partner abusive men who have been studied showed some elevations on the clinical subscales of the MCMI, although there is no consistent profile (Hamberger & Hastings, 1986). Alcoholic partner abusive men were most likely to have clinical elevations on the MCMI (Hamberger, Hastings, & Lohr, 1991). On the MMPI, a study by Bernard and Bernard (1984) demonstrated that the average abuser appears distrustful, isolated, insecure, and alienated; he has a strong masculine identity with which he is overly concerned.

Age

As is the case with other crimes, men who assault their partners tend to be younger than nonviolent men. Men under 30 years of age have been shown to have a rate of partner assault 3 times higher than those over 30, that is, 9% versus 3% (Straus, Gelles & Steinmetz, 1980). Hirschi and Gottfredson (1983) and Gelles (1998) hypothesized that the biological aging process and learning through experience may be explanatory factors. The Latino population is the youngest in the United States; 40% of Latinos are under the age of 20 (U.S. Bureau of the Census, 2006a).

Given the statistics on the general youth of the Latino population, one would expect to see a large percentage of men under 30 in IPV groups. However, our research and experience suggest that this is not the case (Welland & Ribner, 2001; Welland et al., unpublished). The median age of clients in Spanish IPV groups in San Diego is 34 years old, and there are typically few men under 25 in groups. What does this mean? One hypothesis is that their partners have not called the police for previous assaults, bearing up before finally taking action. Another is that the women began to see cumulative negative effects on their children as they developed and this was the crucial factor in the decision to stop the violence. Because only 54% of men in an anonymous survey (Welland & Ribner, 2001) had been violent to their partners on at least one previous occasion before their arrest and subsequent treatment, we do not really know if either of these hypotheses would hold up under empirical scrutiny.

Anger

Anger is not consistently related to violence, in that measures of anger do not show that assaulters are angrier than nonassaulters (Tolman & Bennett, 1990). However, measures that are maritally specific reveal that in certain situations with a woman, an abusive man may be angrier than a nonabusive one. Saunders (1995) suggested that such men displace their anger onto women or become angry when a woman breaks patriarchal rules. The inconsistent relationship of violence to anger may be a result of individual differences between subtypes, such as the Type I batterer who does not show signs of anger as he engages in severe, instrumental violence (Jacobson et al., 1995), as compared to a Type II partner abusive man who becomes overwhelmed by emotional discomfort, or the Type III partner abusive man who struggles with affect regulation and engages in uncontrolled outbursts of anger. When treatment is discussed in later chapters, it will be seen that anger management strategies are a common component of IPV programs for both men and women. Nevertheless, because anger is not the principal contributing factor in episodes of IPV, anger management programs alone are not sufficient to diminish or eliminate it.

Stress

Barling and Rosenbaum (1986) suggested that work-related stress may be as important a factor as family-related stress in violent relationships. However, studies on this factor have produced conflicting results regarding the salience of stress. Saunders (1993) showed that men displace their anger and frustration from work onto those least likely to retaliate, their family. Perilla et al. (1994) defined stress in five different domains: occupational, parental, cultural/family conflict, marital, and immigration; they found that a higher level of stress among abused Latina women was positively correlated to higher levels of abuse perpetrated against them. This research has not been replicated with Latino men to date.

Depression and Low Self-Esteem

Abusive men score above the norm on measures of depression (Tolman & Bennett, 1990); however, it is unclear whether the depression is the due to arrest, separation, and adverse legal consequences or to premorbid factors (Saunders, 1995). Hotaling and Sugarman (1986) showed that men who batter have low self-esteem; again, the causal role is difficult to untangle. Welland et al. (unpublished) found that the violent Latino men they studied had significantly lower self-esteem than their nonviolent counterparts and that low self-esteem was correlated to history of childhood abuse and insecure attachment styles. This finding suggests that low self-esteem may be premorbid to the abusive behavior rather than related to arrest and separation only; however, more research is needed. Perpetrators of the dysphoric/borderline Type III, as mentioned above, are most likely to demonstrate symptoms of depression, frequently of a long-standing duration (Holtzworth-Munroe et al., 2000).

High Levels of Marital Conflict

When there is a high degree of conflict in a marital relationship, there is greater likelihood that there will also be violence, and that the violence will be ongoing (Aldarondo & Sugarman, 1996). Aldarondo et al. (2002) found that the most stable risk factor for IPV across a sample of Latino men from different ethnic groups was a high level of conflict in the relationship. High-conflict relationships are more likely to be violent when the female dominates the couple's decision making (Coleman & Straus, 1986).

Husbands who abuse their wives are more likely to report the husband demand/wife withdraw interaction pattern than nonviolent men

(Babcock et al., 1993). In this interaction style, which is the opposite of the gender-stereotyped pattern, the demand role is seen as less powerful because it implies wanting something, whereas the one to withdraw wishes to maintain the status quo. When the couple's communication skills are poor, violence is likely to increase as male demand/female withdraw increases and the male's decision-making power decreases. Violent men may respond with aggression to compensate for this lack of marital power (Prince & Arias, 1994).

Generalized Aggression/Antisocial Traits

Men who batter severely are likely to be violent outside the home as well; they may have a criminal history. These men have been categorized as the Type I, or "generally aggressive" subtype; their psychological profile is most likely to reveal antisocial traits or antisocial personality disorder (Saunders, 1993, 1995).

Severely violent antisocial men are infrequently seen in the clinical population of Latino men who are mandated to treatment groups in San Diego. Clinicians hypothesize that perhaps they are incarcerated for a more severe crime of partner abuse or for some other crime, or that they have managed, true to their antisocial/narcissistic personality style, to evade detection or prosecution. Because men of this type have been observed to be most likely to want to monopolize the group, to bash women, and to ridicule therapists and clients, other men in Latino groups are generally relieved when such men are forced, by their lack of compliance with court rules (such as payment and attendance), to leave the group.

TRADITIONAL GENDER ROLES:
A NON–RISK FACTOR?

Cross-cultural studies by Levinson (1989) and Yllo (1983) have shown that, on a macrosocial level, patriarchal norms and male dominance are risk factors for violence. However, in six studies reviewed by Hotaling and Sugarman (1986), traditional sex role attitudes did not distinguish partner abusive men from non–partner abusive men, except when women reported their assailant's attitudes, where they tended to identify dominant male gender roles (Smith, 1990; Walker, 1984). This discrepancy may be due to studies of the more rigid gender role beliefs of Type I partner abusive men, who are also the most likely to cause severe injury, and whose partners are most likely to seek refuge in a shelter (Saunders, 1993). This is the population that Johnson (1995) called "patriarchal terrorists." In research with the general population of abusers, traditional gender role beliefs have not been shown to be a risk factor, as counterintuitive as this may seem (Saunders, 1993, 1995). One reason for this may be that the measures of gender role behaviors may not be sensitive to the type of gender-related beliefs that are likely to result in violence.

However, Olona (1993) found that power and control motives in Latino male partner abusive men, as measured by the Abusive Behavior Inventory (Shepard & Campbell, 1992), were significantly related to abuse, including psychological abuse. Nevertheless, the measure Olona used did not examine the motivation of the abusive incidents but merely their content, leaving the interpretation of motives to the theory of the researcher. Welland et al. (unpublished) found that violent Latino men did not differ in their gender-related relationship and family behaviors from nonviolent Latino men. The only significant difference between the groups was that nonviolent men were more likely to endorse the factor labeled *Fostering Values and Unity*, which included fostering emotional stability, maintaining respect and family unity, teaching moral values, and establishing a dialogue with children. The control group did this significantly more than the violent men, but all groups scored well above the theoretical mean. Given that Latina women regularly report machismo as a source or trigger of IPV (Belknap & Sayeed, 2003; Coffin-Romig, 1997; WHO, 2005), research results in this area continue to mystify. Qualitative research may be the most effective means of obtaining an accurate picture of the effect of traditional gender roles, specifically machismo, on family life and the incidence of IPV.

Acculturation/Immigration and Cultural Change

In one study of Latina women abused by their partners, level of acculturation, measured by English-language competency, was not shown to be associated with their high levels of depression or their low levels of self-esteem (Perilla et al., 1994). However, acculturative stress is frequently hypothesized to be a factor in the state of mental health of immigrants (Falicov, 1996). Perhaps the measure used did not discriminate sufficiently in addressing the complex issue of acculturation. In fact, the stress subscales mentioned in the Perilla et al. study suggest the presence of acculturation stress, for example, cultural/family conflict, and immigration stress.

PROTECTIVE FACTORS

The work of Werner and Smith (1992) has shown that in general, about one-third of individuals at risk for psychological or developmental problems do not, in fact, develop them. Vanderbilt-Adriance (2006) showed that, among a sample of low-income boys, child IQ, nurturant parenting, parent–child relationship quality, and quality of the parent's relationship measured in early childhood were all significantly associated with low levels of antisocial behavior and high levels of social skills at ages 11 and 12. No studies to date have examined the role of ethnic factors and values in promoting resilience against risk factors for involvement in IPV.

Hill et al. (1994) theorized that ethnic culture may serve as a protective mechanism in several ways. The group may provide norms and values that influence behavior under stressful circumstances, such as knowing how to achieve in the mainstream culture as well as in their own, knowing how to work through racism, and knowing how to deal with cultural conflicts. A positive sense of personal and group identity may be provided by the ethnic culture, which can counteract discrimination and may reduce the risk for violence and self-destructive behaviors (Helms, 1990; Holinger et al., 1994, cited in Hill et al., 1994). Closeness to extended family may serve as a protective factor for abusive men, providing them with a support system to assist them in diffusing stress and reminding the abusive man of his responsibilities in the culture. Extended family may also serve to protect the abused partner and to offer shelter, economic assistance, and emotional support to the woman and frequently her children as well (Vega, 1990).

Hawkins et al. (cited in Hill et al., 1994) theorize that the development of bonds to traditional agents of socialization within the minority culture, such as school, church, and community agencies, may serve as a protective factor for the involvement of youth in gangs. Church attendance was shown in Calhoun's study (1991, cited in Hill et al., 1994) to be a primary variable in protecting youth from serious involvement in violence, due to religion's function as a means of bonding them to the social contract. Ellison, Bartkowski, and Anderson (1999) found that regular attendance at religious services was inversely associated with self-reported perpetration of domestic violence for men and women. This protective factor did not apply to those men and women who only occasionally attended services. To our knowledge, protective factor hypotheses have not as yet been specifically applied to Latino IPV.

In the next chapter, we enter specifically into the characteristics of Latino culture in the United States as described by theorists and clinicians, with special emphasis on areas that are important to the understanding of IPV, such as gender role socialization, immigration, acculturation, and treatment issues for Latino men.

NOTE

1. Judge Susan Finlay of the Superior Court of San Diego County (Lightman & Byrne, 2004) and we, through our clinical experience, have noted that in nearly every case of treatment failure for men in IPV programs who recidivate, alcohol or drug abuse is the principal factor in relapse.

CHAPTER 3

Latino Culture: Approaches to Therapy

Whenever a discussion of culture arises, it is always necessary to begin with a disclaimer: No culture is so homogeneous that a certain set of beliefs or behaviors can accurately be said to apply to all members of the culture. There are multiple dimensions of belonging for every person in a culture, as a cursory reflection on our own membership, ours and yours, the reader, in the culture of the United States will demonstrate. Nevertheless, there are certain features of cultures that can be said to be noticeable to "outsiders" and that lend themselves to research and analysis, even though there is plenty of heterogeneity within the culture. It is not our intention to stereotype Latino culture. This is particularly difficult given that there are 21 countries in Latin America, each with its own history, literature, music, and culture. Nevertheless, before we begin our discussion on treating Latino men for IPV, it seems essential to summarize the many research efforts that have been made to define Latino culture to some degree.

DEFINITION OF CULTURE

The multicultural model of psychotherapy emphasizes values and is based on the assumption that each cultural and environmental set of circumstances or conditions produces a unique set of coping techniques, or cognitive styles, crucial to personality development and functioning (Ramírez, 1991). If culture has such a broad effect on personality functioning, its importance when developing a treatment model for partner abuse cannot be overemphasized.

Triandis (1994) defines culture as follows: Culture is a set of human-made objective and subjective elements that in the past have increased the probability of survival and resulted in satisfaction of the participants in an ecological niche, and thus became shared among those who could communicate with each other because they had a common language and lived in the same time and place (p. 22). From the "multidimensional position," family theorist and therapist Celia Falicov (1995) defined culture as

> those sets of shared world views, meaning, and adaptive behaviors derived from simultaneous membership and participation in a multiplicity of contexts, such as rural, urban, or suburban setting; language, age, gender, cohort, family configuration, race, ethnicity, religion, nationality, socioeconomic status, employment, education, occupation, sexual orientation, political ideology; migration and stage of acculturation. (p. 373)

Triandis's definition views culture and resultant ethnicity as more of a static reality, whereas Falicov addresses the complexity inherent in groups whose identity is defined by simultaneous membership in multiple contexts. For this reason, it is difficult and often inaccurate to make generalizations about any ethnic group, because the many contexts of each person's and family's life produce a more "varied, fluid, unpredictable, and shifting" concept of group membership than the ethnic-focused approach (Falicov, 1995, p. 374). In the literature on Latinos, mention is always made of the fact that there are large cultural differences between one Latin American country and another (Paniagua, 1994). Furthermore, individual differences are greater within any given culture than between cultures (Sue & Sue, 2002). The danger of stereotyping and overgeneralization is always present if too much credence is placed on "normative" behavior in a given group. There are enormous individual differences in one's own ethnic group depending on the multiple contexts in which one lives; no statement that is made will apply to everyone. However, in our survey (cited in chapter 4), we found that the Latino men mandated to treatment had many cultural contexts in common. The in-depth interviews provided a window into several Latino men's experience of their own abusive behavior, in the cultural context in which they move and make meaning for themselves. Understanding this commonality of experience and to some extent, of worldview, can help therapists to explore with them the reasons behind partner abuse and to codiscover culturally congruent ways to reduce and eventually eliminate violent behavior in their relationships. This discovery was the principal reason for our research with Latino partner abusive men.

Research on Latino culture has identified certain global values or beliefs that characterize the cultural worldview of the Latino population in general (Marín & Marín, 1991). Because of the close proximity of Latin America, and Mexico in particular, including continuous contact and immigration, the forces acting to preserve the culture of origin are strong (Bach-y-Rita, 1982).

Interdependence

Interdependence versus independence as a central component of worldview has been studied in many cultures (Markus & Kitayama, 1991). Interdependent, or allocentric, societies place a high value on the needs, objectives, and points of view of the ingroup, while individualistic cultures select their behaviors on the basis of personal objectives, attitudes, and values that may not be at all similar to those of the ingroup (Marín & Triandis, 1985). Triandis (1989) suggested that collectivism (versus individualism) is a major dimension of cultural difference in social behavior. The collectivist view has been shown to prevail in the Latino population (Marín & Triandis, 1985; Hofstede, 1980), in contrast to the competitive, achievement-oriented dominant culture of the United States. The interdependent view of reality is also congruent with Catholic principles and values, which provide a foundation for living for many in Latino culture (Bach-y-Rita, 1982). Strong pre-Hispanic influences are also present, which, like those of Native Americans in the United States, place a high value on interdependence, self-sacrifice for the benefit of the group, and family cohesion (Bach-y-Rita, 1982; Sue & Sue, 2002).

Interdependence as a construct includes conformity, field sensitivity, readiness to be influenced by others, mutual empathy, willingness to sacrifice for the members of the ingroup, and trust of ingroup members (Marín & Marín, 1991). Field sensitivity refers to the tendency to personalize communication, to focus more on nonverbal than on verbal communication, to be outgoing, warm, and informal in interpersonal relationships, to seek to achieve for the group rather than oneself, and to be more focused on relationships than on tasks or goals (Ramírez, 1991).

Familismo

Researchers have shown in several studies that the importance of family is central to Latino values (Alvirez & Bean, 1976; Marín & Marín, 1991), although Baca-Zinn (1982) challenged the idea that *familismo* is a cultural entity and proposed that it is a structural one instead. As a cultural value, *familismo* involves strong identification with and attachment to nuclear and extended family and strong feelings of loyalty, reciprocity, and solidarity among family members (Triandis, Kashima, Hui, Lisansky, & Marín, 1982). *Familismo* helps to protect individuals from stress and provides a natural support system. It includes a perceived obligation to provide emotional and material support to extended family, reliance on relatives for these supports, and the perception of relatives as sources for advice on behavior and attitudes. Identifying the ways in which a behavior change may positively affect an individual's family has been shown to be a powerful motivator in therapeutic interventions (Marín, Marín, Pérez-Stable, Otero-Sabogal, & Sabogal, 1990).

Research has shown that even after three or more generations from the time of immigration, a highly integrated kinship network persists among Mexican Americans and that the extended family is the primary source of coping with emotional stress (Vega, 1990). Assumptions that Mexican families would eventually "evolve" away from traditional kinship networks to the modern, industrialized model of more independently functioning nuclear families was not shown to be inevitable in Vega's review of Latino research, where it appears that any type of kinship structure is compatible with urban society.

Immigrant Mexican Americans participate in large kin networks and engage in high rates of visiting and exchange. Latinos migrate toward, not away from, their kin networks (Mindel, 1980). However, first-generation immigrants tend to have smaller social networks than families who have been in the United States over generations. This is suggestive of a lack of the culturally normative social support (Vega & Kolody, 1985). However, in chapter 4, we will discuss our finding that the partner abusive men in our study did not appear to suffer from a lack of extended family support as a particular stressor contributing to partner abuse.

Values in Interpersonal Relations: *Respeto, Personalismo,* and *Simpatía*

Hofstede (1980) suggested that "power distance" is another important variable in differentiating cultural groups. This is defined as the measure of interpersonal power or influence that exists between two individuals. High power distance societies, such as Latino culture, promote deference and respect (*respeto*) toward certain powerful groups, individuals, or professions. Thus, many Latinos, especially if they are less powerful in the culture, value conformity and obedience and are very hesitant to disagree with those in power. A cursory examination of the social and political history of Latin America, with widespread oppression of the poor and of dissidents, would serve to explain the adaptiveness of these traits (Keen, 1992).

Respeto "dictates the appropriate deferential behavior toward others on the basis of age, social position, economic status, and sex" (Comas-Díaz & Duncan, 1985, p. 464). *Respeto* is a core concept found at every level of society, including between members of the family; it is especially expected toward authority figures such as parents and elders. The father of the family expects deference from both his wife and his children. Connected to *respeto* is *educación*, which refers to the level that respect is practiced interpersonally (i.e., good social graces) rather than to level of schooling (Paniagua, 1994). The importance of conducting social relationships with *respeto* and *dignidad* (dignity) cannot be overemphasized (Triandis, Lisansky, Marín, & Betancourt, 1984).

Personalismo refers to the Latino tendency to be more oriented toward people than toward impersonal relationships (Bernal & Gutiérrez, cited in Paniagua, 1994). The expectation of a more personal relationship can lead to a feeling of coldness if the other remains at a distance, refuses hugs, or avoids sharing personal information (Paniagua, 1994). Sharing of personal information allows Latino persons to feel connected to the other, although Comas-Díaz and Greene (1994) reported that professional Latinos will also be affected in their choice of a therapist by a scrutiny of professional credentials.

Closely related to *personalismo* is *simpatía*, which has been empirically shown to be a cultural script for Latinos (Triandis et al., 1984). A cultural script is defined as a pattern of social interaction that is characteristic of a particular cultural group. Sometimes translated as "likeableness" or "congeniality" (Simon & Shuster, 1993), *simpatía* actually has no equivalent in English (Triandis et al., 1984). It denotes a permanent personal quality where an individual is perceived as likeable, attractive, fun to be with, and easygoing. Such a person shows certain levels of conformity and empathy for others, is respectful, and strives for harmonious interpersonal relations.

Harmony implies the general avoidance of interpersonal conflict and the tendency for positive behaviors to be emphasized in positive situations and for negative behaviors to be de-emphasized in negative situations (Triandis et al., 1984). Mexican Americans stress politeness, agreeableness, keeping one's temper, and passively enduring stress; they prefer not to directly question another's beliefs or to engage in direct, offensive criticism. There is an attempt to make social relations at least appear to be harmonious. Mexican Americans will tend not to disagree unless doing so can be done tactfully. Falicov (1996) pointed out that it may be necessary for the therapist to specifically give permission to clients to disagree with the therapist. It goes without saying that such striving for harmony disappears in a violent relationship, but perpetrators can be very adept at practicing this behavior outside of the home.

Consonant with the ideals of *respeto* and *dignidad*, criticism and insulting behavior are perceived by Latinos as an assault on the other's personal dignity and self-respect. Latino respondents are more likely to stress harmony and good relations in social situations than non-Latinos (Triandis et al., 1984). However, although the expression of anger is perceived as unacceptable by both Latinos and non-Latinos, Latinos have more tolerance for it in interpersonal relationships (Triandis et al., 1984). Triandis and his associates interpret this as a higher tolerance for blowing off steam, so as to allow the reestablishment of good social relationships, versus bottling anger up, which is perceived as undermining relationships over time. Intimacy, however, is seen as less appropriate for Latinos than for non-Latinos when they are in a subordinate role in the relationship. Triandis and his associates attribute this difference to the high-status versus low-status power distance maintained in Latino relationships (Hofstede, 1980), which was empirically shown to have more power than *simpatía* in social interactions of this nature.

Simpatía includes the following behaviors: (a) greater emphasis on talking with friends; (b) high value placed on loyalty, respect, duty, and courtesy; (c) emphasis on cooperation; (d) willingness to sacrifice self for the sake of family; and (e) preference for services received from professionals who are friends, regardless of competence (Triandis et al., 1984).

Importance of Religious Beliefs

Only 0.37% of all Latinos surveyed in the Hispanic Churches in American Public Life national survey (Espinosa, Elizonda, & Miranda, 2003) were atheist or agnostic. Seventy percent of Latinos are Catholic, 23% are Protestant or "other Christian," and 85% of all U.S. Latino Protestants identify themselves as Pentecostals or Evangelicals. One percent of Latinos identify with a world religion, such as Buddhism, Islam, or Judaism. It is evident that religious or spiritual beliefs are very important in Latino culture. In spite of theological differences among denominations, the basic Christian framework as a way of giving order to existence and bestowing meaning on existence remains common to all. The apparent chaos of pluralistic American society can pose enormous problems to the rural Latino immigrant, who may suffer when his or her moral framework and past experiences are insufficient to make sense out of the chaos (Bach-y-Rita, 1982). Some families migrating from rural environments may seek out small Evangelical churches as a means of recreating a religious and family support system amidst the urban amorality that they perceive in their new American environment. Even if the behavior of Latino immigrants is seen as unacceptable to American society, these immigrants can feel reassured that their behavior is regulated by a set of universal Christian or Catholic principles that conform to the group ethos (Falicov, 1996). Immigrants who are monolingual Spanish-speakers are more likely to report that religion is very important to them and to attend church services regularly (Edgerton & Karno, 1971).

Joy is attached to both suffering and service, especially among women (Bach-y-Rita, 1982). Suffering is seen in Christianity, or in a faith context in general, as an integral, inescapable fact of life that can be an element of fulfillment, as postulated by Frankl in his logotherapy theory and treatment (1969). A woman's culturally sanctioned role is to be good, strong, and dedicated to her duty. The concept of charity, sacrificing for an ideal, and acceptance of suffering are particularly adaptive to families who live a marginal existence. The altruistic behaviors that result from such beliefs are an important element in the survival of the poor. Religious figures who are idealized are virtually all associated with service to God and the human community. Selfish or self-centered behavior is met with mixed feelings.

Religious values may be important motivators to help abusive men alter their behavior. In fact, Shupe, Stacey, and Hazlewood (1987) have shown that men in the United States who subscribe to some religion and attend services are less likely to be abusive than men who do not. Straus et al. (1980) found that men who profess no religion make up the highest percentage of abusers. On the other hand, Ellison et al. (1999) found that there was no significant difference between men professing religious beliefs and their nonreligious counterparts in terms of perpetration of IPV. Both groups were equally likely to be perpetrators. They did find, however, that men who attended services once a week, versus less frequently, were less likely to be violent. Welland et al. (unpublished) found that, among Latino men arrested and mandated to treatment in IPV groups in Southern California (n = 54), 9% professed no religion, compared to only 0.37% of Latinos in the 2003 survey mentioned above, which suggests that further studies similar to that of Shupe et al. could yield interesting results for this population. Of the perpetrators in Welland et al.'s study, 65% were Catholic (versus 80% Catholic in an earlier survey [n = 159], as reported in Welland & Ribner, 2001). Of Catholic men, 36% reported that they frequently heard that domestic violence was wrong at their churches, and 39% said that it was sometimes mentioned. Thus, 75% of the Catholic men in those IPV groups knew that their behavior was out of line with the teachings of their church, but this did not stop them from becoming violent. Men who were non-Catholic Christians (20% of the sample) reported that their churches either frequently mentioned that IPV is against their beliefs (45%) or sometimes mentioned this (36%), a total of 81%.

This suggests that Christian churches of several denominations in the United States are making a good effort to educate their members regarding IPV as it relates to their religion, but there is still much to be done to bridge the disconnect between knowledge and actual behavioral change. Nevertheless, churches and synagogues are increasingly seeing the importance of assisting and intervening in families who are plagued with this problem (Fortune, 2007; Weaver, Larson, & Stapleton, 2001). Prevention strategies that begin in early childhood are more likely to be effective in stopping IPV before it starts (APA, 2006).

In a social context, among Latinos religious rituals serve to consolidate social ties with others in the spiritual community, by the selection of *compadres* and *comadres* who serve as coparents to the children, beginning with baptism. Compadres are an essential element of Latino culture, serving as a means to strengthen the family and protect the children. When these religious customs are not maintained they can serve as a source of both conflict and guilt (Falicov, 1996).

Mexican immigrants may have difficulty adjusting their moral and religious values to the less interpersonally committed American lifestyle. Loss of contact with one's faith can be traumatic. Community activities provided by churches fill the role of social support groups and are readily acceptable to the Latino immigrant who is familiar with such networks (Bach-y-Rita, 1982). Because of the familiarity and acceptability of the local church as a resource, an important component of ecosystemic treatment for IPV may be the provision to clients of information regarding spiritual activities available in the community. Although not all denominations have made a clear stand against IPV in recent decades, most have. As a result, churches can be of real assistance to their members who are involved in IPV. In our treatment program we have included a section on spiritual beliefs and the prevention of IPV, which we describe in more detail in chapter 8.

An inner locus of control is assumed to be the most adaptive for mental health (Rotter, 1975). However, Latinos who are poor, uneducated, and of rural background have little control in reality over many aspects of their life, due to factors such as social class and economic necessity. There is adaptive value to believing that one is in the hands of a greater power under such adverse circumstances, otherwise life would become unbearable. Such core concepts relating to life and death are not easily changed by immigration (Bach-y-Rita, 1982). In this context, an existential component to therapy may be meaningful to Latino men, who may place a high value on spiritual principles. These principles may be explored in the service of transformation of abusive behaviors. In later chapters we will discuss our findings in this regard.

Molina, Zambrana, and Aguirre-Molina (1994) reported that Catholicism considers the maintenance of the family unit as primary even at the expense of a woman's safety or well-being. Although this may have been true in the past, it is no longer so in the United States (United States Conference of Catholic Bishops, 2002). However, it is uncertain to what degree church authorities and pastoral workers in Latin America agree with current trends in the Roman Catholic Church in America and Canada to denounce IPV, to offer shelter and resources to victims and children, and to help victims seek annulments of their marriages when the situation demands it.

Gender Roles

Machismo

Access to social and economic resources in the United States is critical to defining a man's worth and sense of identity. By competing for and maintaining a good job, earning a reasonable income, managing his affairs, and maintaining a stable home and family, a man defines himself in this country (Inkeles, 1983). Education and a job are basic to the attainment of a sense of personal power and control of one's life. And yet, in ethnic groups plagued by low socioeconomic status, the "violent subduing of others may be their only significant achievement. Their capacity to perpetrate violence is the great equalizer in a world characterized by great inequalities" (Hill et al., 1994, p. 72). Regarding partner violence among Latino men, Espín (1994) theorized that

> for poor and working class men of color, asserting dominance over women and children may be nothing but a last desperate gesture to "prove their manhood" in a world that both expects all men to achieve a certain success and systematically destroys the chances of some men to achieve that position. Domineering, aggressive, and sometimes violent behavior towards women on the part of these men may be understood as this desperate gesture. However, this understanding does not in any way diminish or justify the suffering it causes women and their children. (p. 266)

Falicov (1996) asserted that although in general a patriarchal view of gender roles persists among Latinos, more complex dynamics are evolving. There does exist a double standard as regards gender socialization and sexuality, but decision making is frequently shared equally, and is often largely the domain of the mother of the family (Falicov, 1996). In a review of the literature on Latinos in the 1980s, Vega (1990) concluded that Mexican American family life is characterized by a wide range of structures, from patriarchal to egalitarian. Thus, it is vital to note, as we will do in later chapters, that there is great heterogeneity in gender role socialization among Latino men, and not all Latino men who are violent are necessarily *machista*.

Machismo as a concept in Latino culture does not only refer to a man's attitude about women (Bach-y-Rita, 1982). Casas, Wagenheim, Banchero, and Mendoza-Romero (1994) defined machismo as "the strong and strict adherence to masculine gender identity" (p. 315). Machismo has to do with how a man perceives himself, his relationship to his environment, and his gender role in general. It refers to the role of provider and protector of his family, as well as to a man's strength, his ability to restrain his emotions, and his stoic capacity to endure pain and adversity. Latino men learn not to cry from an early age and to endure and suffer in silence. Given the harsh life circumstances of many Latinos, immigrants or otherwise, the admission of pain and vulnerability can be maladaptive.[1]

The Latino male is socialized to expect deference and *respeto* from others, especially from his wife and children, who are expected to submit to the authority of the man in the home. Other qualities of machismo are sexual attractiveness, aggressiveness, and the ability to consume an excessive quantity of alcohol without getting drunk (Comas-Díaz, cited in Paniagua, 1994). Machismo places extreme pressure on the male for constant sexual readiness and heightened expectations of sexual performance (Cullen & Travin, 1990).

Differential gender identity exists in all cultures, and most cultures subscribe to constructs of manhood similar, if not identical, to Latino machismo (Casas, Wagenheim, Banchero, & Mendoza-Romero, 1994). It is a paradox that the men who most succeed at meeting cultural expectations regarding masculinity may harm themselves in the process, because high male gender role stress is positively related to high consumption of drugs and/or alcohol, outbursts of violence toward self and others, unsafe sex, and restrictive emotionality leading to psychosomatic illness. Men who are socialized to validate their masculinity through control, power, and competition are theorized to be more likely to engage in IPV because they have learned to endorse the use of physical force to achieve their ends (Finn, 1986).

There is considerable disagreement among researchers as to the validity or prevalence of the construct of machismo among Latinos and Mexicans in particular (Casas et al., 1994), ranging along a continuum from "very pervasive" to the position that Mexican society is actually matriarchal, and that the whole culture is oriented to the love of the mother. Lara-Cantú (1989) described the Mexican "machismo syndrome" stereotype as characterized by extreme aggressivity and intransigence in male-to-male relationships and by sexual aggression and contempt in male-to-female relationships. Mirandé (1997) also found in his sociological research with Latino men in the United States that machismo is a pejorative construct. He differentiates between *machista*[2] and *macho* as negative and positive constructs respectively. Some of the adjectives that describe the *machista* man are violent, irresponsible, disrespectful, selfish, loud, seductive, abusive, chauvinistic, and dishonorable. The macho Latino man, on the other hand, is described as brave, responsible, respectful, altruistic, humble, protective, and honorable, to mention a few characteristics.[3] Gutmann (1996), in his anthropological study of men's evolving gender roles in a working-class neighborhood in Mexico City, found that gender roles have been in the process of change over the past decades. Men there do not wish to be categorized either as machos (making no differentiation between macho and *machista* as Mirandé does) or as *mandilones*;[4] they find themselves in the midst of a cultural transformation where their role as men is no longer set in stone. The men and women he interviewed over the course of a year of study did identify machismo with male physical abusiveness.

> Not only nationalism but also class, ethnicity, generation, and other factors deeply brand Mexican male identities. Mexican machos are not dead any more than are their Russian or North American counterparts, but claims about a uniform character of Mexican masculinity, a ubiquitous *macho mexicano*, should be put to rest. (Gutmann, 1996, p. 263)

Cultural prescriptions and expectations about appropriate gender behavior are well known by all members of a given culture (Bem, 1981). The gender schema becomes linked to one's self-concept and self-esteem, and as such becomes an internalized motivational factor. Machismo among Latinos is considered to make men responsible to uphold the honor of their family, to deal effectively with the public, and to maintain the integrity of the family unit. A manly Latino is the head of the household, but also listens to, respects, and protects women; he demonstrates courage and virility. Machismo provides the male with much more sexual and sociopolitical freedom than the female (Casas et al., 1994). As we stated before, this conception of Latino masculinity is in accord with the positive male gender role for Latinos in research studies, but the designation *machismo* has a specifically negative connotation, and as such, referring to male honor in these terms is likely to cause confusion and discord rather than clarification.

Marín and Marín (1991) found that a small percentage of Latino men in research studies refused to allow their wives to participate, or that some women were reluctant to give an interview without their partner's permission. This type of rigidity in gender roles is more commonly seen among the rural population of low income and few years of education (Mikawa et al., 1992).

Marianismo

Marianismo,[5] or the Latino female gender schema that is also labeled "the self-sacrificing woman syndrome" (Lara-Cantú, 1989), is characterized by dependent, submissive, and passive attitudes and behavior. Lara-Cantú's research suggests that gender role stereotypical behavior diminishes with age in Mexico, for both genders. Latina women socialized with these gender schemas are expected to be obedient, timid, docile, sentimental, gentle, and to remain a virgin until marriage (Comas-Díaz & Duncan, 1985). Women are expected to dedicate themselves to the home, to serve the man and the children, and to pass on cultural values to the next generation. The word *marianismo* derives from the name of Mary, who is venerated by Catholics as both virgin and mother of Jesus, and as a model for all women. *Marianismo* also implies that women are spiritually superior to men, but that they endure much suffering at the hands of men (Comas-Díaz & Duncan, 1985, cited in Paniagua, 1994.)

GENDER SCHEMAS AND IMMIGRATION

Some evidence shows that the traditional male gender schemas thrive in a stable agrarian environment, where the male head of the family is expected to control his emotions and provide stability to the family (Casas et al., 1994). Women are expected to care for the husband, the children, and the home, and to mediate between the family and the community. Children are expected to be respectful of their elders and to assume traditional gender roles without question. As long as the environment remains constant, the family remains in balance, or homeostasis.

However, once a family migrates from the rural environment to an urban community, especially if that community is in the United States, gender schemas come under constant challenge. What was adaptive for a male in the village becomes maladaptive in the new setting. The mother finds it necessary, and possible, to work outside the home to keep the family financially solvent. Working gives her previously unknown economic possibilities, new skills, and interactions with others that may subtly influence her traditional female gender schemas. His wife's development and the children's role as brokers of the new culture, because they learn the language and culture more rapidly, are threatening to the man's prestige and control. The woman may be earning more than her husband and have work benefits he does not enjoy. His previously unchallenged role as head of the household is severely compromised, but machismo dictates that he not share his anxiety or confusion with anyone. The man may respond by exaggerating the male characteristics of authoritarianism and control, by excessive drinking or high-risk sexual behavior, or by taking the steps necessary to accommodate his rigid gender schema to his new situation (Casas et al., 1994). In line with this, in a study on condom use among Latino males in the United States, Mexican immigrants with the least education were most likely to have negative attitudes toward women and to display *machista* characteristics of invincibility and strength, and the least likely to share decisions regarding condom use with the female (Mikawa et al., 1992).

Immigrant Mexican women tend to work for pay outside the home in the United States because family survival requires it, even though entering the work force remains a culturally anomalous behavior (Kelly & García, 1989). Understanding Latino partner abusive men's experience and concerns regarding changes in gender role schemata is an important component to address in treatment and will be considered in later chapters.

SOCIOECONOMIC STATUS VERSUS RACE

There is great diversity and heterogeneity in Latino cultures, varying from people who are wholly indigenous, to the mestizo, or mixed indigenous and European population, to those who trace their ethnic origins only to Europeans, whether Spanish or otherwise. The indigenous population of Mexico is the most varied of any country in Latin America and comprises 11% of the population (Comisión Nacional para el Desarrollo de los Pueblos Indígenas, 2002), although 36% of municipalities have at least partially indigenous populations.[6] The purely indigenous Mexican population is likely to be rural, with a primary education or less, and of low socioeconomic status. The mestizo population makes up 60%–75% of the population and tends to belong to the lower or middle class. European-descent Mexicans, approximately 15% of the total population, are by and large urban, educated, and of upper-middle or upper class. Fifty percent of the population of the country lives below the poverty line designated by the federal authorities (Schreiner, 2006), and many immigrants to the United States come from rural and relatively isolated areas and so lack the skills necessary for early adaptation to U.S.

culture (Bach-y-Rita, 1982). However, with changes in Mexico's economy over the past 2 decades, many immigrants to the United States now come from urban areas and have somewhat more education than immigrants of previous generations. This was noted in the two demographic surveys conducted by the authors; the results are reported in chapter 4. The educated, urban Mexican or Latino of the upper-middle class is likely to have much in common and share much of the worldview of the educated, urban American.

Racial and ethnic discrimination is a fact of life in Mexico and other Latin American nations as it is in the United States (Falicov, 1996). However, because most Mexicans are dark skinned, there is less of a stigma attached to skin color and more of a stigma attached to socioeconomic status, which is correlated with membership in particular ethnic groups, as stated. In countries where there was a significant population of African slaves during colonial times, there is corresponding discrimination against people of African descent and of mixed blood. The word *indio* (Indian) in Mexico refers to someone who behaves in a stupid or neglectful manner in common speech, demonstrating the low esteem in which indigenous peoples have been held throughout the centuries since the Spanish conquest.[7] *Racismo*, which Shorris (1992) translated as "internalized self-loathing," is compounded many times over for many poor Latinos who immigrate to the United States, where because of their darker complexion, they are easily singled out for discrimination and deportation (Falicov, 1996).

THE IMMIGRATION EXPERIENCE

> Perhaps the most fundamental dislocation of migration is the uprooting of a structure of cultural meanings, which has been likened to the roots that sustain and nourish a plant. (Falicov, 1996, p. 170)

Exposure to new life constructs may subject the immigrant to psychological distress caused by culture shock, marginality and social alienation, psychosomatic symptoms, anxiety, depression, and posttraumatic stress, if the migration involved trauma, as it frequently does for lower status Latino immigrants who face many dangers crossing the border, and much more so since the border crackdown beginning in the mid-1990s (U.S. Customs and Border Protection, 2005).

Frequently, the migration of Latino families is accomplished in stages, with the father coming first, followed by the wife and then the children (Falicov, 1996). This arrangement requires the husband to be gone for months or even years at a time, which results in a situation similar to the incorporation of a stepfather when the family is reunited. Women who migrate with their families often remain isolated in their homes, unable to take advantage of the opportunity to learn English, which their partner may acquire from outside work. The opposite is sometimes true as well, because schools offer ESL classes that the woman may be able to take while the father of the family has less time. As well, studies demonstrate that first-generation Mexican immigrants have less social support from extended family or other social networks than second- or third-generation immigrants, leaving them more vulnerable to stress (Vega & Kolody, 1985).

Illegal immigration status is a constant source of anxiety for many of these families, for even if the male has a work permit, it may not extend to his family, and processing immigration documents takes years and is frequently impossible due to current immigration policy. The fact that a woman and her children do not possess legal immigration status, and the consequent fear of deportation, is a frequent deterrent to the reporting of partner abuse. Eighty-six percent of the apprehensions of undocumented immigrants at the southern border in 2005 were Mexican nationals, with 82% of all arrests being of men. Other leading countries of origin included Honduras (4.4%), El Salvador (3.3%), Brazil (2.6%), and Guatemala (1.9%). Mexico was also the leading country of origin for apprehensions at the northern border (55.6%) and coastal borders (33%). Cuba was the next leading country (30.1%) for coastal border apprehensions (as cited from the Department of Homeland Security in Wu, 2005).

Under the Violence Against Women Act renewal, signed into law on January 6, 2006 (National Coalition against Domestic Violence, 2006), women who are married to a U.S. citizen or a permanent resident may qualify for residency and eventually citizenship even if they are no longer with their spouse, if abuse can be proven. For such women, taking action against an abusive husband increases their chances of changing their immigration status and being able to create a new life for themselves and their families.

ACCULTURATION AND ACCULTURATION STRESS

Acculturation is defined as the process of incorporating the customs from alternate and native societies. It involves the interaction of at least two cultures and is a multidimensional process, meaning that people may be similar in their degree of immersion into the alternate culture, while very dissimilar in the degree to which they have retained their native culture (Mendoza, 1989). Migration is regarded as a stressful event for individuals and families, because it requires a measure of flexibility that will enable them to change and adapt to new circumstances. Migration can also affect family cohesiveness and effect a loss of cultural values, more so if the differences between the host culture and the immigrant culture are very great (Ben-David, 1995). Latino immigrants, especially those from Mexico, tend to retain a strong ethnic identity over generations, perhaps because of continuous immigration that keeps traditions strong in the ethnic community and because of the geographical proximity of their country of origin (Bach-y-Rita, 1982). They may develop a cultural bifocality, retaining their own culture while simultaneously becoming adept at functioning in American society (Falicov, 1996).

Among Latino immigrants, the fact that women are sometimes able to find permanent employment faster than men and may earn a larger salary is sometimes cited as an additional risk factor for partner abuse, presumably because the male's self-esteem, which is closely connected to his gender role identity, is threatened by her increase in status (Yllo & Straus, 1990). Ybarra (1982) has shown, however, that machismo is not the only variable to be accounted for in changing Latino gender roles. She found that Latino families are adaptive and that gender roles change as social conditions require. Social context, therefore, is vital in understanding and tracking gender role transformation and the consequent effect on partner abuse.

Some of the factors that require assessment in determining an immigrant's level of acculturation include language spoken at home and at work; retention or loss of native customs; importance of religion for ethnic identity and experience of discrimination against their religion; number of people living in the home and proximity of extended family; expectations regarding who is the head of the household and appropriate gender roles; age at immigration; ecological fit of native values with host culture values; level of acceptance by host culture and/or level of discrimination experienced; strength of ties to native land and intention to return there or not; and loss or gain in socioeconomic status on immigration (M. Barón, personal communication, February 1997). The stress of acculturation and disagreements over parenting, finances, values, and gender roles within the marital dyad and between the family and the exosystem, such as school, peer group, and work (Falicov, 1996), can be particular risk factors for partner abuse in Latino immigrant couples and will be explored more fully.

PERCEPTION OF MENTAL ILLNESS AND ATTITUDES TOWARD TREATMENT

Access to treatment for themselves and their children is problematic for many Latina victims of IPV. Often, if they are of low socioeconomic status and monolingual, it is difficult or impossible for them to locate a victims' support group in Spanish that is free of charge and is accessible by means of public transportation. Frequently, the victim is unaware of services and/or lacks health insurance or the financial means to pay for individual therapy out of pocket. If there are custody issues, the perpetrator may make it very difficult for the Latina woman to involve the children in the therapy they need to recover from the trauma of witnessing IPV. If the victim is undocumented, she may be afraid to access services, and those she does access are limited by her immigration status, as noted above. As with many victims of IPV of any nationality or ethnic origin, many Latinas go without the mental health services they need to overcome the negative effects of IPV (Orloff & Little, 1999).

Less educated Latinos from rural backgrounds come into treatment with no prior understanding of psychotherapy or the therapeutic process, because psychotherapy falls outside their economic and social reality (Bach-y-Rita, 1982) even in spite of its current popularity in the media. They may experience ambivalent feelings such as inherent distrust of institutions and a fear of being labeled as crazy. They may also feel positive sentiments such as gratitude for receiving needed assistance. Such clients may expect treatment to resemble procedures in a medical doctor's office, that is, for the doctor to ask questions, to know the solution, and to do something. Their role may be perceived as showing respect for authority, cooperation, and obedience. Educated, urban Latinos, on the other hand, may be expected to present with a level of understanding comparable to their American counterparts. Therapists should carefully explain the difference between a physician and a therapist, indicate the role of both therapist and client in therapy, discuss goals for therapy, and choose techniques that are appropriate to the client's cultural norms (Sue & Sue, 2002).

Cultural factors that shape the worldview of Latino clients mandated to IPV treatment may be used to assist in designing and carrying out interventions, or they may be an obstacle to progress if therapists are unaware of their importance. Effective treatment with this population should include sensitivity and understanding of the ways that Latinos interact with each other and with authority figures in a socially acceptable manner, the spiritual beliefs that may form the basis of their worldview, and the ecosystemic realities of their lives as immigrants that shape their experience as individuals, couples, and family.

> The behaviors within a culture may change more readily than the thoughts and emotions that underlie them; these are long-lasting. When a second culture is acquired, the original culture may seem lost and forgotten until an individual is in crisis. Sickness, birth, death—these are

apt to sweep away the topsoil of an acquired pattern of living to reveal the earlier culture beneath. Cultural roots are planted in childhood and grow deep. (Tseng & McDermott, 1981, pp. 6–7)

Researchers in the Latino population have shown that there are several culturally specific areas that need to be addressed during therapy with Latinos in general in order for therapy to be maximally effective. This consideration takes on particular importance in the case of court-mandated treatment for partner abuse offenders, as Williams and Becker (1994) pointed out that the attrition rate for Latino and other minority clients in such groups is higher. They hypothesized that it is the lack of development of culturally sensitive intervention strategies that makes treatment less effective for men who belong to minority groups.

ECOLOGICAL CONTEXT

Therapists should inquire about the ecological context in which the client finds himself and his family, because the family is but one in an "interactive set of systems" (Falicov, 1996). As stated above, many Latino immigrants lack financial resources and have less of a social network in the first generation than later on in their immigration history. They work hard for low pay at jobs with little prestige. Many immigrants experience depression and disappointment over unfulfilled dreams of success and having to lower their expectations of what life in the United States would offer them (Rouse, 1992, cited in Falicov, 1996). The challenge of adapting to a new way of life places strain on intimate relationships, which require more companionship and understanding than before (Sluzki, 1989). The ever-present threat of discrimination and sometimes deportation affects all family members and contributes to disempowerment. Social ills that frequently affect minorities who are discriminated against are also widespread in many Latino populations, such as drugs, alcohol, teen pregnancy, IPV, gangs, and AIDS, particularly in the second and third generations (Padilla, 1995). The parents of these troubled young people may be confused and disappointed at their children's unexpected behavior, which is totally dissonant with the parents' high expectations for their offspring after all the sacrifices they have made to offer them a better life.

Therapists might explore such issues as the quality of the neighborhood (housing, safety, gangs, crime), racial acceptance, employment (income, occupation, job stability), extended family and friendship networks, connection to local church activities, and parent–teacher relationships (Falicov, 1996). Therapists can serve as social intermediaries, assisting their clients to access communal networks of which they may have been unaware (Falicov, 1988). Informing clients of exosystemic resources or pointing them in that direction, depending on the case, can be an important violence prevention strategy.

FAMILY ORGANIZATION

Many Latino families are large and have relatively flexible boundaries, meaning that they expand easily to include grandparents, uncles, aunts, or cousins as well as the nuclear family (Falicov, 1996). The process of separation/individuation so prized in American culture is de-emphasized, while a "familial self" dedicated to family unity and honor is preferred. Parents enjoy high status, while children's status, even that of adult offspring, is low. Decision making is often shared by partners, especially at the present time when more complex gender dynamics are evolving. However, a hierarchical, patriarchal view of gender roles is the norm.

Machismo can be an obstacle in treatment. However, the positive masculine gender role can be used as a bridge in therapy if the therapist stresses the duty of the father to care for his children and for the family's general well-being. Therapists should not hesitate to engage the client-as-father in interventions (Falicov, 1996). In situations where Latino men are mandated to therapy, the therapist needs to make explicit the desirability of expressing feelings and personal details to the group, because *machista* beliefs will dictate that the client present a stoic facade that precludes emotional disclosure (Bach-y-Rita, 1982).

Migration patterns, where the male leaves the home for extended periods, effectively leaving his partner as head of the family, have affected and continue to affect gender role conflicts in Latino families (Carrillo, 1982; Falicov, 1996). These conflicts are further exacerbated when the woman comes to the United States and experiences new freedoms by obtaining employment. The man may feel he has lost some of his traditional authority in interacting with agencies and individuals outside the family, while his partner and children take on greater responsibility. Feelings of isolation and depression, augmented by living in a different and sometimes hostile culture, are difficult for the traditional man to express, out of fear of appearing weak. Seeking security by being consistent in his position as a Latino man, he may increase his anxiety by adhering to more rigid gender roles. Finally, he may experience anxiety over questions of sexual potency. The degree of desirable change in gender roles should ideally be left to the client (Green, Trankina, & Chávez, 1976), because too much change may render the client unacceptable to his or her ethnic group, thus increasing the risk of alienation.

Therapists should be careful not to impose their values regarding appropriate gender roles on their clients; to do so could be counterproductive. Just as immigrants are willing to accept many new customs in the host country and to adapt to them, they may also be willing to examine more flexible gender roles if they are able to see the long-term benefits to themselves, their relationship, and their family (O. Espín, personal communication, November 1995). One of the pitfalls of cultural sensitivity is the potential for the therapist to collude with the family in overemphasizing cultural explanations for the purpose of rationalizing dysfunctional behavior (Martínez, 1994).[8] Culture should not be used as a mask that explains all behavior, nor can it be dismissed as superfluous in understanding behavior. The therapist needs to maintain an informed perspective, balancing awareness of sociocultural and spiritual issues with sound clinical judgment. This is especially true in cases where abuse is present and may be rationalized with such cultural explanations as *respeto* and family honor. Spiritual beliefs held by the family may also maintain a dysfunctional behavior pattern. A positive reframe of the functionality of the belief will assist the therapist to treat the family from within its own context. To do otherwise may add to the client's sense of cultural mismatch, consequent dissonance, and even despair (Martínez, 1994).

MIGRATION HISTORY AND ACCULTURATION

A "migration narrative" is a useful tool for entering into the Latino immigrant's experience. It should include length of residence in the United States, order of immigration of family members, who was left behind, particular stresses that have come about as a result of immigration, and strengths and resources the client has discovered (Falicov, 1996).[9] This technique helps clients to find meaning in their uprooting as a part of their personal history and contributes to the perception of gains as well as losses.

For first-generation immigrants, Falicov (1988) listed several areas of ecosystemic exploration that may be linked to acculturative stress. On the societal level, there is very likely to be cultural dissonance with the dominant culture's values. On the community level, therapists can explore the influence of legal or illegal immigration status and low economic status brought on by unemployment or underemployment. The therapist will take note of language ability (frequently monolingual in the first generation), limited or excessive use of institutions, fear and alienation from society, and residence in an ethnic community. The immigrant's ethnic identity may be split, either idealizing the culture of origin or denigrating it, as a way of coping with the external or internal pressure to acculturate. In the microsystem or relationship level, which is the arena of partner violence, there may be tensions of adaptation, such as culture shock and situational problems, difficulties with migratory separations and reunions, very low or high social support networks, fluctuation of traditional family hierarchies to cope with immigration (e.g., closer marital proximity), and differential developmental norms, such as a shift in the dominant family dyad. Whereas in Mexico and other Latin American countries the mother–child dyad is often the strongest over the generations, in American culture the spousal dyad is considered to be the foundation of healthy family life. Exploration and discussion of these issues in group therapy with abusive men can assist them in identifying some of the areas of stress that are specific to their experience as immigrants and can help them to gain perspective.

Alternative resource theory suggests that Latinos prefer to use family, friends, folk healers, the clergy, and general medical providers rather than mental health professionals when they have emotional problems (Sánchez & King, 1986, cited in Leong, Wagner, & Tata, 1995). However, Reeves (1986) showed that when mental health services are culturally responsive, utilization by Latinos increases. Culturally sensitive treatment programs for Mexican male abusers should, therefore, show decreased rates of attrition, which is usually a problem with court-ordered clients. Furthermore, such a treatment approach is likely to be more efficacious in preventing recidivism, thus protecting family members from future violence.[10]

EFFECTIVE THERAPEUTIC MODES FOR LATINOS

Family therapy has been proposed as the treatment mode of choice for Latinos because of the importance of extended family and interdependence as a cultural value (Paniagua, 1994; Sue & Sue, 2002). Structural family therapy (Minuchin, 1974) has been used effectively, as it stresses the importance of family hierarchies. It is most effective to use this approach in concert with an ecosystemic consideration of socioeconomic and cultural factors (Canino & Canino, 1982, cited in Paniagua, 1994). However, because family or couples therapy is not considered to be an acceptable mode of therapy when there is partner abuse, due to the increased risk of exacerbating conflict between the partners and placing the victim at risk of further violence, we will focus on the appropriateness of group therapy for Latino clients. Nevertheless, the possibility of involving a close extended family member in the intake process, and of suggesting couples or family therapy once the 52-week treatment is completed as a means of solidifying progress, are certainly areas of interest that could be fruitfully examined elsewhere.

Group Therapy for Latinos

The Association for Specialists in Group Work (ASGW) defines group work as "a broad professional practice that refers to the giving of help or the accomplishment of tasks in a group setting. The four group work specializations are task/work, guidance/psychoeducational, counseling/ interpersonal problem solving, and psychotherapy/personality reconstruction" (ASGW, 1992, cited in Corey & Corey, 1993). Yalom (1985, p. xv) divided the experience of group therapy into 11 primary factors: instillation of hope, universality, imparting of information, altruism, the corrective recapitulation of the primary family group, development of socializing techniques, imitative behavior, interpersonal learning, group cohesiveness, catharsis, and existential factors. Effective group treatment for Latino partner abusive men should ideally include all of these factors. An ethnically homogeneous group, composed of members of the same ethnic minority, is sometimes called a culture-specific group (Merta, 1995). Homogeneous groups are perceived as having less conflict, being more cohesive, providing more support, being better attended, and providing more rapid relief of symptoms than heterogeneous groups, although they may be more superficial and less productive.

Avila and Avila (1988, cited in Merta, 1995) advocated group work for Mexican Americans because of their cultural orientation to groups, and they state that homogeneous groups promote better self-understanding. Therapists should take within-group differences such as level of acculturation and ethnic identity development into account, as well as the many between-group differences that exist among Latinos from diverse cultural heritages in Latin America. Although the Latino men who attend IPV treatment may be from diverse cultures, the cultural similarities are greater among them than if they were to attend a non-Latino group.

Paniagua (1994) recommended group therapy for Latinos, with the caveat that a problem-solving approach is likely to be most effective. As regards time orientation, Latinos tend to emphasize the "event" rather than exact scheduling (Sue & Sue, 2002); therefore flexibility is recommended for group therapy. However, such flexibility is not an option in court-mandated therapy for partner abusive men. There are strict attendance and punctuality guidelines set by states and by region. These must be emphasized as court regulations at the outset of group treatment, so that members will be well aware that the inflexibility is not a characteristic of the therapist himself or herself. Otherwise, such a culturally incongruent rigidity is likely to compromise the therapeutic alliance.

Durst Palmer, Baker, and McGee (1997) showed that written, cognitive pretraining for new group therapy members is effective in increasing levels of self-disclosure, as well as levels of group cohesion over time. Such an orientation for new group members is of special value to Latino clients of low socioeconomic status who have little or no experience with the concept or practice of therapy in general (Acosta, 1982; McKinley, 1987), and who may view psychologists as professionals who treat mental illness, rather than behavioral problems (Paniagua, 1994). A clear explanation of confidentiality, goals, and methods employed in group treatment may greatly enhance their participation. However, the level of literacy of the client should be ascertained before a standard, written explanation of expectations of group members is offered to the client. A brief verbal or video presentation may be preferable.

Gutiérrez and Ortega (1991), in their study of the effectiveness of group therapy for Latino students, found that cohesive groups, consisting of similar others, strongly influence individual behavior and provide an environment that encourages risk taking. They found that the group was a fruitful territory for developing new attitudes and exploration of the possibility of social change. Such empowerment is essential if the burden of oppression and discrimination is to be explored and eventually challenged. Such exploration in an IPV group may help abusive men to develop empathy for the oppressed position of their partners. The group may also perform the function of a training ground where new gender roles and new behaviors can be rehearsed in a safe setting.

McKinley (1987) described the particular difficulty that Latinos from lower socioeconomic levels have in expressing themselves in therapy.

> The therapist's speech system creates the expectation that the patient will be able to communicate personal feelings, experiences, motivations, intents, and goals. The speech system of lower socioeconomic Latinos [socialized to be obedient to authority figures without expressing opinions or feelings] discourages such communication. Their language is characterized by a restricted vocabulary, with relatively few qualifiers, particularly those that describe feelings, and a preference for concrete or functional as opposed to abstract thinking. Language is used primarily as a social organizer, which helps to sustain group solidarity, and not as a vehicle for the communication and elaboration of the unique differences of its members. (p. 260)

McKinley found that, in group therapy, patients are able to stimulate each other to share common experiences at their own level. The fact that the authority of the therapist is shared among many members also frees up the patients to invest in group work. The Latino patient expects the therapist, as authority figure, to be active and directive. Out of a desire to be respectful, the patient may adopt a passive and dependent attitude, staying silent and avoiding eye contact. In group work, some of the expected dependency on the therapist is diluted by the presence of others. The culturally congruent expectation that the therapist will give advice is met in psychoeducational group work, as well as the advice and experience shared by other group members. Thus, the patient's expectation of receiving advice is not frustrated, as it frequently is in individual therapy.

Because of cultural taboos regarding the direct discussion of sexuality, explicit permission should be given by the therapist to discuss sexual concerns (McKinley, 1987). Although this is much more of a concern in women's groups than in groups of male abusers, when the facilitators of IPV groups are a mixed-gender dyad or there is a single, female facilitator, it seems advisable to give such explicit permission.[11]

McKinley (1987) has found that group therapy offers the Latino client a much needed corrective family experience, breaks a pattern of social isolation and suffering in a strange culture, and offers the opportunity to learn new skills such as assertiveness and self-reliance, which are necessary for survival in American society. The multiple sources of feedback available in the group reduce the common experience of alienation often brought on by acculturation difficulties, family breakdown, and discrimination. The group may become a symbolic family, providing support and cohesiveness, with the facilitators initially supplying the role of parents (Dunkas & Nikelly, 1975). Group therapy for men, even mandatory treatment for partner abuse, although initially culturally dissonant for most participants, has the potential to be a very positive and life-enhancing experience for the Latino client.

EFFECTIVE THERAPEUTIC TECHNIQUES

Merta (1995) recommended structuring group work with ethnic minority clients so that ambiguity and anxiety are minimized. Members who are unfamiliar with therapy may prefer groups that are problem focused, behaviorally oriented, and highly structured with planned exercises. The facilitator should interrupt the group process when it becomes apparent that a member is confused or anxious, to provide clarification and support. Conflict should be acknowledged rather than avoided, using the technique of consensual validation of perceptions of conflict by other group members (Greeley, García, Kessler, & Gilchrest, 1992). Even in what may appear to be an ethnically homogeneous group of Latino partner abusive men, given the diversity of the population even within subcultures,[12] the group facilitator should be aware of potential conflict over values and ethnicity.

Most mental health professionals who specialize in work with Latinos recommend the use of techniques that are active, concrete, and solution focused (Sue & Sue, 2002). Juárez (1985, cited in Sue & Sue, 2002) recommended the use of behavior therapy, utilizing direct intervention and specific guidance on the part of the therapist. Montijo (1985, cited in Sue & Sue, 2002) theorized that cognitive-behavioral work can help to eliminate self-defeating thoughts and promote more accurate perceptions for clients from the Latino population. Latinos expect therapists to employ a directive approach in therapy and are more likely to rate the therapist as high in knowledge and credibility and to return to treatment when the therapist is directive and uses probing techniques as opposed to nondirective, reflective techniques (Borrego, Chávez, & Titley, 1982; Kunkel, 1990; Pomales & Williams, 1989; all cited in Sue & Sue, 2002).

Research with Latinos has shown that they are more responsive to cognitions related to the survival and benefit of their collective even in individual therapy, for example, the negative effect of smoking on others, including children (Marín, B., Marín, G., Pérez-Stable, Otero-Sabogal, & Sabogal, 1990). Thus, behavioral motivation may be effectively linked to the interdependent values of Latinos, such as the effect that partner abuse may have on men's children, their extended family, and their ethnic group in general, as well as the effect that it has on themselves and the victim.

Falicov (1996) recommended subtly eliciting feelings by utilizing an intense emotive tone in the therapy, rather than expecting clients to "bare their soul." To establish an atmosphere of mutuality, Falicov also recommended explicitly encouraging the client to express both positive and negative reactions to the therapy. It is important for the establishment of the therapeutic alliance to show genuine interest in the client (*personalismo*) and to avoid being excessively task oriented. Latino culture values serendipity, chance, and spontaneity in interpersonal relationships.

Approaching a problem as if it will be necessary to coexist with it rather than to control it is more syntonic with the Latino worldview, which encourages acceptance of difficulties rather than confronting or struggling against them (Falicov, 1996). This is not to be interpreted, however, as meaning that violent behavior should be accepted because it cannot be modified and stopped. Tseng and McDermott (1981) emphasized that showing empathy, providing hope, taking a firm and positive approach, and utilizing the client's personal and cultural strengths are universal precepts that facilitate healing across the boundaries of culture. The effective group leader acts as a positive role model for all members, assisting clients to feel valued and understood and sharing the clients' worldview without being critical or judgmental (Corey, 1990; Yalom, 1985).

CHARACTERISTICS OF THE CULTURALLY AWARE THERAPIST

The degree of cultural competence of a therapist working with an ethnic minority population has been shown to be an important factor in the outcome of therapy, as well as whether a client continues in therapy past the first session (Atkinson & Lowe, 1995). For this reason, therapist characteristics when working with the Mexican population is a vital factor to be examined. Flaskerud (1986) found that Mexican Americans were more likely to continue in therapy when the language and ethnicity of the therapist was matched to the client, and Sue, Fujino, Hu, Takeuchi, and Zane (1988) found that ethnic match alone was related to better outcome as measured by the Global Assessment of Functioning (GAF). However, Sue and Zane (1987) pointed out that a match in ethnicity does not necessarily mean a match in language or ethnic cultural values.[13]

Although Latino psychologists in the United States are very active in the recruitment, training, and mentoring of psychologists of Latino origin (http://www.apa.org/monitor/jan05/leading.html, 2005), there continues to be a critical shortage of Spanish-speaking psychotherapists in the United States (http://www.mspp.edu/images/files/mspp_2005_annual_report.pdf, 2005). The American Psychological Association states that the 2.1% of Hispanic members of APA clearly demonstrates the under-representation of Hispanic psychologists, as well as of other psychologists of color, within the organization. The APA's Guidelines on Multicultural Education, Training, Research, Practice, and Organizational Change for Psychologists (APA, 2002) states that psychologists are encouraged to recognize the importance of multicultural sensitivity/responsiveness, knowledge, and understanding about ethnically and racially different individuals. Atkinson and Lowe (1995) found that the cultural competence of a therapist is an important outcome variable in therapy. Atkinson and Lowe, as well as Maramba and Nagayama Hall (2002), found that responsiveness to and knowledge of cultural content were more important to Mexican Americans and ethnic minorities in general in therapy than the client's level of acculturation or the therapist's ethnicity. Culturally responsive counseling results in greater willingness to return to therapy, greater satisfaction, and more self-disclosure (Thompson et al., 1994, cited in Atkinson & Lowe, 1995).

Several studies (Greene, 1982; Lopez, Lopez, & Fong, 1991; Sanchez & King, 1986, all cited in Atkinson & Lowe, 1995) have found that Mexican Americans with a strong commitment to Mexican culture prefer an ethnically similar therapist. However, paired comparison studies show that the majority of ethnic minority participants rank other therapist characteristics as more salient than ethnicity, such as similar attitudes and values, similar personality, more education, and older age (Atkinson, Poston, Furlong, & Mercado, 1989, cited in Atkinson & Lowe, 1995). Level of acculturation, cultural commitment, and ethnic identity development appear to be related to preference for therapist ethnicity (Atkinson & Lowe, 1995).

Therapists may, with the best of intentions, display "unbridled ethnocentrism" (Atkinson & Lowe, 1995) when they attempt to impose their cultural values on their clients. Corey (1990) recommended that group leaders be open to expressing their own values while not assuming a superior stance that belittles the cultural values of others. This can be particularly challenging when the beliefs of the group regarding gender roles, basic human rights, and the use of violence are divergent from one's own. We prefer to explore the values in Latino culture that support the stance that is taken by the U.S. legal system vis-à-vis IPV, in order to utilize those common values as springboards for discussion, rather than imposing values that may seem self-evident to the therapist but are culturally dissonant to Latino clients raised in markedly different environments. For example, to make our interventions regarding human rights more acceptable to our Latino clients, we quote material from the Web site of the Mexican Commission for Human Rights that details women's rights as regards domestic violence, but from the Mexican standpoint. Although their stance is not substantially different from the statements of the United Nations or major women's rights groups in the United States, the mere fact of it being stated by a Mexican entity seems likely to make it less threatening to our male clients. Our clinical experiences demonstrates that the men in our groups are very receptive to this information over time.

THERAPIST CREDIBILITY

Credibility on the part of the therapist is defined as the client's perception of the therapist as an effective and trustworthy helper (Sue & Zane, 1987). Sue and Zane maintain that credibility is a more salient variable in treating ethnic populations than mere "cookbook" cultural knowledge. Social psychology research has shown that the ability to influence is a function of perceived credibility, which is composed of expertise, trustworthiness, and attractiveness (Sue & Zane, 1987). Sue (1988) proposed that ethnicity is a distal variable in therapy. Credibility is a proximal variable, that is, more closely related to treatment effectiveness. Ethnic matches can result in cultural mismatches if therapists and clients from the same ethnic group show very different values, whereas therapists and clients from different cultures may share similar values, lifestyles, and experience and be better matched (Sue, 1988). Cultural match in treatment can be studied in terms of conceptualization of the client's problems, means for solving problems, and goals for treatment. Falicov (1988) theorized that a moderate degree of cultural distance is optimal, because the therapist is able to introduce alternative world-views by virtue of belonging to a different culture. A moderate range of consonance–dissonance allows for the perception of difference between what is cultural and what is dysfunctional. Sue and Zane (1987) stated that the "primary purpose of therapy is to provide clients with new learning experiences" (p. 40), even experiences that run counter to cultural or personal beliefs and behaviors.

Sue and Zane (1987) defined ascribed credibility as the status that one is assigned by others, by virtue of external characteristics such as age, education, expertise, and gender. Lack of ascribed credibility of the therapist may be one of the primary reasons for underutilization of mental health services. Achieved credibility, on the other hand, refers to the therapist's skills, through which clients come to have faith and confidence. Achieved credibility includes both culturally consistent interventions and general skills, such as empathy and the ability to conduct an accurate assessment. Sue and Zane believe that this variable better explains premature termination.

TREATMENT OF PARTNER ABUSIVE MEN

Erich Fromm (1973) theorized that violence is a reaction to a prior blocking of spontaneous, constructive life energy and that destructiveness is the outcome of a life that is not fully lived. Treatment for men who have been violent to their partners serves to assist them in examining and altering the destructive patterns in their lives, thereby unblocking some of this creative life energy that remains unexpressed.

The most widely used mode of treating partner abuse in North America is in psychoeducational, psychotherapeutic groups. The group approach is economical, decreases social isolation for the abusive man, provides coping skills and peer models, reduces the stigma of treatment, and bolsters self-esteem (Geffner & Rosenbaum, 1990). Interventions are usually highly structured and directive.

Groups are ideally led by a male–female cotherapist team, which models the functioning of an egalitarian couple for group members. Power is shared and the female is seen in a professional role, intentionally contradicting the female stereotypes many abusive men hold. Because group therapy is also meant to provide a positive reparenting experience for group members, the male–female dyad can also represent the parental dyad.

All programs, regardless of their structure, share the primary goal of eliminating violent, coercive, and intimidating behavior in the relationship between partners. Other goals of therapy usually include the acceptance of responsibility by the abusive man for his aggressive behavior, an appreciation of the negative consequences of his behavior on the whole family, the development of empathy for the injured partner, anger management skills, improvement of self-esteem, and the replacement of maladaptive conflict resolution skills with constructive, nonviolent ones.

The three major models of treatment are cognitive, behavioral, and feminist (Dutton, 2003; Wexler, 1999), although in recent years there has been more recognition of the need to acknowledge issues of attachment, shaming, and trauma precursors in treatment. Cognitive treatment consists of interventions that focus on irrational or automatic thoughts that produce anger arousal. For example, Novaco's (1979) adaptation of Meichenbaum's (1977) stress inoculation work is used to help men distinguish between self-defeating and self-enhancing statements. Self-talk rehearsal becomes an important component of helping men to reshape their inner dialogue. Rational emotive therapy (Ellis, 1977) helps clients confront their irrational beliefs about themselves or their partner. Beck's analysis of cognitive distortions (as discussed in Bedrosian, 1982) is used to assist clients in identifying where their attributions of their partner's intentions or their own competence misfire. Problem-solving techniques are taught as a means of resolving conflictual situations. Behavioral interventions such as contingency management (the application of legal sanctions so that men will attend therapy and avoid further violence), positive reinforcement for skills learned, relaxation training, and systematic desensitization using anger-producing scenes are used in many programs (Saunders, 1991).

The feminist approach (Pence & Paymar, 1993) consists of educational interventions that teach men to identify and subsequently alter rigid gender role beliefs and expectations that have led them to abuse their partner. Cognitive restructuring can help men to transform scripts of possessiveness, competition, and achievement into more flexible behavior. Behavioral modeling and rehearsal are important techniques used in skills acquisition and generalization of new gender role perceptions and behaviors.

These models are not based on the assumption that violent behavior is the result of an underlying mental disorder or relationship problem, because they are mostly based on social learning theory, which posits that self-control can be learned and that there is hope for change. However, the fact that a large percentage of abusive men report childhood trauma or witnessing family violence in the family of origin suggests a need for methods that also attempt to treat trauma, as stated above. The cognitive-behavioral methods mentioned above do not address these issues (Saunders, 1991). There is more attention to issues of trauma recovery and building up damaged self-cohesion in the Wexler model (Wexler, 1999), which forms the foundation of the treatment program we created based on our research.

Clinical research (Murphy & Baxter, 1997) indicates that the direct confrontation of denial and minimization often practiced by those who advocate reeducation of men's patriarchal views of power and control is ineffective, and that a supportive strategy produces better results. Miller (1985, cited in Murphy & Baxter, 1997) found that empathic therapists are more successful than confrontational ones in helping clients to comply with and succeed in treatment for substance abuse. An intrusive, authoritarian, and aggressive stance on the part of the therapist is most highly correlated with clients who drop out of group treatment or whose condition worsens (Yalom & Lieberman, 1971, cited in Murphy & Baxter, 1997).

Because most men mandated into therapy as partner abusers have been shown to have low self-esteem and frequently have a history of witnessing violence and/or being victims of severe childhood abuse, they are more at risk for becoming therapeutic casualties. Henry, Schacht, and Strupp (1990) found that clients move toward affiliation and autonomy when therapists pass their "tests" by consistently disconfirming their clients' expectation of rejection. A therapeutic setting where premature confrontation abounds is not a safe environment where clients may encounter a corrective emotional experience. Murphy and Baxter (1997) theorized that the negative effects of controlling, hostile therapist behavior may be compounded when the client is of a different race or ethnicity, given their mistrust of the therapy situation. The exploration of appropriate or useful therapist styles was an important part of the data we collected in our interviews with Latino men in this study.[14]

It is difficult to establish a strong working alliance with men who are aggressive and angry, such as is frequently the case with court-ordered men who have abused their partners. Bordin (1994) outlined the components of the working alliance: shared understanding of treatment goals, shared understanding of the tasks required to achieve those goals, and a supportive and warm bond between therapist and client. Murphy and Baxter (1997) proposed that a stronger working alliance will enhance interventions with partner abusive men. They suggested use of the motivational interviewing technique developed by Miller and Rollnick (1991) to establish a strong alliance. The method is designed to work supportively with the client's ambivalence about change, as well as to help clients accept a disquieting self-image and commit to a difficult process of change by eliciting the client's own concerns, instead of imposing the therapist's concerns on the client. Strategies include raising consciousness about the need to change; enhancing the perceived benefits of change and resolving ambivalence; choosing, planning, and committing to change strategies; initiating and carrying out behavior change; and identifying and coping with the potential for relapse. In the work with Latino partner abusive men, empowering clients by establishing a strong working alliance and demystifying the therapeutic process by clarifying strategies and goals are likely to be important components of treatment efficacy.

Harway and Evans (1996) proposed a model of the cycle of violence that focuses on "feeling avoidance." The abuser experiences tension and unacceptable emotions, which lead to an overload on his deficient coping mechanisms. There is a crisis of overwhelming emotions such as hurt, shame, helplessness, fear, guilt, inadequacy, and loneliness, which the man believes are signs of unacceptable weakness. The abuser then defends against the feeling by placing blame on his partner and denying responsibility, controlling everyone around him, using alcohol or drugs to anesthetize the pain, and/or seeking negative excitement to distract himself. Harway and Evans theorized that it is the cycle of feeling avoidance in dealing with one's central issues by being abusive that is the core issue for partner abusive men. If this behavior pattern is not changed, the abuse will continue. They propose that the most successful intervention process is a mixture of therapy and education, including cognitive-behavioral techniques, traumatology, feminist analysis, and psychodynamic approaches, while always keeping the most important goal of behavior change in mind. Feldman and Ridley (1995) pointed out that programs that address diverse factors at the intrapersonal, interpersonal, and societal levels more adequately capture and treat the multidimensional nature of the problem of partner abuse. Such an ecosystemic approach is more likely to effectively impact the problem.

Addressing the clinical implications of working with Latino men who have a strong male gender identity, Casas et al. (1994) pointed out that these men avoid all situations in which they perceive themselves as helpless or weak. The parallel of Casas et al.'s clinical findings to the feeling avoidance model proposed by Harway and Evans is striking. Masculine self-esteem in the case of these men is tied to the ability to cope and problem solve independently. Such clients look upon therapy as a humiliating admission or accusation of weakness and dependence, which is only compounded by the therapeutic focus on expression of feelings. Casas and his associates suggest that the therapist be aware of the wounded self-esteem of such clients, their lack of motivation, and their mistrust of therapy. They recommend redefining a truly strong person as one who admits to difficulties and obtains temporary assistance for his own and his family's best interests. In later chapters, we address the issue of mandated therapy and how considerably more resistance is to be expected from Latino men, or any clients for that matter, who find themselves in a therapy group in spite of their often heartfelt belief that they do not belong there. Because the abuse that men perpetrate is often patterned on the abuse they suffered as children (Straus et al., 1980), Harway and Evans (1996) suggested that retraining is inadequate as a means to change partner abusive men. Partner abusive men need healing and recovery, like any other victim, before they can stop using the coping patterns affected by their own victimization.

DOES TREATMENT FOR PARTNER ABUSIVE MEN WORK?

Whether or not intervention for partner abusive men is actually effective and reduces IPV is a controversial issue. The relatively few outcome studies that have been conducted empirically tend to produce mixed results that make it difficult to answer this question. Babcock, Green, and Robie (2004) found in their meta-analysis of the effectiveness of IPV interventions (using psychoeducational or cognitive-behavioral treatment models) in 22 studies that the overall effect size was small. The programs included in the study were typically of short duration, 12–16 weeks.[15] Taft, Murphy, Elliott, and Morrell (2001) reported attendance-enhancing procedures, such as reminder phone calls and short notes after intake and when clients missed a session, that resulted in strong effect sizes in their outcome study, regardless of the intervention model. This technique appears to have increased client investment and reduced attrition. We will expand on outcomes in our work with Latino partner abusive men in later chapters. Strong backup from the legal and judicial systems is essential in treating partner abusive men, because as a mandated population, their initial investment in treatment is low or nonexistent. There continues to be a pressing need for more specific research regarding treatment outcomes as they are related to duration of treatment and intervention model used.

Latino Men and Treatment for IPV

The National Latino Alliance for the Elimination of Domestic Violence (la Alianza) is very active in promoting information, research, and events to raise consciousness regarding IPV in the Latino community. Their research director, Julia Perilla, who created a family intervention program for IPV in Georgia (Perilla & Pérez, 2002), writes on the Alianza Web site:

> Domestic violence is a serious and damaging problem for Latino communities throughout the United States, one that requires an honest look at a range of factors that perpetuate this violence within our communities, as well as outside our communities. Domestic violence within Latino families occurs in a context of communities suffering from a legacy of multiple oppressions, some of which go back for centuries, both here and in our countries of origin. Among these oppressions are colonization, discrimination, racism, long-term poverty, and governmental oppression and violence. Latino men who batter are influenced by oppressive patriarchal traditions and models of masculinity and manhood that are widespread in our cultures and in society. In addition, the multiple oppressions that many men in our communities experience intensify oppressive conduct in intimate relationships and complicate the change process for them. (http://www.dvalianza. org/pdfs/r_analytical_framework.pdf, 2007)

In summarizing some of the research on IPV and specifically within the Latino community, we have come full circle. From the worldwide theoretical approach of the World Health Organization to researchers in the field of IPV among Latino immigrants in the United States, there is consensus that IPV cannot be perceived or treated as a problem of the individual alone, whether perpetrator or victim. The reach of IPV extends from individual to family to community to society and back. Effective interventions must take this into account, and policy must be developed from an ecosystemic perspective if any serious, long-lasting change is to be effected.

In the remainder of this book, we will explore the world of the Latino partner abusive men mandated to treatment for IPV. Based on the research in this chapter and on their own words, we will formulate some answers to the question, What elements should culturally specific treatment for Latino partner abusive men include, and how should it be delivered?

NOTES

1. These attitudes are readily observed among young Mexican migrant workers who risk their lives to cross a dangerous border and subsequently withstand deplorable work and living conditions far from the simple comforts of home, in order to be able to provide some financial support to their parents and siblings, or to their young wives and children in Mexico. Crossing the border and enduring the hardships of the migrant agricultural worker's life has become somewhat of a rite of passage into genuine masculine adulthood for many young Mexican and other Latino men of low socioeconomic status.

2. *Machista* is the adjective for the noun *macho*. In Spanish, *machista* denotes a man who demonstrates machismo. Macho, although a noun, can also be used as an adjective, with different meanings depending on the context and the speaker, as is explained in the following pages.

3. In our chapters discussing the participants' views of machismo, it will be apparent that they agree in large part with Mirandé's findings. Under the heading of therapeutic interventions we will also discuss the importance of clearly understanding how male gender identity is currently understood by Latino men.

4. This word can be loosely translated as *wimp*.

5. It should be noted that, unlike *machismo*, the term *marianismo* is not used in common speech and is a useful invention of cultural researchers. Thus the mystified look on clients' faces should a therapist decide to use it.

6. Statistics are given for Mexico. However, similar heterogeneity is the norm in all Latin American countries, to varying degrees depending on history and pre-Columbian distribution of indigenous peoples or the use of African slave labor during the colonial period. The nations with the highest percentages of indigenous populations in Latin America are Guatemala (40.3%) and Peru (45%), per World Factbook (Central Intelligence Agency, 2007).

7. Indigenous peoples in Mexico have since reclaimed the word *indio* to refer to themselves, as the native peoples of the United States have done in recent years by using the name Indian.

8. In our experience, partner abusive men can be particularly successful at convincing Child Protective Services workers that their abusive behavior toward their children and spouse is culturally normative. Not wishing to appear insensitive, some workers fail to follow up on clearly abusive and inappropriate behaviors that would not be acceptable among their professional colleagues in the country of origin.

9. Although an evaluation of this nature is usually impossible in an IPV intake interview for group therapy, the issues mentioned here are excellent ones to keep in mind when discussing the phenomenon of immigration with the group as it comes up or in specific interventions.

10. Our study of attrition rates for the IPV program we piloted is briefly described in chapter 9.

11. Strategies for bringing up sexual content are discussed in later chapters.

12. In every culture there are regional, linguistic, social, and economic differences, to mention only a few characteristics of which a therapist may be unaware.

13. Take, for example, the potential mismatch of a wealthy, privileged psychologist of European descent from Mexico City with a Mexican client in the United States who is undocumented, of indigenous and rural origin, poor and unemployed, and whose first language is not Spanish. Both may be Mexican, but this does not make them a natural fit for empathy and cultural understanding.

14. Therapeutic successes and failures are described by our research participants in chapter 6.

15. In our clinical experience, IPV perpetrators have usually made very little progress in changing long-held beliefs about gender, conduct, or the need to change at all in 12–16 weeks. Outcome studies that are conducted at this stage of treatment, or treatment that is of such short duration, may show little effect.

CHAPTER 4

Who Are the Men
Being Treated for IPV?
Results of a Survey

No single survey can capture the demographic profile of all Latino men who are currently in treatment for IPV across the United States. Nevertheless, the Bureau of the Census does inform us that over 60% of Hispanic men in the United States are of Mexican descent, either as first-generation immigrants themselves or as children or grandchildren, and so forth, of those immigrants (U.S. Bureau of the Census, 2006). There are several states in the United States where the concentration of Latinos is highest: California, Texas, New York, Florida, Illinois, Arizona, and New Jersey. Colorado and Washington State also have significant populations (Baradello, 2006). However, Latinos are moving to populate most regions of the United States, wherever they can find employment. In the northeastern United States, Puerto Ricans form the majority of Latinos, and in Florida, Cubans are the Latino majority. In every other state, Mexicans are the Latino majority. It is quite probable that, were surveys similar to ours to be conducted in those states, a comparable demographic profile would emerge. However, because no such surveys are accessible in the literature as yet, firm statements cannot yet be made.

When we began our initial research (Welland, 1999), we communicated with several agencies in the San Diego region, attempting to collect demographic data regarding Latino men in treatment for IPV. We found that neither these agencies nor the Department of Probation keep separate descriptive statistics for Latino IPV offenders. It became clear that, in order to establish the demographic profile of the Latino population of IPV offenders, it would be necessary to conduct a survey of agencies that provide IPV therapy for men in Spanish. We developed a survey form, adapted and expanded from the demographic survey used by Olona (1993), who conducted research with a Latino population of IPV offenders in Los Angeles. The survey also included items that pertain to the major risk factors for male-to-female IPV in the American population (see CDC, 2006, for a current list). It was a 50-item, paper and pencil instrument given to participants at the beginning of one of their weekly group therapy sessions.[1] All of these men had been convicted of IPV and had been mandated to 52 weeks of group treatment by the courts in San Diego County. Based on an expected low level of literacy for some, from personal experience conducting IPV groups with Latino men in the San Diego area, special measures were taken to ensure the maximum participation of all group members who wished to complete the survey. Assistance was given to willing men who were unable to read the items, taking care to humiliate no one. The sample for the survey consisted of 159 court-ordered members of IPV treatment groups conducted in Spanish in the San Diego region. At the time, there were 9 agencies providing such groups, treating a total of 400 Latino men. Thus, our sample made up 40% of the total population of Latino men in Spanish groups in San Diego County and as such may be considered representative of the total population. Currently there are 15 agencies that conduct Spanish-language groups in San Diego County.

Four agencies provided participants for the study. The survey was administered anonymously, so as to eliminate participants' potential fear of disclosure. Those who were interested in participating in the in-depth interviews were given the option of filling out a two-page form separate from the survey, which included identifying data as well as information that would assist the researcher in selecting the interview sample.

The major results of the survey provide a sketch of important personal characteristics and historical factors of Latino men who are mandated to IPV groups in Southern California, and may perhaps be applied to other

---

The information we gathered in our survey is important for clinicians to know about their clients at intake. We suggest incorporating items that target these factors into the intake packet given to Latino clients as they enter treatment. Being aware of major demographic and risk factor information from the outset can alert a clinician to potential issues that clients may have, past and present, as well as to possible typology based on history of abuse, substance abuse, and history of violent crime.

Latino men across the country, as stated above. Where relevant, we also include statistical information from the interview respondents. We hope that future surveys will expand on this information and provide data specific to various geographical regions where the concentration of Latino ethnic groups is different.

ETHNICITY OF SURVEY RESPONDENTS

Eighty-five percent of respondents were first-generation Mexican men, representing all geographic regions of Mexico. Central Mexico, including Mexico City, was the most highly represented with 40% for the survey respondents. There were few indigenous Mexicans responding to the survey, an unexpected finding, because it is well known among those who work with Latinos in North San Diego County that there is a substantial indigenous population working there, mostly of the Mixtec nation of Oaxaca in southern Mexico. We hypothesize that perhaps their partners are not willing to call the police during IPV incidents, or that they lack education regarding resources available to them.

Four percent of survey respondents were second-generation Mexican Americans, who, although they were fluent in English, preferred to be in a group with other Latinos. The remainder consisted of 6% Central Americans (from El Salvador, Guatemala, and Honduras) and 2% Cubans. The interview respondents were selected to be 100% Mexican in origin for the purposes of the survey.

Needless to say, it is very important for therapists to have a working knowledge of the principal Latino ethnic groups in their region to be effective in the group. Asking members for cultural clarification is always acceptable, and often the preferable approach, because it demonstrates openness and a willingness to learn. Therapists must also guard against one particular group stigmatizing or making fun of another and must clarify the ground rules from the outset. Often humor, but never at any one group's expense, is the best way to defuse tension. Stereotypes abound in every culture, and the group is a good place to unravel them, when appropriate and when time constraints allow.

URBAN VERSUS RURAL ORIGIN

Sixty percent of the survey respondents in the present study were from urban areas of Mexico, an unexpected finding. In the older literature on Latino immigration it is assumed that many Mexicans migrate to the United States to seek opportunities in American cities that were not available to them in their villages. Only 40% of the survey respondents came from a rural background. However, 7 of the 12 interview participants were raised in a rural environment. Urbanicity of residence is considered a statistical risk factor for Latino violence in general by American researchers, although the interview participants expressed the belief that IPV is more likely in rural areas of Mexico than in the cities. No Mexican statistics are available to verify this belief. However, the WHO's Multi-country Study (2005) found that sexual, but not physical, IPV was significantly more prevalent in a rural population in Peru than in urban settings. Generally, this study did confirm that IPV is more prevalent in rural areas around the world.

> The group setting is an ideal place to confront members' and therapists' stereotyped beliefs about violence and its relationship to demographics and risk factors. When we are exploring, for example, the concept of rural/ urban differences or machismo in chapter 5, we are confronted with participants' generalizations in their interview comments. These are excellent starting points for group discussion and for uncovering assumptions that may be blocking progress or contributing to within-group discrimination.

NUMBER OF CHILDREN IN FAMILY OF ORIGIN

An unexpected demographic finding among the interview participants was the large number of children in their families of origin. Because this factor was not mentioned in the IPV literature, it was not included in the survey questions. However, 7 of the 12 interview participants came from families of at least eight children. The men from families with 12 or more siblings were among the most severely abused as children. The positive correlation of family size and incidence of child abuse has been noted by social workers in Mexico (Deckenback, Smith-Resendez, & Wakamatsu, 1978) and may be an added risk factor for this population.

HISTORY OF ABUSE AND NEGLECT

Fifty-one percent of survey respondents stated that they had been physically abused by their parents. The qualifiers were of a more serious nature, such as hit, slap, punch, and kick, as well as "otherwise abuse you." One of the men who volunteered for the interview answered "No" on this question, but during the course of the interview described very severe, if infrequent, abuse by both his parents. This fact raises the question of reliability of the other survey responses. The survey question was focused mainly on frequency rather than severity of abuse, so the percentage reported offers only a glimpse of the abuse scenarios in the respondents' households. Nine out of 12 of the interview participants reported being abused by their fathers. Of these, 6 described brutal, unreasonable violence perpetrated on them, usually when they were under the age of 8. Eight of these same men reported frequent, damaging emotional and verbal abuse as well. All of the abused men reported feelings of hurt, fear, and anger toward their fathers. A smaller number, 4 of the 12, reported physical and emotional abuse by their mothers as well. These men were more likely to weep during the interview, to suffer from symptoms of PTSD, and to report a complete lack of social support and protection during their childhood. Five of the men, including 2 of the 3 who were not themselves victims of child abuse, described witnessing violence in their community or being abused by other relatives. The 3 men who were not abused all received corporal punishment at some time during their childhood. Suffering child abuse is a risk factor for later IPV, as seen in chapter 2.

HISTORY OF WITNESSING IPV

Forty-four percent of the survey respondents reported that their father had beaten their mother either frequently or on occasion. The description of IPV that was used in the survey was mostly of more severe abuse, such as slapping, punching, and kicking. Of these, 14% reported that the abuse was frequent. Seven of the 12 interview participants (60%) had witnessed IPV in their homes, and in six cases, the violence was frequent. Two of their fathers perpetrated serious violence with injuries that should have been medically treated but were not, due to lack of access and resources. All the abuse was male-to-female. All of the interview participants described conflicted and painful emotions related to these incidents. Anger and helplessness were the primary feelings. As stated in chapter 2, witnessing parental partner abuse is the strongest risk factor for adult perpetration of IPV.

FATHER'S ALCOHOL ABUSE OR ALCOHOLISM

On the survey, 49% of the men responded that their fathers drank sometimes, and 28% reported that their fathers drank frequently, a total of 77%. Half of the men interviewed (6 out of 12) had alcoholic fathers based on their detailed descriptions of their fathers' behavior. Five of them stated that their fathers were frequently drunk during bouts of IPV and child abuse.

> Group sessions where child abuse, witnessing violence, and their fathers' alcoholism are discussed are invariably laden with emotion. Signs of trauma reactions among some members of the group are common.

MOTHER'S STATUS IN THE FAMILY OF ORIGIN

Fifty-one percent of survey respondents reported that their mothers were equal to their fathers in power and authority. Ten percent stated that their mother had more power and authority than their father; only 10% responded that their mother had no power in the relationship at all. The question may have been interpreted to describe the considerable authority Mexican mothers enjoy in the home with their children; however, this may not translate to equality in the marital relationship.

In the course of describing gender roles, 7 of the interview participants volunteered that their mother held an inferior position to their father. In the cases where there was more severe partner abuse, their mother was treated like a servant and had no authority in the marital relationship. This treatment appears similar to Type I abusers in the United States, who are known to hold more rigid gender roles and to have more contempt toward women; they have been classified as "patriarchal terrorists" (Johnson, 1995).

RELIGIOUS IDENTIFICATION

Ninety-five percent of the survey respondents self-identified as Christian. Of these, 80% were Catholic. Only 3% of respondents claimed to have no religion. Eighty-nine percent of respondents stated that their religion was important in their daily life, and for 51% it was very important. No survey respondent replied that religion had no importance to him. In the demographic portion of a more recent study (Welland et al., unpublished) 65% of Latino partner abusive men were Catholic, 20% other Christian, and 9% reported no religion. Seventy-four percent stated that religion was important to them, and for 35% it was very important. Only 0.04% of respondents reported that religion had no importance to him.

It may be that a smaller sample size in the second study was responsible for the difference in this statistic.

Of the 12 interview participants, 11 were Catholic, and 1 was Evangelical. Nine of the interviewees identified their religion as important or very important to them. In response to the researcher's question regarding the teaching of their church regarding IPV, the participants unanimously agreed that their church is against spousal violence and endorses such values as respect for others, peace, love, and caring for one's family. Most of them had heard something at church about avoiding IPV, usually at churches in the United States. Only 1 participant related that his village priest in Mexico spoke explicitly against IPV. These responses are comparable to our more recent study (Welland et al., unpublished), where we found that 75% of Catholic IPV offenders and 81% of non-Catholic Christian offenders reported that IPV was sometimes or frequently mentioned and condemned in their churches in the United States.

> Not unexpectedly for those who work with Latino clients, religious and spiritual beliefs turned out to be very important for clients. The ability to approach these issues comfortably and respectfully in the group is an important asset to therapists.

MARITAL STATUS

Seventy percent of the 159 survey respondents were either married or cohabiting at the time of the survey. Twenty percent were separated; only 5% were divorced. Five percent of the men reported that they were not in a relationship at the time of the survey. The average length of time with their partner was 10 years.

Ninety-four percent of the survey respondents responded that they had children, and 31% had stepchildren. The average number of children per family was 2.6.

IMMIGRATION STATUS

Sixty-three percent of the men had permanent residence. Only 12% were citizens, although the average length of time the survey respondents had been in the United States was 15 years. Thirteen percent of the men were undocumented.

EMPLOYMENT STATUS AND UNEMPLOYMENT

Ten percent of the employed survey respondents were in technical or retail occupations, and the remaining 90% of the employed men were in blue-collar occupations. Of total respondents, 15% were unemployed, and 8% did not reply to the question. The level of unemployment reported is almost 4 times higher than the average annual rate of unemployment in San Diego, which is 4.2% (San Diego Association of Governments, 2002). Unemployment is seen as a demographic risk factor for IPV in the general population (Straus & Gelles, 1980). Hypothesized connections are economic stress due to low income, marital conflict, and emotional stress on the man because he is not providing for his family and living up to his expected gender role (Perilla et al., 1994).

Seventy percent of the survey respondents' partners were not employed outside the home, indicating that the Latino cultural value of staying home and caring for the children was mostly intact in this sample of first-generation immigrants. Further study may determine whether or not rigid male gender roles play a part in the spouses' decision to stay at home, or how the rate of 70% of spouses not working compares with nonviolent Latino men. Of the 30% of women who were employed, 5% were in professional occupations, and the remainder worked at service jobs.

ALCOHOL ABUSE BY RESPONDENTS

Eighty-four percent of the 159 survey respondents reported some alcohol use. Twenty-five percent of the respondents stated that they drank heavily. A measure of the severity of their alcohol problems, and an indication of severe impairment of judgment as well as ignorance of or disregard for the law, is the high percentage of survey respondents who reported having been arrested for driving under the influence of alcohol (DUI). Twenty-five percent of the survey respondents had been arrested once, and another 12% had more than one arrest for DUI, a total of 37%. Eighteen percent of respondents reported illegal drug use before treatment. Ten percent of men admitted to marijuana use, 11% reported use of crystal methamphetamine, 5% used cocaine, and 2% used heroin. Six percent of drug users were polysubstance abusers. Forty-two percent of the survey participants reported that they were drunk at the time of the IPV incident. Ten of the 12 men interviewed reported problems with alcohol, in some cases clearly alcoholism. Nine had abused only alcohol, and 1 had abused both alcohol and several drugs. Four of the 12 men interviewed reported being under the influence or drunk during the IPV incident. As Olona (1993) found in his study, not all the alcoholics were drunk at the time of the incident, and not all the perpetrators who drank were alcoholics. Recent research, including the WHO fact sheet on IPV and alcohol, published in 2006 and cited in chapter 2, emphasizes the importance of assessing for and treating alcohol abuse as a factor in IPV. All of the 12 interview participants who drank had witnessed and/or experienced violence in their childhood, and 8 of them (75%) reported that they drank explicitly to forget childhood trauma and/or to cope with stress. Two gave their reason for drinking as purely social and to fit in with others. All of these men stated that their chronic alcoholism or occasional abuse caused relationship stress because of economic deprivation to the family and/or conflict with their partner over their drinking habit. Fully 8 of the 12 interview participants had been arrested and mandated to treatment for DUI. Two of the men had been arrested and treated on two occasions.

We can never stress enough the importance of assessment for alcohol and drug abuse at intake. Some men, as they were not intoxicated at the time of arrest, will not have been mandated to alcohol treatment by the court. Usually the only reliable way to assess for an alcohol or drug problem, given the strength of clients' denial, is to obtain collateral information by telephone from the partner. When illegal drugs are involved, the partner may also be using; thus drug information may be harder to obtain. Therapeutic errors and treatment failure, as well as repeat offenses, can result from not taking the time to evaluate ongoing alcohol impairment.

AGE OF RESPONDENTS

The third demographic risk factor proposed by Straus and Smith (1990), youthfulness of IPV offenders (i.e., under the age of 30), was not borne out in this study, which was an unexpected finding, given the overall youthfulness of the Latino population. The median age of offenders surveyed was 34, and the large majority of men who are mandated to groups begin treatment within a few months of the offense. Only 29% of the total survey respondents were under 30. Forty-eight percent were between 30 and 40, and 18% were between 40 and 50. Only 4% were over 50. The median age of the 12 interview participants was 39, and only 1 of the interview participants that met criteria for the interview, that is, 40 weeks or more in treatment, was under 30 years of age. It would appear that many first-generation Mexican immigrants continue to assault their partners even when they are middle-aged. Absent any empirical research data to explain this phenomenon, and noting that 54% of the men surveyed had been physically violent to their partners on at least one other occasion prior to their arrest, we can only hypothesize that their spouses had chosen not to report their prior violence, perhaps for lack of knowledge of IPV laws in the United States, out of fear of deportation if the police were to become involved, or out of concern for the financial consequences. Perhaps as their children grew older and they saw the damage the violence was doing to the family, the spouses finally decided to take action, and by this time the man was in his 30s. We can only speculate at this time. But "reaching their limit" is a tempting explanation, and one that has been reported in qualitative studies with Latina victims (Coffin-Romig, 1997).

DEPRESSION

On the survey, only 4% of respondents admitted to being depressed most of the time, although 58% reported being depressed sometimes.

Of the 12 interview participants, 2 reported that they were depressed at the time of the interview. Five others reported that they had been depressed around the time of the IPV incident, but that they had recovered since then. Three of the men reported depression (and subsequent alcoholism) as a result of their marital separation, after the IPV incident. Depression has not emerged as a consistent risk factor for IPV in the general population, and it appears not to have had much salience in the Latino population we sampled either, at least not based on the self-report of participants without the use of standardized measures. It has also been remarked (Saunders, 1995) that, using standardized measures or simple questionnaires, it is impossible to tell whether the depression men report was premorbid to the violent incident or whether it flared up after the arrest, with all the negative consequences due to the IPV, including incarceration, probation, community service, loss of income, and often separation, divorce, and/or loss of visitation rights with children.

Men may deny depression but may admit to a past alcohol problem at some time during their treatment. Based on our research and clinical experience, as well as the very high rates of both alcohol abuse and history of trauma in the population of IPV offenders, symptoms of depression may be denied and self-medicated by alcoholism. Some of our clients may consider depression an unmanly state for someone who should be able to "snap out of" whatever is bothering him (Casas et al., 1994).

RELATIONSHIP CONFLICT

Only 3% of 159 survey respondents reported frequent arguments with their partner, while 53% stated that they sometimes argued. Six of the men interviewed (50%) reported a chronically high level of conflict in their relationship before the IPV incident. In some cases, the conflict was ongoing, although the violence had stopped.

GENERALIZED AGGRESSION

On the survey, 14% of the men reported being arrested for crimes other than IPV and DUI, but the question was not specific enough regarding violent crime to determine a history of antisocial behavior. In Welland and colleagues' quantitative study (unpublished), 24% of the violent Latino men in treatment groups and 15% of the control group admitted to a history of arrest for nonviolent crime, not including minor traffic violations. Less than 8% of the men in treatment groups endorsed the item referring to a history of arrest for violent crime. This percentage of violent crime is very low, given that up to 20% of batterers in typology research are classified as generally violent (Jacobson et al., 1995). This may be the result of social desirability responding. In future research, more sensitive measures that include commission of violent crime, without necessarily being arrested for it, will be helpful for clearer descriptions of this subset of the population. It is also possible that there are fewer generally violent men in treatment, because antisocial men are more likely to be incarcerated for the higher level of violence perpetrated, or to have escaped arrest or treatment, due to manipulation of the legal system and/or threats to their partner (Jacobson et al., 1995).

In our clinical experience, the majority of clients who present for treatment with antisocial personality disorder or features do not complete the program. They are usually unwilling to observe the strict attendance and payment rules set by the courts, and thus are "terminated" within a couple of months at most. The other men in the groups are frequently relieved when such men drop out of treatment, as their negative attitude and narcissistic traits impede the progress of the whole group.

Only 2 of the 12 men interviewed reported that they had been violent outside the home, when they were younger. Neither of them recounted severity or frequency of aggression or lack of remorse that would suggest an antisocial personality. It stands to reason that men with antisocial features such as generalized aggression would have little interest in participating in the in-depth interviews.

EXTENDED FAMILY AND SOCIAL SUPPORT

Sixty-five percent of the survey respondents reported that they had extended family living in the region. Seventy-three percent reported compadres[2] and close friends in the area. Eight percent of the survey respondents had their or their partner's parents living with them, and 18% of respondents stated that other relatives shared their living space. Eighty-eight percent of respondents stated that they were satisfied with the level of social support they enjoy. Thus, isolation from extended family does not appear to have played much of a role in protecting from or in contributing to the IPV, as is sometimes speculated in the literature on Latinos. Because we did not survey their partners, we do not know if women in these relationships feel isolated from family or support. Clinical experience would suggest that they do in at least some cases of IPV.

The interview participants identified their extended family as a source of moral support in most cases. Almost all of the men interviewed had parents or siblings living in the region, and 7 had frequent contact with them. Most of the men reported that their families were upset with them because of the IPV incident, even some of the fathers of the men who had been extremely violent themselves. Many of the men did not expect financial help from extended family. In a few cases, extended family was a problem, exacerbating marital conflicts and contributing to alcoholism by excessive drinking when socializing.

LEVEL OF ACCULTURATION

Level of acculturation, which may be an indication of how well immigration is being handled, can be assessed through language, proximity of extended family, importance of religion, and clarity of gender role expectations (Falicov, 1995). The survey respondents, when asked about language use, reported speaking Spanish at home in 71% of cases; 8% used mostly English, and 19% spoke a mixture of Spanish and English. Only 28% of survey respondents reported relative fluency in the English language, an indication that a Mexican immigrant living in Southern California is able to make a living without ever fully acculturating into the dominant group. However, when asked directly about their level of comfort in the United States, 98%

reported that they had attained an acceptable comfort level living in this country. The level of acculturation of the survey respondents is difficult to assess absent specific norms with which to compare their responses. However, it would seem that subjectively, they are satisfied with their decision to emigrate. The 12 interview participants reported socializing and doing business almost entirely with other Mexicans or Latinos. They all reported being more or less content in the United States and recognized many benefits from residence here. Only 1 man was still considering the possibility of returning to Mexico. Even when men want to return, their partners and children often do not.

SUMMARY OF SURVEY FINDINGS

It is thought that most IPV goes unreported, and the fact that only 400 Latino men were in treatment for IPV, a small fraction of the population of over 500,000 Latinos in San Diego County at the time of our survey, appears to corroborate this theory. Based on the demographic profile of San Diego County, we expected most Latino IPV offenders in treatment to be of Mexican origin, and in fact 89% of the men in treatment were.

The survey results present a demographic profile of Latino men in domestic violence treatment that is not readily available. Most of the findings were expected and were predicted by the literature, such as low socioeconomic status and a low level of educational achievement. Some of the findings that challenged our expectations warrant further discussion.

The National Violence Against Women Survey (Tjaden & Thoennes, 2000) reported that 30% of women injured during their most recent assault received medical treatment. However, only 5% of the 159 survey respondents' partners received attention at a hospital, and another 4% saw a doctor. Because it is unlikely that their injuries were less serious than their non-Hispanic counterparts, their failure to seek care may be due to lack of access or insurance (Leong et al., 1995) or inaccurate information provided by the men. More research is needed to ascertain the reason for the low level of medical attention afforded to these Latina victims. Women may also be influenced by expected family loyalty (*familismo*) to refrain from calling the police or seeking medical or therapeutic attention (Coffin-Romig, 1997). Economic issues, fear of reprisal, and illegal immigration status are other potential reasons that immigrant women may fail to report domestic violence (Orloff, Jang, & Klein,1995). For Latinas, more public education on this issue is needed, especially as regards available services and the long-term cost to the family if violence is not halted.

Fifty-seven percent of the survey respondents reported that their children were exposed to IPV. This indicates a high rate of potentially serious emotional abuse and trauma being perpetrated on the Latino children growing up in violent families. The fact that a high percentage of the survey respondents (44%) were exposed to domestic violence in their family of origin has already been mentioned. There is an urgent need for policy to be determined and acted upon for the mental health of Latino children and to prevent the evolution of future generations of abusive men and abused women. Latino individuals have been shown to be most responsive to behavior change when the positive impact of the change on their families, especially the children, is stressed (Marín et al., 1990).

In the literature on Latino immigration in past decades, it was formerly assumed that many Mexicans migrate to the United States from rural settings (Bach-y-Rita, 1982). However, as noted in chapter 2, migration has changed since the early 1990s. In our survey, 60% of the respondents came from urban backgrounds, which suggests the need for therapists who work with this population to be able to discuss both urban and rural issues and to utilize metaphors to which both populations can relate. We found only a very small percentage of indigenous men in treatment, in spite of the fact that up to 50,000 members of the Mixtec and Zapotec nations of Oaxaca, Mexico, reside in San Diego County and Baja California (Share International Archives, 1994). It may be that calling the police is so culturally inappropriate for women in these groups that they do not obtain the protection they need and their partners do not obtain necessary treatment, which suggests the need for a particular effort at education for Latino indigenous groups. Because often the women are monolingual in their native tongue, public education presents a challenge for health care workers.

In the present survey, it was found that up to 70% of the Latino domestic violence offenders in treatment live below the poverty line, based on their reported income and number of family members. The low socioeconomic status of the respondents has important repercussions when one considers that the great majority of men mandated to treatment pay $20 or more per session and that treatment lasts for up to a year in some states. Treating agencies need to be aware of the possible hardship that weekly fees place on the families of men mandated to treatment. Community resource lists can be provided to clients to ease the financial strain many families experience. Another efficacious way to ameliorate family finances is to verify that alcoholic domestic violence offenders receive appropriate treatment and follow-up, as heavy drinking habits place economic strain on families. Moreover, an abused Latina woman who, with her children, suffers the consequences of income reduction during her partner's therapy because she called the police, is likely to hesitate to call again should her partner reoffend.

ADDITIONAL FINDINGS FROM THE SURVEY: MAJOR RISK FACTORS

The three major risk factors for domestic violence in the general population are being exposed to and/or experiencing violence in childhood, low income and education, and alcohol use, especially alcoholism (Saunders, 1993; Tolman & Bennett, 1990). It has already been shown that most of the men in the sample live under the poverty line. Geffner et al. (2000) and Straus et al. (1980) found that exposure to parental violence compounded with physical abuse in childhood are the strongest predictors of domestic violence in adulthood. The results of the survey reveal a clear pattern of child abuse and exposure to domestic violence in the histories of many participants. Clearly, exposure to violence in the home and the community was a large part of the respondents' lives. For Latino domestic violence offenders, then, it would appear that the research on this major risk factor that has been done in the general population could be applied to them as well. To this end, an empirical study was conducted that is currently under review for publication (Welland et al.). Alcohol use and abuse emerged as very prevalent in the lifestyles of the survey respondents, as well as in their own fathers' lifestyles. Drug abuse was less prevalent as a problem, but was nevertheless present. The rate of alcoholism or alcohol abuse signals the need for further public education on alcoholism for Latinos, including the consequences of drunk driving. Agencies will benefit Latino families tremendously if they screen carefully for alcohol abuse and ensure that their clients are treated for it. Although no standardized measures of alcohol use were used in this study, it is evident from the responses to the survey that a very high percentage of Mexican immigrants arrested for domestic violence have alcohol problems. In our empirical study, the Michigan Alcoholism Screening Test scores showed a significantly greater presence of alcohol problems among the treatment group, even when we controlled for marital status, employment, and education. The control group did not score in the clinical range of alcohol abuse, although the sample was demographically matched, except for IPV.

In summary, the majority of respondents met criteria for all three of the major risk factors in the U.S. population: history of exposure to violence, low income and education, and alcohol abuse. Because no previous demographic survey has been published to delineate the characteristics of the Latino population of IPV offenders and such information is vital for future research, the English text of the survey is reproduced in appendix B.

NOTES

1. The English text of the survey can be found in appendix B.
2. *Compadres* and *comadres* are close friends, sometimes relatives, who are godparents or sponsors of religious rites of passage such as baptism of children, confirmation, first Holy Communion, or marriage. Accepting this responsibility creates a special bond between adults, not only of friendship but also of economic and spiritual assistance when it is needed or requested. There is an extensive anthropological and sociological literature on this essential relationship in Latino culture.

CHAPTER 5

The Qualitative Method: Researching Gender Roles, History of Family Violence, and Coping Skills in Partner Abusive Latino Men

Qualitative research, instead of quantifying observations of behavior by statistical analysis, examines people's words and actions in narrative or descriptive ways that are closer to the situation as experienced by the research participant (Maykut & Morehouse, 1994). Qualitative research is based on phenomenological principles; that is, the focus of study is on understanding the meaning that events have for the person who is the participant. Qualitative research stems from the position that knowledge is constructed, formed from multiple sociopsychological realities, and that the knower cannot be separated from the known. Research cannot be value-free, because the values are embedded in researchers themselves, in the research question, and in the manner that research is conducted. Causality is not central to this alternative paradigm, because multidirectional relationships are found within situations. Qualitative researchers value context sensitivity, seeking to understand complex phenomena within a particular situation and environment. This type of research is not designed to be generalized to a large number of subjects and experiments, which is the subsequent task of empirical research. It is oriented toward the discovery of salient propositions, by careful inspection of the patterns that emerge from the data.

Because phenomenologists see the world as complex and interconnected, the research must maintain this complexity to be able to offer trustworthy explanations. Information is seen as a web of meaning, a three-dimensional image whose parts are all interconnected. The researcher has a singular perspective on the data but does not perceive himself or herself as objective. The difference between the two paradigms can be stated as the difference between proof and discovery (Maykut & Morehouse, 1994).

The qualitative researcher seeks to understand and interpret the words of the participants, requiring that she or he have an empathic understanding for the feelings, motives, and thoughts behind the actions of others (Bogden & Taylor, 1975, cited in Maykut & Morehouse, 1994). The use of words captures the particulars and the meanings of individual people's lives (Bruner, 1986).

The purpose of qualitative research is to discover the world of the participant, attempting to enter his or her subjective reality. Because the researcher also has a perspective, the research includes the researcher's views, as well as that of others. In qualitative research, the goal is to discover patterns that emerge from the data after thoughtful and painstaking analysis. Contextual findings, not sweeping generalizations, are discovered.

The researcher's role is that of human-as-instrument, which means that all the researcher's skills, experience, background, and knowledge, as well as biases, are the primary source of data collection and analysis (Lincoln & Guba, 1985). This means that the researcher is able to obtain clarification of idiosyncratic responses on the spot, something quantitative researchers are unable to achieve with standardized measures.

The qualitative researcher is a person who has the ability to be with others, to share in their reality. Recognition of the human connection between researcher and participant enables the researcher to focus on individuals in detail, so as to see differences in similar situations and similarities in different situations. He or she needs tolerance for ambiguity and the ability to wait to discover which of the various potential interpretations of the individual is best explained by the data. Qualitative research presupposes reflective thinking.

For identifying how to deliver culturally appropriate treatment to Latino male immigrants living in Southern California who have been arrested for IPV, qualitative inquiry was better suited to this purpose than an empirical study. Because there is so little research in the literature on this population, this research study is somewhat in the nature of an expedition into the unknown. Attempting to conduct quantitative research with this population when so little is known about it would have been counterproductive, although areas of future quantitative research did emerge from our work.

The men we interviewed were mostly low-income immigrants with few years of education. These are people who have never had a voice in their country of origin and who have so far had limited political influence in the United States. One of the strengths of qualitative inquiry is its emphasis on words and experience, on giving a voice to the research participant (Gilligan, 1982). Some of the men interviewed for this study were functionally illiterate. They would not be able to take part in quantitative research because of its reliance on reading and responding to measures in writing. In qualitative interviews, on the other hand, they were able to speak, unhindered by their lack of educational opportunities.

The first author's experience with Mexicans and Latinos of low socioeconomic status since 1976 both in urban and rural Mexico and in San Diego has prepared her to enter into and understand the experience of the participants in a unique way. Her years working with men mandated to domestic violence treatment and with abused Latina women is another asset that helped her to be open to the participants, as well as to empathically guide the interview questions when an area of potential interest was being explored. Such an empathic stance may be the only way that a violent man can be reached, as mentioned in chapter 2. The same might be said of a marginalized population living in an atmosphere of discrimination and intolerance, as is the case for many Latino immigrants, who are under suspicion because of their ethnicity regardless of their immigration status, during the current period of intense social debate and the apparent inability of lawmakers to reach a consensus on effective ways to deal with illegal immigrants residing in the United States.

QUALITATIVE IN-DEPTH INTERVIEWS

A qualitative in-depth interview is a purposive conversation that is characterized by depth and by the rich discussion of thoughts and feelings (Maykut & Morehouse, 1994). Because such an interview lasts approximately 90 minutes to 2 hours, there is an opportunity for prolonged engagement with the participant, which enhances rapport and fosters a climate of trust. Questions are open-ended and designed to reveal what is important about the topic being studied. Because there are several key questions that we believed would be fruitful to explore, an interview schedule was developed and utilized. This format consists of a detailed set of questions and probes that may be modified by the researcher during the interview, depending on the direction the interview is taking.

Sample

Twelve persons were interviewed altogether. This is the standard number for a qualitative study, usually considered sufficient to reach the saturation point, or the point at which no new information is being accumulated (Maykut & Morehouse, 1994). We interviewed men who had completed 40 weeks or more of the 52-week cycle of domestic violence treatment. The posttreatment men, it was hoped, would be able to articulate what was beneficial or detrimental/culturally dissonant in the program they attended.

The method used in the selection of the sample was maximum variation sampling (Lincoln & Guba, 1985), where the widest range of experience of the phenomenon being studied is desirable. Participants were selected based on their context and setting, as well as on the length of time in treatment criterion. Examples of demographic data that affected the researcher's purposive sampling were level of education, income, experience of family of origin violence, alcohol consumption, region of origin in Mexico, years since immigration, and presence of children during the violence. By seeking out persons whose contextual experiences were different and by seeking to maximize the contrast between them, we gained a wider understanding of the phenomenon. We selected some participants who demonstrated a high number of risk factors for domestic violence, as well as some participants who endorsed fewer or no risk factors, in the group of 12 participants. This purposive, nonrandom sampling approach is called theoretical sampling, because it allows the researcher to build and broaden theoretical insights in the ongoing process of data collection and analysis (Glaser & Straus, 1967).

DEVELOPMENT OF THE INTERVIEW SCHEDULE

The interview schedule was developed from an extensive review of the literature, some of which is cited in chapters 2 and 3, as well as from our clinical experience. Both theory and risk factors were explored, as well as cultural issues that were expected to be of importance in treatment. By grouping similar ideas and concepts together, we brainstormed areas to be explored, then decided which categories best captured the focus of inquiry, the culturally appropriate treatment components. We elicited from the participants responses to questions that explored their understanding of the nature and reasons for the violence; the differences, if any, between their experience of conflict in the relationship in the United States versus in Mexico; major areas that they would be willing to or want to explore and problem solve in group therapy, including the issue of childhood abuse or witnessing parental violence; whether their perception of gender roles had changed and how that had affected their relationship; what they believed would be helpful in group treatment and what would not; whether and how the treatment would be different if it were delivered in Mexico rather than in the United States; whether they believed that their cultural and gender identity was under attack, and if so, how they experienced this; and what they would add or subtract from the group treatment curriculum so that it would better suit their needs. Their experience of the group facilitator(s) and of the treatment group was also included in the schedule questions, for the benefit of the therapists who work with this population.

The schedule included a personal introduction, a statement of purpose that underscored the important contribution that participants were making to their community by agreeing to be involved in the research, and informed consent, including explanations of confidentiality, the limits of confidentiality, for example, reporting of child abuse, and permission to audiotape.

The research questions that we sought to answer in the two-part study were the following:

1. What is the demographic and risk factor profile for Latino IPV offenders in the San Diego region?
2. What was their subjective experience of IPV?
3. What was their subjective experience of court-ordered IPV treatment?
4. What cultural components, both of content and process, should be included in IPV treatment programs for first-generation Latino immigrants?

Translation and Back Translation of the Interview Schedule

The interview schedule was then translated by the first author, who is qualified and experienced in this area. Two native Mexican Spanish speakers were then consulted to make any needed revisions to the questions, assuring that the language would be easily understood. Following the revisions, a bilingual native English speaker back-translated the document to ensure that the documents were equivalent (Brislin, Lonner, & Thorndike, 1973).

Pilot Study of the Interview Schedule

Following the revisions, an informal focus group of 8 Mexican migrant workers fine-tuned the document with the first author, to determine whether the questions and sequence were understandable and whether they elicited the information that was being sought. Revisions and adjustments were then made to the final draft of the interview schedule.

DATA COLLECTION

We audiotaped the interviews using an audiocassette recorder, after obtaining the written consent of the participants, with the assurance that all identifying material would be altered when the research was written up. The location of the interviews varied depending on the circumstances of the participant. Once the preparatory remarks, informed consent, and entire interview schedule had been completed, the first author also took note of observations such as facial expressions, body posture, and mood of the participant, as well as of her own feelings and thoughts about the material presented. These observations formed field notes that contributed to the data analysis (McCracken, 1988).

TRANSCRIPTION OF THE INTERVIEW

Interviews were transcribed as soon as possible after meeting with the participant (Maykut & Morehouse, 1994), directly into English for the purposes of the study. The original Spanish audiotapes were kept in a secure location in order to preserve the original words of the participants for use in publications in Spanish.

DATA ANALYSIS USING THE CONSTANT COMPARATIVE METHOD

Using the constant comparative method of qualitative data analysis (Maykut & Morehouse, 1994), we made triplicate copies of the transcripts, then color- and number-coded all the transcripts. Units of meaning were culled from the data by reading and rereading sections of the transcripts. We then cut two of the transcripts of each interview into units of meaning based on exposed themes, that is, a word or phrase that fell into a larger category based on the meaning it represented. The meaning units were then glued to large index cards containing category headings based on topics explored in the interview. These units were compared to the categories in the focus of inquiry and divided into sections that reflected emerging themes. Data piles were reviewed to determine whether any amendments or condensation should be made. A discovery list was then created from the themes that developed out of the data. Main categories were decided on, depending on the literature. From the discovery list, we made provisional categories, developing theoretical parameters and deciding on rules of inclusion. Categories that were not included in the study were set aside as areas of future research, to be communicated at the end of the document. At this point, we summarized our findings in theoretical notes (Strauss & Corbin, 1990).

We then observed the patterns that emerged from the data and made an integrative diagram of the main categories. A mind map followed (Maykut & Morehouse, 1994), where the data was organized for the written document (Feldman, 1995), using a computer spreadsheet as the final step.

COMMUNICATION OF THE OUTCOME OF THE STUDY

Having completed the analysis of the data as stated above, we had a rich body of information to present. The outcomes that emerged from the data were then prioritized according to the focus of inquiry and also by their prominence in the data (Maxwell, 1996; Polkinghorne, 1994; Rubin & Rubin, 1995). Representative data excerpts were selected for the illustration of each proposition. The outcome propositions were then ordered into a meaningful sequence with the representative data samples included as embedded quotations. We then wrote up the research outcomes section, weaving together a narrative from the topics mentioned by the participants. At the end of this process we were able to delineate the components of culturally relevant treatment that our research had uncovered (Welland, 1999; Welland & Ribner, 2005).

In presenting our findings, the themes that emerged from the interviews are briefly described, then illustrated with a few of the clearest quotations from the interviews. Because many quotations are lengthy, and there is considerable redundancy, as is to be expected and hoped for in a qualitative study, only a few of the men who responded to each theme are quoted. A theme is defined as prominent if 7 or more of the 12 men mentioned it during the course of the interview, although many of the themes were, in fact, mentioned by 10 men or more.

Sin Golpes, Cómo Transformar la Respuesta Violenta del Hombre en la Pareja y la Familia (Welland and Wexler, 2007)[1] is the treatment program for Latino men that resulted from our research. In it, we use many quotations from the participants, embedded into the material being presented in that session. These quotations lend themselves to discussion among group members. They also give credibility to the material, as group members hear about the issues from the standpoint of men who share much of their experience and who were able to take responsibility for their behavior and make the necessary changes.

VIOLENCE AS A WAY OF LIFE

This section presents the justification for the abuse from the participants' perspective. We wanted to understand how the men experienced the moment that they were abusive to their partner and how they made sense of it at the time, as well as after a year of treatment. They gave many explanations for their behavior, which are described below, with the themes that were most salient to them listed first. It will be clear that their responses correspond to most theories of the etiology of IPV, as well as to research on risk factors in the general population, all of which we discussed briefly in chapter 2.

Violence in the Family of Origin: Normalizing the Experience

Most of the men (10 out of 12) believed that they learned to be violent by being frequently exposed to violence in their families and communities.

The theme of witnessing violence and becoming desensitized to it was a common one among the interview participants. Only 2 of the men stated that spousal abuse was seriously frowned on by the whole community; in both cases these were small villages. All the men mentioned that corporal punishment of children at the very least, and frequently child abuse, was the norm in the society in which they were raised. People were violent to each other on the street as well, so that aggression toward others surrounded the majority of the participants in their childhood and youth. In the previous chapter we noted the sobering statistics regarding the frequency of child abuse and witnessing domestic violence among survey respondents and interview participants. The interview participants frequently mentioned the power that their abusive father's violent behavior had for them as a learning experience. Learning violent behavior through modeling by adults, especially authority figures, is the basic tenet of social learning theory as applied to domestic violence. As Rogelio stated,

> I learned that from my father. That you have to hit women to teach them that you're a man.... You use force because, to start with, you have that tradition that that's the way to educate her. By force. To the wife, but also to your children. To both. That's the mentality you have. That's the way you teach people, by hitting them, shoving them, and shouting at them.

Gregorio commented,

> My father was violent. My uncles also, his brothers. I saw one or another of my uncles hitting his wife almost every day. The kids too.

They used a belt or a rope or a horsewhip on them....I think Mexican men use force, violence, because they're brought up that way. They've always seen it. They think there's no other way to discipline their wife, or the children. The man was, like, the boss.

Raúl, who was raised in a rough neighborhood in Mexico City, stated,

In the community you live in, the strongest child is the one who survives. In the *colonia* [neighborhood] where I lived, if you let people step on you, you'd get crushed. It was the street....In my experience I used force a lot as a child because it was used on me.

Many of the men (8 out of 12) attributed the abuse and violence they grew up with to ignorance and poverty.

The participants tried to explain to us why their parents and relatives had been violent, either to themselves or others. They excused their parents on the grounds that they lacked education and had themselves been raised in poverty, without access to better relationship skills. Research has shown that IPV is most common among populations with lower educational achievement and lower socioeconomic status. It was important to the interview participants, in most cases, that we not come away with a negative image of their parents. To quote Rogelio,

I'm not blaming my parents because no one taught them anything either. No one has the opinion that domestic violence is wrong, because they don't know how to live either. If this had happened in my village, they wouldn't have tried to stop me. The opposite. They'd be saying, "Give it to her good."

Juan recounted,

My father was really very harsh. I don't know if it was the poverty. I've talked to him, like I said, "Remember how you used to beat us a lot?" And he says, "Yeah, but..." My dad never went to school. He can't read and write.

José, seeing the need for change, explained,

In my village, the people are very closed-minded. They don't know anything about not being violent....People just don't know. A person from there can learn just as well as I can. It's very important.

And Hilario, who initially denied being abused and later disclosed severe, if infrequent, physical assaults, reflected,

I think about it sometimes at night and I analyze it. I ask God to forgive my parents because they were ignorant. They didn't know what
they were doing.

Being in the group is an important way to empower violent men to change
themselves and to be agents of change in their social circle. "Normalizing" the violence they have grown up with, not justifying it, can be a step
toward recognition that they can help break the cycle of intergenerational
violence in their families, nuclear and extended, by modeling adaptive
skills to their partners and children and by intervening or sharing their
knowledge with relatives and friends.

TRADITIONAL GENDER ROLES AS THE BEDROCK
OF VIOLENCE TOWARD WOMEN

Ways to be male and female are highly codified in Mexican society, as in
all societies. We have already quoted Mirandé's (1997) and Gutmann's
(1996) research on machismo to illustrate this. The men effortlessly identified both positive and negative ways to be a man that were part of their
upbringing. The positive aspects of their expected role were not the problem in the violent incident. In fact, these aspects of manhood would have
helped them not to be violent. As a result, positive aspects of Mexican
manhood will be discussed in the next section as a protective factor.
    What did emerge from the interviews was the consistent view that
a large part of their decision to be violent was based on their destructive idea of what a man should be and do, and of what a woman should
be and do. This topic had major salience for the interview participants.
The premise of sociocultural theory, that IPV is the natural product of
a patriarchal, oppressive society, is supported by the views of the participants. Dutton and Golant (1995) have noted that although all men in
a given society are socialized in basically the same gender roles, not all
are violent. We have expanded on this above. Nevertheless, in spite of
the psychological and personal history explanations that are cited later
and are likely to convince the reader that more than just machismo was
involved in their violence, many of the men we interviewed were clearly
comfortable with the idea that there is a one-to-one relationship between
machismo and IPV. Often unaware of the negative effects of more personal variables (exposure to violence, alcoholism, insecure attachment
and resultant jealousy), they bought into the cultural stereotype that
machismo was the sole culprit for their behavior.

All of the men identified the negative male gender roles with which they were socialized and connected them to the attitude that makes IPV acceptable.

The participants differentiated between male gender roles and machismo, which is mentioned next. The following quotations are a small sample of a theme that came up continuously in the interview participants' narratives, namely, that men are looked upon as superior to women and that the woman is expected to serve the man.

Rogelio described his attitude as head of the household:

> So she comes to the door and, of course, she says, "I'm not going to let you in," and I said, "What do you mean you're not going to let me in? I pay the rent, and this and that. It's my house, I pay for it, I have the right." So then I saw she wasn't letting me in, so I tried to open the window, and when she saw I was getting in, she opened the door.

Hilario was uncomfortable with his wife's decision to practice massage therapy for male clients:

> According to her she was now doing massages for people. And I didn't like it. I told her, "I don't want you massaging anyone." I felt bad that she would be making money rubbing some man's body. So I told her not to.... That's when I got angry, and I said, "I don't want you massaging any men. If I see you with some man lying there under you, I don't know what's going to happen. It's wrong," I told her.

Juan described his father in these terms:

> The problem for my mother was that my father always had to be right, and not her. She used to say, "Why are you drinking, why are you going around like that?" And he would say, "I'm the man. I'm in charge here, not you."

Ignacio described the traditional Mexican man as follows:

> Suppose that person, maybe me or anyone, if he works and he's a demanding person, he comes home, he's tired, he wants to eat, and nothing is cooked or if he's used to—people have always done it for him—to have clean clothes, or that the clothes are placed in the bathroom and everything is ready for him to take a bath, and suddenly he doesn't see that anymore, of course he's going to shout because he notices the change. He doesn't feel respected, he thinks, *Something's missing here.* And that's where the violence begins. What's missing is attention, or communication.

Blas regretted the poor example he received from male relatives:

> What happened was I was behaving badly. I thought that that was
> the way to show her that I was a man. I thought the way I touched
> her was good. But on the contrary. I didn't realize, everything I did,
> everything was wrong. [*tearful*] No one ever taught me, I never saw a
> good example of how to treat a woman. If I had seen it, I would have
> done it, but I never did. [*sobs*]

Ceferino recalled his parents' arguments:

> I remember Dad would come home drunk and shout at my mother. He
> would insult her. He wanted her to be his servant. Mom would shout
> at him, "Where's the money?" And he would say he didn't earn very
> much. And then she would say that he just spent it all at the whore-
> houses downtown (La Cahuila) and that he had another woman. And
> it was true.

Leonardo spoke thoughtfully about how he used to view his duties as
husband and father:

> I thought by working and bringing home money that was enough,
> but it really isn't. It's ignorance, not knowing that children need more
> than money. Or to my wife, I'd give her the money, "Let's go to the su-
> permarket," and we'd go shopping together. After that, I thought I'd
> fulfilled my entire obligation. I didn't have to do anything more to
> collaborate with her.

He elaborated further on the way he was brought up:

> That's something that you get like an inheritance, you understand? The
> woman is for the home, and the men should be in the field, working.
> She's always looked upon as less. That's the way it was, a long time
> ago. It's part of the culture—not machismo, that's even worse—but
> that is tradition, the same custom is repeated over and over. But that
> doesn't include that the man is *machista*.

Raúl felt threatened by his wife's behavior in public:

> I was more possessive, rather than jealous. Because I was really against
> the idea of my wife talking to a man, or just hanging out on the street
> with her female friends. I didn't like it. I would tell her that if she
> wanted to talk to her friends and waste her time, she could take them
> over to our house, not talk to them on the street, parading up and
> down there.

Ramón felt pressured by male gender role expectations to show his wife who was in charge:

> So the next day I was thinking about it, while I was drinking and drink-ing. I felt really bad that she did that to me in front of my brothers and her cousin. And they kept asking me why I let myself be treated like that, and they called me *mandilón* [wimp]. And I told them, "Right now I'm going home and I'm going to give it to my old lady. It's my right." And they laughed. I think they didn't believe me, and the next day when they came to look for me, I was already in jail.

Discussing gender roles in the group is a delicate balancing act, requir-ing experience and knowledge of the clients' resistance. We learned a great deal about this from the men in our study. They resented the macho stereotypes that they felt some therapists imposed on them. At the same time, they frequently reported that machismo was a pervasive problem in their relationship and in the culture of their family or neighborhood. Our technique is to let them talk about it among themselves and to use the quotations from the men in our study to broach the topic and stimulate changes in perception. Clients often have the expectation that their thera-pist feels contempt for their *machista* beliefs. Thus it is important to "pass their tests" and not fall into stereotyping. Sometimes we use a paradoxi-cal intervention, taking the side of the *machista* man in a discussion and allowing the men to argue against it. A grave therapeutic error, according to several participants' comments, is to appear to be an angry *feminista*. This puts clients off completely and will cause the group to shut down self-disclosure out of fear of saying the wrong thing. We prefer to let them challenge each other.

Eleven of the 12 men described machismo as a special case of traditional male gender roles.

We did not use the word *machismo* in our interview schedule, to minimize social desirability. We waited until the men brought it up, which they unfailingly did. The great majority of the men made a distinction between the negative aspects of Mexican manhood and machismo. In their opinion, machismo is considerably more negative than the standard male gender role.

The following are some of the ways that the *machista* man is described by the participants: the *machista* man is closed-minded, violent to his wife and frequently his children, has to be in charge, has extramarital rela-tionships, gives orders, does not care for the children, lacks relationship skills, is always right, is verbally abusive, believes he must solve his own problems, drinks to excess, forces sex on his wife, wants to have many children, sees women as property, treats his wife like a child, is overprotective, expects his wife to obey him, is likely to be ignorant and of rural origin, is jealous and possessive, is aggressive, authoritarian, and full of himself. The *machista* man doesn't share his feelings except when he's drunk, and he is easily recognized by his "puffed up" actions, posture, and demeanor.

Rogelio explained that his father taught him by example

> that you have to hit women to teach them that you're a man. That the man is in charge in the house. That you have to have more than one woman, more than just your wife....Machismo is that the man has to give orders, that's all. He just says, "Make me something to eat." He never takes care of the children. He really has no training in how to live, how to have a relationship. Even my father would say, "Look at the neighbor, he's taking his own corn to the mill to grind. What an idiot. You'd think he doesn't have a wife."

Leonardo gave an eloquent description of the macho man:

> A macho man is always right. If you say, "This is red," he'll say, "No, it's white." Even if it isn't. What he says has to be right, and there's no power on earth that can contradict him. He believes he's the ultimate, he even believes himself. Even if it's a lie. He knows it's a lie, but he'll never say so. Like he might have five or six women, but he'll swear he doesn't even have one. For me, being *machista* is to claim something that isn't true. He's rude, but he knows who to be rude to, not to everyone. Especially not to his drinking buddies. The majority of machos are also heavy drinkers. Because if they weren't they wouldn't be machos. It's very difficult for his wife and children to live with him. The wife will probably get in the habit of doing whatever he wants to avoid having problems with him. Because the macho man isn't going to say, "Oh sorry, forgive me," if he's wrong. He would never say that, or accept responsibility for some mistake he's made. A *machista* person shouldn't exist. The person who says, "I'm macho, I do whatever I want." That person is poor, uneducated. The macho man comes out of the environment of ignorance.
> Researcher: So there are no rich machos?
> Leonardo: Yes, there are. But I don't think they think they're machos [*laughs*].

Ramón recounted how his father is *machista*:

> In Mexico, men beat their wives because they believe that they rule over them in every way. Like my father came here and wanted to hit

my partner. And I told him, "This isn't your village!" And he said, "I beat my wife at home and they don't do anything." And I said, "That's why; this isn't your village. Here, we're better off."

Speaking of stereotypes, Lucio commented,

> I think they're ashamed, afraid, they feel embarrassed to talk in the group. Shame, because Mexican men are famous for thinking that we're real men, real machos, that nothing touches us, that we should never cry. But those are just words. Even so, those words take root in people, so they think things like, *OK, well I don't need to tell my problems to anyone. I can solve my own problems.* But really ninety-five percent of us, ninety-nine percent of us can't solve our problems by ourselves. We need help....If the woman doesn't want to have sex, the man hits her, so she'll do what he wants. Even if the man isn't drunk, just because [unclear] he's in charge. But he has it because the woman lets him have it.
>
> The man who has more children is more of a man. If he has a lot of women he's a real man. The man who drinks is a real man. That needs to end. All Mexican men are famous for that. Even if we don't do it, we still have the reputation.

Gregorio described his experience with the rural/urban difference in gender roles:

> The people who live in the country are more ignorant. So if you work with city people in Mexico, they aren't so ignorant. The people who live in the city are mostly like people here, couples work, all that. Not in the country. In the country the people are *machista*, they don't let their wives work, the men think they can do it all—if the woman works, she'll find someone else; but in the city, no, the people are more, more civilized. Men who want to be in charge are always complaining, but they cause it themselves. So if you ask them, "Why are you carrying all the weight? What's your wife for? She's your companion. She can help you too." [*Imitates macho voice*] "No, she's my wife, I'm the man around here."

Many of the participants (8 out of 12) identified machismo as being involved in their domestic violence incident.

It is noteworthy that not all the men identified themselves as *machistas*. By their definition, machismo is one step removed from the mere negative aspects of manhood. It is a state further along the continuum that destroyed their relationships.

Gregorio described himself before he came to the United States and was mandated to treatment:

> In those years men believed, I believed too, that the woman was like an object, your property. If I got married to a woman, she had to do what I told her. If she didn't obey, I had the right to hit her and no one could say anything. Because then I didn't realize, now thank God I know, that the woman is a companion, not an object that belongs to you. I learned that in the programs I've been in. When I came to the United States I had those same ideas, machismo, all that. That the woman belonged to you, that she was an object, not that she was a companion, a person.

Blas was one of the men who regretted his former machismo the most, to the point of tears:

> I think the Mexican man should erase machismo from his mind. Because machismo doesn't lead to anything good. I think machismo is to be aggressive, authoritarian, to be proud of what they do when they do bad things—they are proud of shouting and beating and feeling superior to others, dominating others—and I realize that all those things are so wrong. They're things that, instead of taking us to a happier place, to union with each other, we're throwing ourselves away. [*Amazement in voice*] We lose what's most important to us. My uncles were *machistas*. You can tell just by how someone speaks. When they're talking about something they always mock other people, they puff themselves up, it's like they're full of themselves and what they're saying. I was like that until my eyes were opened, when this problem happened. The second time I was arrested. The first time I didn't realize. It wasn't till the second time that I realized why she left me. Because I've talked to her since then and she has told me how I was, how I killed the love she had for me bit by bit, and the affection. All those things made me think, they opened my eyes. Machismo is present in all cases of domestic violence. Machismo is the culture of the Mexican man. I'm Mexican, and I'm changing because people helped me to open my eyes. Because I'm looking at what happened and I'm accepting that I did wrong.

Although Blas readily admitted that he was *machista*, he deeply resented his therapist's "attacks" that made him feel disrespected. He complained that she always took the woman's side and never wanted to hear his side of the story. He felt misunderstood, never a good place to proceed from in a therapeutic setting.

Raúl painted this picture of himself before treatment:

> The negative side [of being a man] is what I was. That look of arrogance, always intimidating my partner, not letting her go out, and controlling

all her actions, always being overprotective. Like if she did something wrong I would take care of it for her—that is the typical Mexican man. If the wife makes a mistake, he doesn't let her take responsibility for her own actions. Instead he goes and fixes it for her. Why? *Because I'm the man.* You treat her like a little child.

He added his thoughts on machismo:

If they're at home and they're arguing, many times the man is the one who gives in, who does what the wife wants, and many times he even gets hit. But as soon as he walks out the door of his house, it's, "No man, my wife does what I tell her." That's the way the Mexican guy acts. But the reality of what happens indoors and what gets expressed outside is very different. So why is the Mexican man known like that? Because he goes around talking like that, and that's the only reason. His experience is actually very different. Here in the United States men don't talk like that so much, but they still have their problems, their differences, and their situations here. The Mexican gets more attention because he looks more puffed up and everything. So people say, "What a great rooster! He's going to fight and win," or whatever. But they get carried away by his strutting, by his appearance, that's the only difference.

His disturbing description of his own threatening behavior follows:

I was used to giving out a lot of verbal abuse. I shouted and was angry a lot. I think the worst occasion for her was once when she was in school, and she was talking to a man, a man who was waiting for his son, and I came to pick her up and saw them talking and I got out of the car and went up to them and I asked her, "What are you doing here?" And she got really nervous when she saw me and that's what bothered me. So I said, "And what are you looking for, or why in the name of your fucking mother are you standing here talking to this son of a bitch?" So then the man turned away and then I said to him, "Yes I'm talking to you, you motherfucker! If you don't like it, let's go outside." I was angry. And then my wife began to say, "He was just asking me..." and I said, "Get out of here, you whore! I don't want to see you talking to any motherfucker here again. Because I'll beat the shit out of both of you, him and you, together!" I was very angry, and I think that was one of the worst things that happened....It was a lot of intimidation. A lot of threat.

Rogelio was one of the men who believed that machismo is to blame for IPV:

Machismo is involved in one hundred percent of domestic violence cases, because the man has to have other women, and the wife isn't

supposed to say anything. She's supposed to put up with it. So when
the woman says, "OK that's it!" and he doesn't like it, there it comes
[*imitates a punch*] and that's what happens. It's common.

Juan described his extremely violent father in these terms:

In my case, my father used to say that he was in charge. He gave out
the money, he paid the rent, so with his privilege he was the king who
ruled there, and my mother—"Bring me this! Cook me that!" And if
she didn't do it right away, he'd raise his voice. Yes, that's the mentality
I grew up with. That I was in charge in my house.

Ceferino was the only participant who described the positive meaning of *macho*, and how it has changed in his opinion:

Macho used to mean a person who took care of his family, who brought
home food to his family, and who was with his family. And now *macho*
is a man who has a lot of women, who fights more, who drinks more,
that is the *macho* of today...now *macho* means all that, the man who
shouts the loudest. The program changed the way I thought. The counselor helped me to see that my way of thinking was wrong. I think
machismo affected my relationship with my partner a lot, since she
comes from the same culture. She grew up the same as me, her father
is very violent too. He defended what I was saying, and that caused a
big conflict between them. It affected her a lot that I might be violent
to her, because she had come here trying to forget, thinking it would be
different. She wanted to have a better life here, but unfortunately she
started living with me, and I did what her father had done, what her
mother had done.

José sounded sad as he recounted his own history of machismo:

Machismo is something that drags men down to perdition. Like you
think, *I'm this, I'm that, and you can't tell me anything*—that's the
really bad part of you. And you're lost because you don't want to listen
to anyone anymore. You're just closed up, and then you get drunk too.
You're drunk and something important comes up and you don't even
realize it. That's where you make so many mistakes.

*Many men (11 of the 12) identified the traditional female gender roles
that they were socialized to expect.*

The gender behaviors mentioned above could not be maintained unless the corresponding female gender behaviors supported them. Of
course, there have been and continue to be many changes in gender role

behaviors in Latin America, the "fallout" of which (from the participants' standpoint) will be discussed under a different heading.

The following are some of the traits and behaviors of the low socio-economic status Mexican woman that the participants described as culturally approved when they were growing up: She should nurture and care for her husband and family; take care of the home by cooking, cleaning, washing (by hand) and ironing; serve her husband upon demand; submit to sexual relations upon demand; put up with his extramarital relations silently; submit to his beatings patiently; and teach her daughters to do the same. She is to be docile and obedient, but possessive of her husband; she should not raise her voice, and on no account may she work outside the home for fear of sexual indiscretions. She is to be the man's property, to protect him and be loyal to him under all circumstances, and to keep his violent behavior a family secret. Her task is to be the servant of her husband and family. According to the participants, the more extreme version of this is to be found in a rural setting, while inroads toward some gender freedom have been made in the cities. In most of the following commentaries, the participants are describing their own mother's role in the family.

Lucio commented,

> Abused women stayed because their mother told them, "That's how it is, you have to stay," or because they don't know how to do anything else...to be independent. I think that's changing now. But it's very hard to change. Others still tell their daughters who tell them, "My husband is treating me like this,"—"Oh my child, just bear it. Bear it. He's your husband. You have to respect him. He supports you. He's the father of your children." That's wrong. That comes from the fact that we didn't get an education about it.

Blas described how the women in his family behaved:

> The house, the home. Taking care of the children, the house, always to have food ready for my grandfather or the wife for her husband. First her husband, then her children and her home. Even now, I never saw a woman who worked outside the home. Who said, "I'm going to work, I'm going to do this." My father and uncles were, I'd say, men enough to make ends meet. To give their wives all they needed.

Ramón made the following observation:

> Many men didn't beat their wives, but if they did, no one did anything to protect her. But you know that in Mexico, women are very quiet, they don't tell the police about things. The Mexican woman just washes

clothes, cooks, and cleans the house. That's it, that's all. You never
see that her husband is taking her out to dinner. The woman is in the
house. The husband is drunk; maybe he works a little. He's in charge in
his house, he does whatever he wants, nothing else. It's no good.

Juan saw that his daughter was in danger but failed to get involved:

> Even now, many women just put up with a lot of beating. They keep
> quiet, even if they're beating them, even if they're killing them, they
> don't say anything. Sometimes my daughter comes here, and I tell her,
> because she lives with her children and this man—he's only twenty, but
> he's a very rough person; he uses really vulgar language. He calls her
> "whore," "hooker," and I don't know what else. She's already put up
> with too much from him. I don't know why. I guess probably because
> she loves him. Otherwise, why? I lived with them for a while and I saw
> everything. But I didn't get involved, I didn't get in the middle of their
> fights, because I felt like fighting with him. I don't think a woman
> should put up with that, not my mother or my daughter.

In many years of doing group work with Latino men, it has been encouraging to note that the great majority of the men in the groups come to see
the benefits of equality and sharing the burden of raising a family in new
ways. Although they often resist it at the outset, over time in the group
discussions, it becomes clear to them that they have more to gain than to
lose from evening up the scale in their relationship.

---

*The men described parenting problems related to their rigid male gender
    roles.*

*All of the men identified problems in knowing how to parent their
children and/or having disagreements with their partner on parenting
issues.* The topic of parenting was extremely important to them. They
frequently mentioned the harsh, uninvolved parenting style of their own
fathers as being the only model they had for being a father, and they realized how defective that model was in many respects. Their sorrow over
their failures as a parent was very apparent, most so if they were separated from their former partner and no longer lived with their children.
    Juan spoke sadly of his former parenting style:

> Sometimes they used to ask me about their homework, and I used to
> say, "I don't speak English." And even later when I knew a little, I just
> said, "No, I don't know." I thought I was important because I was
> providing the food for my family and a place to live, but I didn't give

them the most important things, like communication. To ask them, *How are you, How do you feel? What did you do in school today? Are you sick?*

Researcher: Did anyone ever ask you those things when you were a child?

Juan: No, never. No one ever asked me that.

José commented,

> And if the mother sides with the children, you can't talk to your wife properly, and that's when the violence explodes. Because their problem was that the children weren't doing what their father said, and most of the guys [in the group] would come and tell us that. And for wanting to get their wife and their children to respect them, that's where the problem was. The kids would answer back and the parents would fight, and that's where it started. We talked about that a great deal in the group. And many of the men in the group were reconciled with their children and became good friends, and could get along again, both the father and the child.

Rogelio, who has four children, commented on his difficulties as a parent:

> It's really hard for me. To spend time with them or to teach them. Maybe because I didn't get that love from my father, to play with me, or to carry me on his shoulders and all that. I don't know, it's hard for me to be with them and to teach them something. I don't know how to do it, to spend more time with them....I don't have the experience.

Hilario commented on his attempts to find parenting solutions with his wife:

> And we didn't argue in front of them. I used to say, "Be quiet, let's not talk about this at all right now." That's something I used to always say to her, "Don't shout at the children. At all." And, "Now is not the time to talk about that."

Ignacio deeply valued what he had learned about parenting in his group:

> Now I treat my children better, I communicate better, I talk with them, I didn't do that before, I don't shout at them anymore, like I used to say, "Sit down and shut up!" Things like that. But I've decided to correct that, and to talk to them differently. Many of the men used to abuse their children. You listen to different stories from the guys and

slowly you learn about what's going on in life and that maybe you are doing that too without realizing it. So we learn from each other's experiences. I get along really well with all my children. But it really hurts me that I don't live with my daughters. I live alone here.

The topic of effective fathering was so important to the men in our study that we incorporated an entire parenting section into the treatment program. During these discussions, men bring up current issues with their children or stepchildren, as well as past issues from their own childhood.

TODAY'S PERPETRATOR IS OFTEN YESTERDAY'S VICTIM: CHILD ABUSE AND NEGLECT IN THE FAMILY OF ORIGIN

In clinical research studies, male IPV offenders consistently produce higher scores on measures of psychopathology than control groups. Offenders frequently demonstrate symptoms of posttraumatic stress disorder, related to childhood experience of and exposure to violence. This trauma affects their sense of self, their ability to trust, their view of the world, and their ability to withstand real or perceived stressors. Following are some examples of the abuse received and family violence witnessed, as well as trauma symptoms that some participants continue to experience after many years.

Most of the men (11 of the 12) had some impairment in their functioning consistent with psychopathology, such as posttraumatic stress disorder, depression, poor impulse control, or borderline personality features. These findings provide support for the clinical model, self psychology, and attachment theory. Alcoholism, another major factor in the men's clinical picture, is discussed under a separate heading.

Childhood Abuse

Eight of the 12 interview participants described emotional abuse, and 9 of the men described physical abuse perpetrated on them by their fathers. A smaller number, 4, spoke of emotional and physical abuse by their mothers as well.

These findings were mirrored in a recent quantitative study of Latino partner abusive men (Welland et al., unpublished), where the presence of trauma symptoms was correlated to psychological aggression, minor physical abuse, neglect, and injury by violent Latino men's fathers, but not their mothers. The control group was significantly less likely to have been abused or neglected or to have trauma symptoms. Emotional abuse by their mothers was correlated to insecure attachment on the part of the abusive men.

The main feelings the participants in our qualitative study identified concerning the abuse they suffered were fear, anger, hatred, confusion, sadness, and hurt. In some cases, the participants did not recognize their childhood experiences as abusive. This is consistent with studies that show that many women in regions where IPV is common and where it is not often punished by the law fail to identify their experience as abuse (Orloff & Little, 1999).

Juan described some of the beatings he recalls when he was about 6 years old. The incident cited below happened about 1 year after he was raped by a neighbor, which he kept an absolute secret:

> I went out early to play with some little girls, and when I came back, my father tied me up by the wrists with some wire, onto a pole that held up the roof. And he just kept hitting me in the head and my head was going back and forth, back and forth.... He would get really angry. When he hit me with the belt, the bed would bounce, and I'd go up and down, up and down. Just from the beating.

Ceferino wept as he described what his father and older brother used to do to him:

> My father would send my brother to call me and he'd say, "Dad is calling you." And I would go, and then when I was going home they'd hit me....I don't know why. I tried to get away but they'd hit me with a cable. And they would kick me also. My brother would hold me, and Dad would hit me, or my brother would hold me by the hair and Dad would kick me in the back, here.

Ramón effectively summarized the rage and woundedness of the participants who had been abused:

> Sometimes when the others in the group talked about what happened to them when they were children, sometimes I felt like crying. That happened to me too. When I was saying what my father used to do to me, I wanted to cry, but then I stopped talking about it to the teacher....The day he was leaving [San Diego after a visit] he got drunk...and he wanted to beat my partner. I had so much anger toward him from before, I had been asking him before why he beat my mother like that, why he beat us like that, but he wouldn't say anything. I really wanted to get him, but I controlled myself. He's my

father, but everything I have inside—man, if that gets out, look out. He's done all of us so much harm.

José described how the abuse he received has affected him for close to 40 years:

> It's a problem. And sometimes you argue with your wife because you're really not there, you're thinking about it and you feel the pain, and you get lost in it. At first I used to drink when I remembered all that....I've shared my suffering with my wife a lot, like something will happen to remind me, and I'll tell her. But it doesn't go away. I can't really talk about it because I feel so bad, like all that feeling is still there. It stays in my heart. I don't really want to talk about it much....It never goes away...

It is vital during revelations of childhood abuse that come up during sessions to model empathy to the clients. Developing empathy is one of the major treatment goals for perpetrators of IPV. Some men in the group will feel uncomfortable with the level of emotion that is felt in the group when instances of abuse are disclosed. They may laugh at their companion's tears or may joke to lighten the atmosphere. Therapists can be most effective if they maintain an empathic stance, disallowing by their seriousness any trivialization of the client's pain, expressing sorrow for his suffering, and using it as an opportunity to deepen the clients' commitment to not follow in their parents' footsteps. It is advisable to give explicit permission to clients to shed tears during these revelations and to emphasize that such openness and sincerity is a manly way to express feelings. Sometimes it is advisable to speak to the abused client after the group and to recommend individual therapy sessions, where more time may be spent on resolving past trauma. Normalizing his response to trauma will be an important way to give him permission to seek help. Many Latino men, like many men in general, lack experience of therapy and may feel that seeing a psychologist is tantamount to an admission of "craziness."

Witnessing Abuse

Seven of the participants witnessed domestic violence in their families of origin.

The more severe abuse left lasting scars, but even instances of relatively minor abuse were frightening and confusing for the child.

Ramón described the most severe abuse to his mother of any of the participants:

When my father's drunk he's another person. That's when he'd beat my mother, and beat us and throw us out of the house. I saw my dad rip off all her clothes and leave her naked. To intimidate her. And I remember how I felt. I was about seven. I went in between them and I said, "Leave her alone!" and he hit me, and I ran out crying because he hit me.... My grandmother brought my mother here to get her away from my dad. He broke a glass bottle and cut her arm with it. She has a big scar. He also hit her in the hand with an ice pick, and sometimes those wounds don't bleed, but they get infected and the person dies. If the blood doesn't flow, that happens. And Dad was drunk, but he sucked the wound so the blood would come out. Even though he was drunk, he was able to do that. I was about nine when that happened. It was very traumatic. Since my mother left home, ten years ago, I haven't seen a woman being beaten or attacked like that.

Leonardo explained how he felt when he saw his father throwing his mother against the wall of their home:

At the time I felt sad, helpless. Of course I couldn't stop my father, because I didn't know what they were arguing about, and I wasn't sure whose side to be on, my father's or my mother's. Of course, it seemed obvious to side with my mother because she was the one being assaulted, but I couldn't decide whose side to be on at that moment. You get really confused at a time like that. It's hard....I would have liked to hold my father back.

Group treatment for IPV often includes an educational session on the effects of witnessing IPV between parents. If the therapist has the trust of the clients, the men themselves can tell you all you want to know about how it feels, because about half of them have been in the position of a terrified, angry, sorrowing child watching helplessly while their mother is attacked. A very powerful intervention in our program is to allow men to role-play their child's experience when they attacked their partner, again aiming at developing empathy in the client.

Childhood Trauma and Abandonment Leading to a Fragile Sense of Self

Some of the men reported hypersensitivity to shaming, so much that it seemed intolerable to them. Dutton (2006a) has shown that some men who come from very abusive backgrounds feel extremely threatened and lash out when humiliated, as we discussed under typology in chapter 2. Welland and colleagues (unpublished) found that emotional abuse and insecure attachment were also significantly higher in Latino partner abusive men than in controls.

Blas gave the most powerful example of a man whose sense of self was very fragile:

> [I said to her:] "Enough! Leave me alone, I don't want to argue about this anymore," and I went out. And she was following me and following me and following me, shouting at me and humiliating me in front of everybody. We got to a corner and I turned to her and I begged her, "Please, go home. I can't take any more of what you're saying in front of people, here in the street. Insulting me here in public. Go home, please." I was angry. I got violent. I pushed her. And she said, "I'm not one of those Mexican *pendejas*[2] who put up with this crap." She slapped me across the face. I was very angry. I hit her and she fell back.

A client with this personality profile may be one of the most resistant clients in the group at the outset. He will put you through multiple tests to see if you can be trusted with his emotions, whether you too will abandon him to his pain without empathy for what he has suffered. Because his expectation of you, the therapist, is negative, it may take a while to convince him that he is safe in your group. Once you have won his trust, he may make great strides in treatment and become one of the most effective members for others in the group. Most of these men need additional individual therapy, which can be invaluable to them. Some may also benefit from an antidepressant.

MALADAPTIVE COPING SKILLS

Most of the men explained their behavior by reporting that did not know any other way to deal with problems. They lacked anger management and relationship skills, such as communication, and they frequently allowed arguments and resentments to simmer for a long time before exploding. The abuse of alcohol is mentioned first because of its major salience for the participants and the fact that, in most cases, it was used as a coping mechanism. We have already discussed the major contribution of alcohol as a risk factor for IPV in previous chapters.

Alcoholism

Father's Alcohol Abuse or Alcoholism

Half of the men interviewed (6 out of 12) had alcoholic fathers. Five of them described how their fathers were frequently drunk during bouts of domestic violence and child abuse. The effect of their modeling alcohol abuse and dependence to their sons was evident in the alcohol abuse histories of the participants. Ramón recalled,

> I ran out calling to my grandmother and I was saying, "Grandma, grandma, my dad is beating my mom." And my grandmother went over there right away. I was shaking.... If I go to my village, I remember it. And if I see my dad drinking and I'm drinking, my tears start to come. I don't know why. And it's like I can hear the sounds, "Bam, bam!" And I want to get even with him for all that he's done to my mother, to me, to my sisters and brothers.... My dad used to get drunk and all that. Once a year he'd get drunk for a month. He works like eight or nine months, and then he drinks. He's an alcoholic. When he's not drunk, everybody there respects him. He sells tacos, donuts, ice cream, all that. But when he's drunk he's another person. That's when he'd beat my mother, and beat us and throw us out of the house. He'd break things that my mother liked. He bought them, then he'd break them, then go and buy them again.

Blas, who was raised by his aunts and uncles, saddened as he described one uncle's behavior:

> I was just coming home and he was drunk. It really upset me. He was asking her something, I don't remember what. And they started to fight. He pushed her and he tried to hit her. And I got in the middle. I wasn't afraid, because he and I used to fight like two enemies. He used to hit me like I was his enemy. I felt resentment toward him.

Gregorio, himself a recovering alcoholic, spoke about his father:

> He didn't drink all the time. Sometimes on weekends, but he did drink. People think that when they only drink on weekends or at parties they aren't alcoholics. But when you go into AA they explain it to you. But then, when your mind is closed, you don't know that.

Juan, a victim of severe child abuse, depicted his father's irresponsible behavior:

> He was always drinking. Always drinking. Friday, Saturday, and Sunday. He'd drink until he didn't have any money left.

Ceferino wept as he described his father's abusive behavior:

> My father began to come home drunk. He was always drunk. I was very afraid of him, because he always shouted at me. He scolded all of us; he always shouted at me. He was drunk.

*Alcohol Abuse and Dependence as a Risk Factor
for Intimate Violence*

*Ten of the participants had problems with alcohol, and the 4 who were
under the influence at the time of the violent incident cited alcohol as
a contributing factor to their loss of control.* The high level of alcohol
abuse can be determined from the fact that 8 of the 12 interview participants had been arrested at some time for driving under the influence of
alcohol.

As stated above, one of the three major risk factors for IPV is alcohol
use and abuse. Although alcohol abuse or dependence is not the cause
of IPV, it is frequently correlated to it, due to disinhibition and impaired
judgment. Frequent conflict is also common in relationships where alcohol is a problem. Welland and colleagues (unpublished) found that 50%
of the Latino partner abusive men studied were under the influence of
alcohol at the time of the arrest for IPV. They were significantly more
likely to be abusers of alcohol overall than the control group.

Hilario described his descent into alcoholism:

> So at this point my friend says, "Come on, forget it! Let's go and have
> a couple of beers. Beer takes away sorrow." He started off buying six,
> and we'd drink two each. I'd come home and it was easier to sleep
> with the beer. After that I started drinking on Sundays. So from that
> point I began to drink. . . . I felt that my marriage was falling apart, I felt
> discriminated against, humiliated, desperate, depressed. I didn't know
> what to do.

Raúl, too, used alcohol as an escape for his sorrow over his divorce from
his first wife. Being drunk exacerbated the violence in his second marriage:

> After we separated, I stayed alone for about four or five months.
> Then I started to drink. I wasn't thinking of anything. I just wanted
> to forget about myself, drown myself, forget about my own existence
> completely. . . . All I was interested in was drinking at that time. . . . No
> one in my family taught me by their example. On the contrary, they were
> telling me, "You shouldn't drink when you have problems; you should
> solve the problem." But at that time I didn't want to feel all that pain.

Rogelio completed AA concurrently with his treatment for IPV. He
admitted,

> I'd come home drunk. The last time she wanted to leave, and I was say-
> ing, as I always did, "No, I'm going to change, I'm going to change."
> And no, she had decided to leave me, she had a job. . . . The problem

has been that I didn't know how to live my life, or how to stop my alcoholism. This year I should be able to finish paying off all the consequences of what I did, finally. I started drinking heavily about two years after I got here, so about fifteen years ago. I think my alcoholism had a lot to do with the problems in my first relationship and with my wife. You don't know what you're doing. Alcohol has a big influence in that. I think sometimes you drink without even knowing why. It's like it's a custom, a tradition.

Ceferino fell into alcoholism and drug abuse at an early age, escaping from one violent and uncaring environment into another:

When I was about thirteen, I was going to school and working with my dad, and my dad said I couldn't go to school anymore, so I left the house and I never went back. Then I got a job on Avenida Revolución [an area full of bars in Tijuana] once I had learned some English. That's where I started drinking. I began as an assistant bartender. I became an alcoholic right there.

If your client is still drinking in a problematic way, he will not benefit from therapy, and the violence is likely to continue, if not during his treatment, then in subsequent months or years. Take the time to verify his behavior with his partner. All the men in our pilot program who relapsed, even though the number of relapses was very small, did so under the influence of alcohol.

Lack of Relationship Skills

Cognitive-behavioral theory proposes that one reason why IPV occurs is that violent people lack adaptive skills for conflict resolution and problem solving. Once relationship skills such as open communication and assertiveness are taught, and cognitive distortions that perpetuate negative thinking and behavior have been explored and replaced, violence becomes one option among many, instead of the sole coping mechanism available when faced with conflict.

All of the participants said that they, and in most cases, their partners as well, lacked relationship skills, and this contributed to the abuse. Ten of the men mentioned arguing and poor communication skills. Nine of the men identified their jealousy as a problem; 6 mentioned extramarital affairs, with their partner being involved in five instances. Five men reported that their partner was also violent, in three of these cases out of retaliation. Five of their partners were verbally abusive to them, frequently before they, the men, became violent. Some of the common topics that couples disagreed on were the woman not doing traditionally female tasks such as cleaning and cooking, the man's drinking, the woman's change of religion, and the woman's "excessive" expectations of freedom, or *liberalismo*, as Hilario called it.

Ceferino admitted,

> I always started it, I used to tell her she was crazy, stupid, an idiot, that she didn't know what she was talking about, I used to call her names.... Call her names, insult her, and be unfaithful to her. I was unfaithful to her about three times. One time it was with one of her friends, so she found out. When she accused me I said it was her fault. I always blamed her when I did that. That was part of the verbal abuse. I've thought a lot about the past with her, and I realize that I was the one who started things.

Rogelio recalled,

> In the past we never talked about it. We never used to sit down to talk about a problem. Never. What a thought! No. We just argued and fought. And of course dealing with problems that way we just made them worse.

Raúl had difficulty disclosing mutual violence:

> But it wasn't just that I pushed my wife, and she fell back, and that was it. No, she'd come back at me, and it would have been totally humiliating for me to go outside and admit that she had hit me with the broom in the back, or slapped me. Very shameful. And so the cover-up begins there. So that if we *did* get to arguing or something, and she slapped me, even though I didn't slap her back or do anything—never in my life, I mean *never*, would I admit to someone that my wife had slapped me.

Uncontrolled Anger

Anger management skills are a standard component of most IPV groups, because many violent men come into therapy with very poorly developed impulse control and few skills for self-containment. Many of these men feel helpless and impotent to control themselves. They frequently feel that their anger is justified, and their belief in the use of force coupled with rage is a volatile mix.

Eleven of the participants reported that they were very angry during the violent incident. Their anger stemmed from fear of loss, or from the sense of being disrespected, dishonored, betrayed, or ignored. Six of the men connected their feeling of anger to jealousy over a real or perceived extramarital relationship their partner was having. Their comments show that their anger, in 10 out of 11 cases, sprang from gender role expectations that, in their perception, their partner was violating.

Lucio let himself be mastered by his anger and jealousy:

> Then this person I don't approve of drops her off. A former boy-friend of hers. And she comes in the house with alcohol on her breath. But I was more angry because I saw her arrive with this person. He dropped her off and he left. If she had come home alone, my reaction would have been different. I would have been angry, and asked her why she did it. But this really hurt me, like she had betrayed me.

Raúl admitted that he felt able to inflict more harm on his partner than he did:

> I didn't hurt her then, or do anything more, because there was no time. I was extremely angry, and I think I would have done at least a little more to her—my blood got fired up because she began to call out the name of this friend of hers, and I didn't even know who it was yet; unfortunately I've forgotten his name now.

Leonardo was surprised and dismayed at the power and intensity of his anger:

> In that moment, you know, I've analyzed things, and if she had rejected me or thrown something at me or slapped me, or something like that, who knows if I would have done worse? But she didn't do it. And that's why I felt so bad, because she didn't try to defend herself. I felt so angry because she was walking away without hearing what I had to say. But it's possible something worse would have happened, like I could have slapped her, or broken her arm. I don't know. Sincerely, I was very angry. It's dangerous.

It is vital for men to learn to recognize and control their anger, their negative thoughts, and their standard ways of responding to situations, whether real or imagined. A great part of our treatment program is dedicated to learning such skills, to developing the "tool box," so that clients will be empowered, with practice and fine-tuning, to choose an alternative to violence when the stimulus arises. Learning how to take a simple "time-out" is one of the favorite strategies of the men in our groups.

ENVIRONMENTAL STRESSORS

Financial Stress

The literature and clinical experience both point to stress as a risk factor in IPV. Unemployment and lack of adequate financial resources can place considerable stress on the individual, the couple, and the family. As we have seen, most of the Latino men in the IPV groups surveyed lived below the poverty line, providing an additional stressor in their relationships.

Although only 3 of the men interviewed cited economic stress as a major issue in their relationship, most of the men mentioned the financial need of many others in their groups, and the difficulties it can provoke in the relationship. IPV groups are typically paid for by the perpetrator, unless Child Protective Services is paying, and because it is court-ordered, men must come up with the funds or face probable jail time.

Ignacio was one of the men who identified financial stress as a burden for him:

> I see people—and I feel like I'm one of them—sometimes you don't have money to pay and if you can't pay you can't get into class. I've heard many guys say, "I didn't come last week because I didn't have any money. Why don't you call to see if they can lower my fee?" I pay $25. I don't think they care that it's hard for me.

Rogelio described ways that IPV agencies might help to alleviate financial stress on families:

> A couple of the men in the group mentioned that their fee was taking away from the money they needed to feed their family, but they never gave us a resource list. I think something like that would be indispensable, to give out that kind of information, so you know more about what's out there. A lot of the time, you just have no idea about it. Several of the members used to mention that they had economic problems and that made things more stressful.

Whatever the stressor, stress management techniques are a necessary part of any treatment program for violent men. We use a CD of relaxation exercises that each man acquires at the outset of treatment, for personal use outside the sessions. We also often use the CD at the beginning of sessions. With just 5–10 minutes of such relaxation, the stress in the room melts away, and men and therapists are better able to benefit from the session.

Being an Immigrant, Often Unwelcome: Acculturation Stress

The literature on immigration suggests that the process of immigration itself and ongoing struggles to acculturate contribute to stress in Latino families. Recent anti-immigrant rhetoric and activity makes life uneasy for Latino immigrants, whether documented or not. In spite of this undercurrent of anxiety, all of the interview participants stated that immigration has been a tremendously positive experience. They came to the United States primarily to have a better life and to give their children the education and the future they would not have had in Mexico.

Leonardo mused on his emigration from his home town and its benefits:

> The most important reason for me to come here was to look for a better way of life. I think that's the dream that the majority of Mexicans have when they come. It's better economically and for jobs. More opportunity for our children and a better standard of living for us. I think that's the reason. It was for me anyway. I was twenty-two....If my daughter, for example, was there, I could never have given her the studies she's doing now. She's going for a social work degree. And if we were there, my son wouldn't have been able to study as a chef. For me it's been positive.

Raúl can't see himself returning, even though, as an undocumented worker, his salary was among the lowest of all the participants:

> Sincerely, I don't think it would be the same. I feel that I fit in better here than there, in every way. Financially, and by that I mean stability. Here I can go out and buy a car, and yes, I have to work very hard, but I can have things. I have an apartment. I have a shower. There you have to struggle a whole lot for everything. And more than anything else, what I think I couldn't adapt to, is because of this reason—My children, let's face it, don't know Mexico. They were little when I brought them here. They have done all their school here. When I came here, it was to give my children a better life. And for better or worse, they now have a different mentality, more education than many of us had in Mexico. I could say that I studied for a career in Mexico, but I was never bilingual. And that's another step ahead for them. Those are some of the reasons why I feel that I would not go back.

However, immigration also presents challenges and dilemmas.

Immigration Difficulties

Although 11 of the 12 men identified aspects of their life that are better than if they had remained in Mexico, 9 of them reported difficulties

stemming from immigration and the process of acculturation. Of these
9 men, 4 reported difficulties specifically with their partner, and the way
that she had changed.

At this time, when immigration is such a hot topic in the United States, the participants illustrate for us some of the struggles that Latino immigrants face in this country. The interview participants did not mention unemployment, because the vast majority of Latino immigrants work. They came to the United States for this reason. However, we did note that 15% of the men we surveyed were unemployed; this may have been a seasonal issue for construction and agricultural laborers. The main issues they described were cultural changes in their family life, discrimination, and financial stress.

Leonardo considered covering the topic of immigration essential for effective treatment:

> We talked about it in group and many of the men talked about it. They said their wives were changing after coming here. Many guys say that women, or men too, come here, and they're different people. I think we need to talk about that in the group. It's important—it would be a good topic.

Hilario described what he had experienced and witnessed:

> [The Mexican woman] arrives here and she begins to say, "We're not in Mexico here! Here I'm going to do this," and the husband, because he believes the custom that "I'm in charge, and I'm the head of the family," that's where the problems begin. So it's bad because what each one expects is different. She's going on about how it's different now, that "Now I'm my own person, and now you're not going to get away with what you do." She threatens him. Then the husband gets angry and then the arguments begin.

Ignacio talked about what he has observed:

> I don't think that all Mexican women change. But I've heard a lot of men in the class say, "Ever since I brought my wife here, my wife totally changed. She was no longer the woman I knew when we lived in Mexico. As soon as she got her papers, she wasn't worth a damn." I've heard a lot about how women change, like one guy says, "When my wife lived in Tijuana she was really good. As soon as she got her papers, she changed completely. Her way of behaving, of thinking— like, she used to do whatever I said, we had no problems, now that she's here, I don't know what to do."

Ramón, whose partner is Mexican American, lamented the difference in social and role expectations:

When someone says that they go to work, and then they have to come home and clean up the house and there's nothing cooked, and he has to do it, that's not OK. You know what? It'd be better if I looked for another woman who will do all that for me. You go to work happier if you know there will be food ready when you come home. My wife doesn't have a sense of responsibility. Nothing matters to her. She just blows everything off. She says she doesn't give a crap. In Mexico if your partner doesn't cook or anything, why would you give her money? Here they expect us to give her money when she doesn't do anything. It's very different here.

Blas was confused by the cultural differences between himself and his Mexican American wife. He was blindsided by her response to his behaviors:

My wife speaks Spanish, she has all the habits of Mexican culture, almost, but her ideas were different. She used to always attack me about how Mexican men treated women. She'd say—even though I had nothing to do with it, she was attacking me. And I'd say, "What have I done? I didn't do anything!" "Yes, but your brother, see how he talks to his wife?" When she attacked me in that way I realized she didn't want me to be that way, but even so I was doing what she didn't like. I couldn't understand it.

José explained how careful he has to be to keep the laws because of negative consequences, even though he is a permanent resident:

I've been here for fifteen years. But I've been all over California. After my wife came, we just stayed here. Frankly, you can't get away with much in this country; if you do the wrong thing, you can be deported. I think about the problems I can get into. Sometimes problems like this come up and you lose control, or maybe your wife does, because now I've more or less learned to control myself.... It's not like we're citizens or that we have the right to be here in the United States. No, you see that the laws are really strict for us Mexicans. I mean they just come

When we analyzed the reasons that men gave for becoming violent, they often had to do with jealousy and anger over situations that they considered unacceptable and threatening to their authority as the head of the family. Thus it is of great importance to help clients to adjust to the changes in today's world, and to see the benefits to them and to their family of women's insertion into the workplace and the greater freedoms that women are beginning to enjoy, in Latin American as well as in the United States. Discussions on the topic of changes in gender roles usually have to be timed, such is the interest and passion of the group on this topic.

up and deport you if you don't have papers. There's nothing you can
do about it.

Discrimination

*The majority of the interview participants (7 out of 12) reported that they
had not experienced discrimination themselves since they came to the
United States. Five of the men had, and their experiences varied considerably. However, 11 of the men were aware that many other immigrants in
Latino domestic violence groups had experienced the negative effects of discrimination.* Discrimination or the threat of discrimination has been shown
to be an added stressor in the life of ethnic minorities in this country.

Lucio described his struggles to come to terms with the treatment he
has received:

> Here you go through a lot because you want your children to have
> a better life, to get them things. When you're young you're more
> impulsive, you might want to fight back. When you get older, you have
> to think of your family, your children. You have to put up with it. You
> can complain to personnel, or to the manager. But you don't do it,
> not to be labeled a snitch, second because, they pay no attention, and
> third, because you make enemies. So you don't do anything. You keep
> silent. You let it go in one ear and out the other. Sometimes I think
> the discrimination has affected my self-esteem. Like I ask myself, *Is it
> true?* Just for a moment, then it passes. People don't have that kind of
> power over me.

Raúl recounted his experience of contemptuous treatment:

> Once the *Migra*[3] detained us. There was a woman in the group of those
> of us who were detained, and I don't remember why we were talking
> there, but I said, "I wonder how many American women work for the
> *Migra*?" And a *Migra* officer heard me, and he came up and slapped
> me in the face and said, "American women are for American men, not
> for pigs." I remember it perfectly. He spoke Spanish well, this guy. He
> was American. Some of the *Migra* are really good people, and some of
> them just beat you up the whole time. Just the worst.

These topics lend support to the ecosystemic theory of IPV, which
incorporates influences from the entire society, as well as closer circles,
such as community and family, and the intrapsychic world of the violent man.

In summary, the participants described frequent exposure to violence
in their communities of origin, as well as rigid, dominant male gender

In the groups, we choose not to spend a lot of time discussing men's experience of discrimination. We do not want the session to become a list of grievances, or to divert sessions from the overall theme of taking responsibility for one's violent behavior. Nevertheless, it is helpful for clients to feel understood in their struggles and to acknowledge the legitimate difficulties they experience. Generally, when we introduce the topic of discrimination it is to use it as a springboard for the discussion of discrimination against women.

roles and submissive female gender roles, as the primary reasons they had been violent to their partners. They recognized the lack of positive parenting they had received from their fathers, and spoke about the difficulty they had in being loving and understanding parents. After describing their personal experience of trauma—child abuse and witnessing their fathers' violence to their mothers—they went on to describe their own maladaptive coping skills, specifically alcohol abuse and dependence, poor relationship skills, and lack of anger management. Finally, they described other issues that affected their ability to cope in their families: financial stress, difficulties with acculturation, discrimination, and the changes that immigration had brought about in their relationships with their partners. In chapter 6 we explore the cultural values common to Latinos that might have served as protective factors against family violence, but in the case of our participants, did not. We then go on to explore men's experience in the therapy group, and how this helped them to work on the transformation of their behavior.

NOTES

1. The first edition of this program was titled *Violencia Doméstica 2000* and was published by Health Transformations in 2003 (Wexler & Welland, 2003a, 2003b).
2. *Pendejo* can be roughly translated as idiot, asshole, jerk, fool, and so forth, depending on the context. It is very insulting.
3. *Migra* is an abbreviation of Migración, which denotes the Border Patrol, now known as U.S. Customs and Border Protection.

cultural values as incentives to conform socially and behave in a socially appropriate manner has the potential to be a powerful source of motivation for partner abusive men.

Researchers already cited in chapter 3 have found that the following features are generally held in common by most Latinos, even given the large individual differences between people of any nationality or ethnic group: interdependence, which means placing a high value on the needs, objectives, and point of view of other members of the culture or group; *familismo*, the strong identification with and attachment to nuclear and extended family, and strong feelings of loyalty, reciprocity, and solidarity among family members; respect, or *respeto*, which is defined as appropriate deferential behavior toward others on the basis of age, social position, economic status, and gender; *personalismo* and *simpatía* in relationships, which consist of a tendency to be more oriented toward people than toward impersonal relationships, and a friendly, empathic, and harmonious manner of dealing with others; a spiritual orientation to life, whether Catholicism or other religions, which provides existential and moral principles, as well as social support and rituals that are important in the culture and positive gender roles, specifically the male gender role, which includes protection of the family, the responsibility of providing for the well-being and security of wife and children, and upholding the family's honor.[1]

In this chapter, we focus on the cultural factors that were eventually incorporated into the program, based on the participants' feedback on whether particular cultural values truly had special salience for them. In chapter 5 we explored the men's explanations for why they were violent in the bosom of their family. Even though the sanctions against family violence embedded in their cultural beliefs were apparently not salient enough to act as protective factors for the participants, the men were at least very aware of these beliefs, values, and expectations. It seems that when personal risk factors are present, these cultural values are distorted and may lead to violence, because almost anything that comes up in the relationship can be misinterpreted by a partner abusive man.

Hill et al. (1994) stated that connection to ethnic culture may act as a protective factor in two ways: by providing a sense of identity and closeness, and by reducing the risk of violence. They suggest that reduction of violence may be achieved in two ways: first, through the support of extended family (e.g., offering diffusion of tensions to the couple and protection to the woman), and second, through the family's adherence to ethnic values. Thus we explored the concept of *familismo*, as well as ethnic values such as *respeto*, positive male gender roles, and spirituality in the lives of the interview participants, and to a lesser extent, the survey respondents.

The interdependence and *familismo* (primacy of loyalty to family, family honor, and the welfare of the family versus the individual) of Latino culture have been widely discussed in the literature (Marín & Marín, 1991). Sixty-five percent of the survey respondents reported that they had extended family living in the region, and even more reported close friendships. Over 20% of respondents shared their living space with other relatives. A large majority of respondents stated that they were satisfied with the level of social support they enjoy. As Mindel (1980) found, Latinos tend to migrate toward family, not away from them. Although the men in our study experienced negative learning from their families, the strength of Latino families in general must be emphasized; in our treatment program family is a major focus of interventions.

Many Latino cultural values are also connected to the Catholic faith (Bach-y-Rita, 1982; Falicov, 1996), and as such, spirituality may be seen as a protective factor as well. Ninety-five percent of the survey respondents identified themselves as Christians, and only 3% of survey respondents said they had no religion. A total of 89% of respondents said their religion was important or very important to them. All of the 12 interview participants knew that their religious values are incompatible with IPV and had heard this at church. However, in spite of close family networks and connection to their culture's spiritual values, the respondents had become violent to their partners.

In the following pages, we explore the interview participants' views and experiences related to their cultural values. In each case, we briefly describe how these values were later incorporated into the content and process of the treatment program.

POSITIVE ASPECTS OF MALE GENDER ROLES

We have already discussed the influence of negative male gender roles, machismo, and traditional female roles as increasing the likelihood of IPV for the participants. However, Latino culture also defines the *positive* gender expectations of men in the society. *Eleven of the 12 participants identified some of these positive male roles that they lived or were aware of before treatment.*

Raúl described how he was good at being a Mexican man:

> For me the positive side was taking responsibility that they would always have food to eat, and money to buy food and clothes and to go to school. Provide, protect, give them everything. For me the positive side was, if someone was disrespectful, to go and take care of it

immediately. So that my partner would always feel secure and supported. Also the intention that I had to take my wife out to dinner or the family out for the day when I could, both here and in Mexico. That was my good side I guess.

Raúl attributed most of his adaptive masculine qualities to his father, whom he saw as the ideal role model of Mexican manhood:

When we were old enough to work, he'd say, "I'm going to teach you how to contribute your salary to the family, so that you learn starting right now to be responsible. That's the first thing. And second, I never want you to even *think* about going around here drunk or smoking in the house, either in front of your mother or me, or your little brothers and sisters. I expect you to show respect."

Latino men who leave their countries of origin, unless they are of the upper-middle or upper class, usually do so because of greater poverty at home. As such they could be called "economic refugees." In the United States, they are able to provide more for their families, not only financially, but in terms of educational possibilities for their children and even themselves that they would never have had at home. Even when they struggle financially and feel disappointed that it is so hard to make a living in the country they felt had "streets paved in gold," they still feel they are better off in the United States. In a study comparing self-esteem among partner abusive men in Tijuana and San Diego, Fernández de Juan, Welland Akong, and Candelas Villagómez (2007) found that Mexican immigrant men who were violent to their partners had higher self-esteem than their counterparts in Tijuana. This was attributed this to their greater earning power, because in other respects there were no significant differences. José emphasized the dedication to work that characterizes the positive side of the Mexican man:

He should act right, fulfill all his obligations, help his family to get ahead, to get their education, their studies, their progress—his children, his family. His obligation is to work so that nothing is lacking in the home, to be responsible in every way. When he has done all that, he's a real Mexican man. Of course, sometimes you can't, but at least you try. My father taught me to work and to be respectful. I'm glad he taught me to respect my mother and I'm grateful that he taught me to work. I have never been a good-for-nothing. I've always worked.

When working with Latino men, the culturally enshrined respect for the mother can be utilized as a way to explore the lack of respect for other women, such as the mother of the client's children. It is an issue fraught with emotion. Often men know they should respect their mothers, but some have repressed hostility and resentment toward her, frequently from histories of abuse from their mother and/or lack of protection from their father. Often, these men have been brought up in violent families where their mother was abused emotionally and physically by their father in their presence. This, too, creates a tremendous amount of confusion and pain for clients. If their mother was not respected by their father, while at the same time their father was insisting that they respect her, how do they reconcile this conflict with their own intimate partners and with their children? Normalizing and working through some of this anger, confusion, and negative role-modeling in the group can free a client to see his romantic partner in a new light and to treat her with the respect she deserves. Several of the participants commented on the helpfulness of having a female therapist for their months of treatment and how this constant contact was good training for respecting women in general.

Ramón, who himself received very little in the way of positive modeling from his father, was able to describe the ideal:

How should a Mexican man be? Respectful, understanding, loving, responsible. A good communicator. If a man had all that, and his partner too, wow! It would be great. I'd like to be like the man I just described—the ideal man, loving, respectful, all that.

FAMILISMO

The Nuclear Family

All of the participants identified family as central to their lives and to their self-concept. Loyalty to the nuclear family is also a vital aspect of *familismo*.[2] The participants unanimously declared the importance of their nuclear family to them even before their IPV treatment. Most of them reported being concerned about their children's education. Their main concern was to be responsible men, by providing for the family economically and by protecting their partner and children from outside harm (if not from harm from themselves). These values constitute the core of the positive male gender role for Latinos, as described by Marín and his associates (1990). Casas et al. (1994) described the positive Mexican male gender schema as the fulfillment of the role of protector and provider, while restraining vulnerable emotions and displaying stoic strength in the midst of adversity. The level of variation in roles described by the participants supports Vega's research (1990), in which he presented a wide range of male socialization patterns in Mexican American families. In support of this, some of the participants shared decision making with their partner from the beginning of their relationship. Some were willing and eager for their partner to work when they migrated to the United States. All of them describe a life of hard work with the purpose of being the family's provider.

Contrary, however, to some of the literature (Bach-y-Rita, 1982), all of the men described machismo as a negative phenomenon. That is, the male gender role for Mexican men is not synonymous with machismo. This view is in accord with Lara-Cantú (1989), who found that machismo is a negative construct in modern Mexico, as did Mirandé (1997) and Gutmann (1996).

Understanding the current popular definition of *machismo* has important clinical implications for therapists working with this population. Accurate use of the term will ensure better communication and dispel the sense men in treatment may get of being stereotyped and misunderstood.

Blas described his current life as completely focused on his children's welfare:

> I grew up without my mother and my father. And I never want that to happen to my children.... But for most Mexican men, they'll never understand, until what happened to me happens to them. To understand that in reality, his family is the most important thing in the world to him. To understand that he must love his wife and children and put them first. Then yes, his eyes will begin to open.

Ceferino brightened as he described his relationship to his children:

> I love them very much. I want them to live in a healthy environment, to grow up in a different world from the one I lived in. I want the best for them in every way. I'm not rich, but whatever I have in my pocket I give them. I try to give my family now, my children, what my own family never gave me.

Raúl did not see his children for 3 or 4 years while a restraining order was in effect, but he has now become an important part of their lives once more:

> I don't see my ex-wife when I go to get them. I don't know if she's with someone else. I don't want to ask my children and be investigating all that. I don't want to substitute one thing for another. I go to see them because I love them, because I want to be with them and make them feel good.

Extended Family

We found in both the survey and the interviews that social support and closeness to extended family are largely intact among the Latino domestic violence offenders in treatment in Southern California, and that the men interviewed knew what their culture expected of them as husbands and fathers. This finding, however, does not explain how the supposedly protective factor of *familismo* failed to shield the families affected by IPV. Our explanation of the data is that the negative reality of their family experience, both in the family of origin and in the current stress they experience, outweighed the positive cultural influence of *familismo*, which for many abusive men appeared to be more of a myth than a reality. Furthermore, in almost every case, the positive interactions that the interviewees mentioned were rarely if ever with their fathers, and almost always with their mothers, the cultural protectors of the hearth, and with their siblings.

It will be seen in later sections that learning how to activate the man's positive contribution to *familismo*, as enshrined in the culture but not in the histories of the participants, was one of the greatest gains of treatment. Of course, in working with the men to redefine their gender roles and change their attitude toward women, their idea of family and women's roles takes on nuances that are different from the traditional ideas, even the adaptive ones, that, in their case, had the effect of marginalizing women and making them second-class citizens.

Most of the men (7 out of 12) continue to rely on extended family for support, advice, correction, and protection. The migration network pattern described in the literature, that is, that Latinos tend to move closer to family rather than away from them, was very evident in the participants' depiction of extended family relationships. Some of the men relied on family support in every way; others were hesitant or ashamed to ask for financial help. They felt that they should have achieved more financial security since their immigration than was actually the case. Of the 5 men who did not enjoy a positive or close relationship with extended family, 3 of them came from very abusive homes, and 2 were older and had fewer family contacts. Interestingly, almost all the men described how their family supported their partners and criticized them for their violent, abusive behavior.

Ignacio reported tension in his family over the incident:

They're all against me because they all loved her a lot, they still love her. It really hurts. They're very supportive but they do tell me that I have to change. They help me a lot, not economically, but morally, I get a lot of support. In every way.

Raúl mused on how his parents would have reacted had they been in San Diego when he was violent:

> They didn't allow me to do that kind of thing. The first thing my father would tell me would be, "What kind of little man [*hombrecito*] are you, going around insulting and hurting a woman? God gave you this woman for you to care for her, not for you to hurt her." That's the way he thinks and acts, and that's why he still has his marriage.

Ramón, whose family came to the United States to escape their violent father, described a great deal of interaction and support:

> We all help each other. We're all united here. The ones we're not united with are with my partner's family. Her mother lives here, and her father, her stepfather, and one of her brothers. She only has two brothers. They don't support her at all. [The closeness of my family] is really a help to me, but sometimes we fight because my brothers come over here every day. My partner doesn't want them to come over every day. She says once a week is enough. I tell her, "Just because your brothers and your mother don't visit you doesn't mean mine shouldn't visit me."

Ramón had stated earlier that one of the main reasons his partner disapproved of these frequent visits was that his brothers drank too much. But Ramón was grateful that his family was close to him, regardless of their behavior. Not only that, he expected his partner to tolerate and even appreciate their daily visits. This attitude would be fertile ground for a discussion in the therapy group.

Respeto

Respeto *was mentioned by all the participants as being a core cultural value for the Mexican, supporting the work of Hofstede (1980), Triandis and his associates (1984), and others.* Their parents taught them to be respectful of their elders and authority figures and to expect *respeto* from their partners and children. All the men knew how to be respectful to the therapist and the men in their treatment group, by their own admission, and all of them were very deferential, even gentlemanly, to the first author during their entire interview. *However, 8 of the 12 interview participants reported that they had failed in* respeto *to their partner, but not only during the domestic violence incident.* In most cases, the lack of *respeto* was a chronic pattern, in contrast to their usual deference to others. This behavior is commonly seen in Type II and III partner abusive men, who demonstrate markedly different behavior with strangers and associates than with their family members. Furthermore, they frequently described the conflict between partners, and with their children as well, as deficits in *respeto*. Clearly, *respeto* as a cultural script has major importance. As a result, we have incorporated it as a vital attitudinal and behavioral goal in our treatment program, not as a separate topic, but as a significant ingredient of all human interactions.

Men are briefed from the outset regarding the expectation of *respeto*, and if they fail during their group treatment, it is pointed out to them immediately as a requirement of the program. As a result, we rarely find that this social threshold is crossed by group members, and if it is, they correct each other swiftly. Such practice is an important learning experience, especially as regards respect toward their female therapist, which serves as practice for respect to their partners. Part of our task as therapists is to demonstrate to our clients that even though they learned one way of behaving at home at an early age, they can always change and learn another that is more in line with an adaptive cultural script like *respeto*. This does not apply only to *respeto*, of course, but to all the attitudes and behaviors that are common among partner abusive men. Behavior was learned: It can be unlearned and replaced, although not without difficulty and perseverance.

Eleven of the 12 participants spoke about respeto *and identified it as highly desirable in an intimate relationship.* They mentioned that their own parents had taught them the importance of *respeto*, but in spite of that, they admitted that *respeto* was lacking in their relationship on the part of one or both partners. On the other hand, let us not forget that most of the participants came from violent families, so the *respeto* that was taught was in word, not in action.

Hilario bemoaned the change in his wife after immigration:

Like I used to say to the teacher, "The first thing you lose here is respect." First the woman loses respect for her husband, then the husband becomes a mess, and we're back to the same thing, that's where the problems come from....I think if there's love between a couple, there has to be mutual respect, the two of them, to be respectful in every way, to be equal.

Hilario's characterization of his wife's "loss of respect" in his case refers only to the outward display of respect that is expected of an obedient and culturally appropriate wife in Mexico. What he infers, although he confuses the external with the internal, is that his wife really never *did* respect him, and that she gave up the pretense of it once in the United States. This is by no means true of all immigrant women, and is much more likely to be a reflection of the behavior of the violent man and resultant resentment on the part of the woman than because the immigrant man occupies a lower position in American society. On the contrary, immigrants from backgrounds of poverty in Latin America have more materially and are typically seen as more successful in their culture of origin than the men who stayed behind. In Hilario's case, in light of the entire interview, it was evident that there had been a great deal of conflict in the couple for many years and that respect was absent in their relationship on both sides.

Lucio wished he had given better examples of *respeto* to his children:

So it's really important to teach respect in the family, because if the children see us acting one way, they carry on that chain in their lives. And if we don't change that, it will never be broken.

Leonardo described a mutual lack of respect in his relationship:

At that moment she was lacking in respect to me, when she came in and the way she came in. I was also wrong and lacking in respect to her because I was there drinking with my friends. At that time, I saw it like, *This is my house. I don't want to have to go out to the street to drink.* But it was a lack of respect, because it's bad to get drunk in your home, especially with the children there. Drinking is against her religion. We had argued about it several times before. There were two sides to it. We both failed and were wrong, and we lacked respect.

The treatment program that was the result of this study emphasizes *respeto* both in the content of the material, where it is frequently mentioned and reinforced, and in the group process. Facilitators are encouraged to never fail to respect their clients, in spite of the tests they are put to, and to insist on a respectful environment in the groups. This creates a safe place where men can learn to express themselves appropriately, which is the practice they need if they are to replicate this behavior in their homes.

SPIRITUALITY

Importance of Spiritual Values

Most of the men (9 out of 12) placed considerable value on their spiritual beliefs and stated that they wish to be guided by them in their behavior.

They described their interest in spirituality in various ways, ranging from active involvement in churchgoing to private prayer and reading. Even the 3 men who were not active in any religion identified belief in God as important to them. Some of them described how their religious observance had declined since immigration. For others, it had increased. The amount of religious instruction the men had received was related to their place of origin in Mexico. Central Mexico has traditionally been able to provide much more instruction to Catholics than the north or the south. Eleven of the men were Catholic, and 1 was Evangelical. Ignacio was one of the men who was dissatisfied with his current adherence to spiritual values:

> I think recently Mexican men are very far from spirituality. I speak for myself too. You go by a church and you think, *So many people are going, but at the same time, so many aren't going. There's more people at home than at church.* In my village everyone went to Mass every Sunday. Every little village has its church or chapel, and Mass.

José's approach to religion was simple and direct:

> I'm Catholic, and it's important to me. My parents are Catholic too, and I like to go to church. You get relief from your bad thoughts.

Ramón received little religious instruction, but he prays every day:

> Sometimes, very infrequently, I go to church. Every morning when I get up, I make the sign of the cross. I pray the Our Father and ask him to take care of my partner, my children, my mother, and brothers and sisters. That's what I do. And I ask God to forgive my father for all he did to us.

Spiritual Teaching and IPV

The participants all expressed the belief that their church is against domestic violence and that it endorses such values as mutual respect, responsibility, caring for others, and nonviolence. Most of them had heard at least something at church about avoiding IPV, usually in the United States, and much less frequently in Mexico. In spite of the prevalence of IPV throughout the population, it appears that many churches fail to utilize their moral authority to teach men better conduct and to link this conduct with their faith. Recent efforts by some congregations suggest that this is changing in the United States and some parts of Latin America; however, there is much work to be done. The participants felt very strongly about their church's opposition to IPV and felt that the researchers should be aware of it.[3] However, as with *familismo*, in spite of the personal salience of their religion, and at least a rudimentary knowledge of their faith's teachings, the participants had not refrained from domestic violence. The forces of violence were more powerful in their lives than the sketchy moral teaching they had received, indicating that information is not enough to change behavior when destructive forces are hard at work.

Given the importance of religion and spiritual beliefs to the great majority of the Latino men in our survey and interviews, and the corresponding lack of religious involvement of many psychologists and therapists, there is a potential inherent disconnect here in the group treatment.[4] If a therapist does not feel qualified or comfortable discussing the topic of religion or spirituality as a way of preventing future abuse, or of seeking forgiveness for past abuse, he or she may consult with the group about their beliefs, at the very least. Further education on the importance of spiritual matters with the Latino population for therapists who find themselves unprepared in this area could be an important goal for continuing education. Above all, it is important for rapport building to avoid giving the impression that the therapist considers the men's spiritual beliefs to be primitive, unmentionable, or worse, laughable. Men express relief when their spiritual beliefs are respected by their therapists and the group. It is also a useful way of modeling respect and tolerance in the group. Therapists who feel truly out of their depth might consider calling in a colleague who is more experienced when touching on spiritual matters. Our program includes a four-session educational and practical unit on spirituality and IPV prevention, to which the men typically respond very positively.

Hilario was one of the few men whose parish priest in Mexico spoke explicitly against domestic violence. He had also refrained from IPV in his relationship up until the time of the one incident that led to his arrest and treatment.

> We had one priest named González who used to say that the man who beat a woman wasn't a man. And it's true. I only remember him saying it about twice. It really stuck with me.

Gregorio had a different experience:

> In those days when I was young, in the *rancho* the priest never mentioned domestic violence at all. I mean people knew it wasn't what the church wanted, and you knew it was wrong, but they didn't talk about it. And they didn't change. Here, the priests do talk about it. I learned everything about domestic violence here in the States. It is very important for priests to talk about domestic violence and the family, even though many people go to Mass and don't pay any attention to what he's saying.

Leonardo was adamant that IPV is not tolerated by his church:

> My religious training did affect my beliefs about domestic violence,
> because of course the Scriptures teach us not to be violent against your
> wife, and that we shouldn't be disrespectful to anyone. Of course,
> it's obvious that my church is against domestic violence. I've heard
> the priest here in Escondido speak out against domestic violence in
> public.

José expressed amazement that such a question should even be asked of
him:

> Of course men who don't practice faith are more abusive. If I don't
> have any hope in any kind of Catholicism, as they say, in religion, then
> I'm a person who doesn't have anything good in my mind. So I think
> it's better for people who go to church, or to some religion. A man
> like that is less likely to be violent. It has the same effect as one of my
> classes. Maybe some other religion thinks it's good to beat your wife,
> but not my church. No, never.

For these men, it seems clear that the positive support and teachings
of Latino culture, their religious tradition, and their families were not
powerful enough to override the major risk factors for IPV that under-
mined them. All of the interview participants, and most of the survey
respondents as well, met criteria for several risk factors each, including
demographic factors. It appears that these men had the odds stacked
against them in their task of being men, husbands, and fathers who could
live up to the positive expectations of their culture.

Having explored the adaptive and maladaptive cultural scripts of the
participants, we went on to examine their experience of group therapy,
both as Latinos, specifically, and as men who had been violent to their
partners and were learning a new way to live their masculinity. They also
enlightened us about the qualities of their therapists that they found had
facilitated or blocked change. This information, because it is not usually
available to therapists, was invaluable to us and to all those who work
with Latino men.

WHAT WAS IT LIKE FOR THE MEN TO BE IN
TREATMENT FOR PARTNER ABUSE?

In listening to the participants' experience of group treatment, we learned
a great deal about their personal and group behaviors, as well as therapist behaviors. They also had a considerable amount to say about the

content of the curriculum of the programs where they were enrolled, which varied only depending on the style of the group therapist.[5]

The Experience of Group Therapy: What Made Treatment Work

Themes relating to their therapy experience specifically as Latino men will be described first. They serve as a fitting introduction to the participants' 52-week journey toward change and healing. Subsequently, we will explore their thoughts about group treatment in general.

The Latino Group

Most of the participants expressed a clear preference for being in a group with other Latinos, mostly because of cultural similarity and understanding, as well as the obvious language factor. All of the men felt that group therapy with men of their own cultural group was the best way to tackle the problem of IPV, for several reasons. Support, better and more varied advice, and more opportunity to confront one another and work toward honesty and accountability were the most common reasons mentioned. We did not find this surprising, based on other research into treatment for domestic violence and on the appropriateness of group therapy for Latinos (Avila & Avila, 1980; Gutiérrez & Ortega, 1991). Apart from the cultural appropriateness of Latino groups, many first-generation Mexican and Latino immigrants, due to the extensive ethnic community present in this region, never learn English sufficiently to really benefit from therapy in that language. We found that even after 20 or 30 years in the United States, most of the men had not faced the need to learn anything but rudimentary English.

Seven of the 12 men interviewed mentioned that being in a group of Latino men facilitated their learning and their process of change, apart from their need for therapy in the Spanish language. Because of similar cultural scripts, as mentioned above, there is a deeper sense of being understood and accepted by people who are from your own culture and specific background. Blas completed 40 weeks of English IPV group treatment before reoffending and beginning a Latino group:

> It's so much better when it's in your own language. And it's true, when you see other Mexicans, who don't want to admit that they're *machistas*, but they are. And that makes you feel . . . like I used to counterattack my companions, not to fight with them, but to help them understand that they had a problem. Those of us who had been there longer would give them concrete examples of how to act. I was also receiving help from the same men in other ways.

José commented,

> Everybody was Mexican. For me it's better to be with just Mexicans because they have more problems. And you can talk more freely, because they tell you not to be ashamed to talk about what you feel. We understand each other's problems better. Your own people should be able to contradict you or to tell you what's happening, what's right and wrong, all that. With different people you don't have that kind of trust.

Ramón volunteered,

> I think it's easier with other Mexicans because we know how life is there, the problems we've been through as children...if your father was like mine, you just say a few words and they understand. About half the guys in my group said they'd been traumatized by their fathers when they were children.

Lucio referred to the absence of discrimination in the Latino group:

> If we were with people from this country, there wouldn't be much unity, like all the time there'd be that, I don't know, feeling of being enemies. When you're with your own race, you feel more trust.

- The participants believed that IPV treatment groups specifically for Latinos, in Spanish, were more acceptable and effective for them than heterogeneous (mixed ethnicity) groups in English.

Use of Spanish Videos

Seven of the 12 participants reported that the videos they saw in English were helpful, but only to a point. They had difficulty comprehending the language and relating to the characters. These men thought that audio-visual material should be in Spanish and appropriate to their needs and social class. They also commented that the books some of the agencies used had inadequate and inaccurate translations. Their feedback spurred us to pilot our treatment program for 4 years and to refine the vocabulary so that every word was accurate, intelligible, and defined if necessary.

Rogelio commented,

> I would have preferred Mexican films, of course. Something that's related to our life, because if you see yourself in a film, you realize, *Wow, I really did something wrong.* It would be really great to have Latino films in the group. You'd understand it better. In English you kind of get it, but you miss a lot.

Lucio observed,

> We saw the film *El Chupis* [in Spanish]. It's a film about the middle class. There was no one in the film who was from our level. Just office workers and people like that. There was no one from the working class there. I mean, everyone works to survive, but you identify better with your own class.

Ignacio described the experience of using English videos:

> I'd like the films to be in Spanish. Not all of us understand English, and the counselor has to be there translating. So it gets out of control, some people understand, others don't. It gets confusing.

Efforts are under way in the therapeutic community in Southern California to produce video clips in Spanish that are truly tailored for our Latino clients. Spanish-language movie clips can also be used, with the caveat that the characters match the life experience of the clients to some degree. We also make use of current Latino popular music to illustrate such themes as jealousy, repentance, lack of empathy, and attachment in the lyrics. This music has been noted to touch clients in ways that bypass rationalization and minimization, opening the way for deeper discussion of emotional issues.

- The participants believed that audiovisual material used in groups for Latino men should be in Spanish and appropriate to their socioeconomic status.

Ethnicity of Therapist

Most of the therapists the participants had over the course of 52 weeks of treatment were Latino, though not necessarily Mexican. Some of the men had Anglo therapists. *Eleven of the 12 participants stated that they did not mind whether the therapist was Mexican or not, as long as he or she spoke Spanish fluently and was familiar with Mexican culture, especially the culture of "the lower class."* Two of the men expressed preference for a Mexican therapist but were concerned that it might be difficult for a Mexican woman to be impartial and understanding, due to a supposed inability to forgive Mexican men for the discrimination women have suffered.

Atkinson and Lowe (1995) found that responsiveness to and knowledge of cultural content were more important to Mexican Americans in therapy than the clients' level of acculturation or the therapist's ethnicity.

Atkinson and Lowe's research demonstrated that the degree of cultural competence of a therapist is an important outcome variable in therapy. Sue and Sue (2002) also emphasized the vital importance of cross-cultural awareness for effective therapy, stressing respect for differences, awareness of one's own personal values and heritage, sensitivity to circumstances, and awareness of one's own racist attitudes, beliefs, and feelings as essential factors if one is to be accepted and trusted by clients of different groups. They stated that the culturally skilled therapist possesses specific knowledge of the group they are working with, understands the ramifications of the clients' sociopolitical standing as a minority, and is aware of institutional barriers to accessing services for minority clients. Consequently, therapists who are not of the same ethnic origin as their Latino clients, and/or who are from a different social class or gender, need to be very conscious that their clients will consciously or unconsciously "put them to the test" to see if they can be trusted to be helpful and fair in their case. Therapy is a socially constructed reality, from the postmodernist standpoint, and is a constant learning experience for all parties.

> Cultural competence is not a global, measurable phenomenon but a socially constructed notion created by the therapeutic relationship that is influenced by the social locations of the therapist and clients which vary case by case. Therapy with Latino families will become culturally competent as the therapist and client constantly strive to gain mutual understanding through the countless interactions that take place within the therapy session. (Taylor, Gambourg, Rivera, & Laureano, 2006, p. 430)

Several men were pleasantly surprised that their non-Mexican therapists were so familiar with Mexican history, culture, and customs. This knowledge increased their trust in their ability, thus their credibility, supporting Sue and Zane's finding (1987) that ethnicity is a distal variable in therapy, while it is credibility that is the proximal variable. Credibility is of two varieties: Ascribed credibility consists of status assigned to a therapist due to external characteristics, such as age, education, expertise, and gender. Achieved credibility refers to the therapist's clinical skills. It becomes more important when clients are court-ordered and are not as free to leave therapy based on what they might perceive as low ascribed credibility on the part of the therapist. A therapist who is able to carry out culturally consistent interventions and to demonstrate skills such as empathy and accurate assessment will be much more trustworthy in the eyes of clients. This was clearly the case with the participants, who mentioned that they felt comfortable with their therapists who were culturally and clinically competent and experienced a deeper sense of trust in their interventions.

On the other hand, many of the men felt misunderstood and/or stereotyped by their therapists and mentioned attitudes and behaviors of the therapist that alienated them, such as verbal attacks and blaming, accusing the men of being sexist, accusing the men of lying, and voicing the assumption that "all Mexican men are drunken wife-beaters," to quote one participant. Some of these men felt disrespected and unjustly categorized; they lost trust in the ability of the therapist to help them. Corey (1990) recommended that therapists of an ethnicity other than their clients' should not assume a superior, belittling stance. These findings take on greater importance because of the growing Latino population, coupled with an ongoing shortage of Latino therapists in the United States, and the resultant need for therapists of other ethnicities to be conversant in and comfortable with the Spanish language and with Latino culture and values. Therapists may apply stereotypes to clients of other cultures without being aware that they are doing so, especially if they lack firsthand knowledge of the specific population with whom they work, in this case low-income first-generation Latino immigrants of both urban and rural backgrounds.

When hiring Spanish-speaking therapists of any ethnicity to work with Latino men in IPV groups, agencies should screen candidates carefully to ensure that their cultural competence matches their linguistic ability. Employers should be particularly careful to employ therapists who demonstrate deep respect for Latino culture and for the men they will be treating. Stereotyping in the therapy session is death to disclosure on the part of clients.

Gregorio described the cultural expertise of his therapists:

The therapists knew a lot. They study all that. They knew more than me. It made me feel happy. I felt good that someone who wasn't even from there knew more than I did. It gave me more trust.

Leonardo had a very positive group experience:

María is from Honduras. I felt comfortable with her even though she wasn't from Mexico. I wouldn't particularly have preferred a Mexican therapist. We liked the way she did things, myself in particular. What was important was that she was able to get the information across. That's what I liked. I think it's very important for people working with others, from let's say Asia or wherever, how wonderful to know that

that person knows the culture of that country, how people live there. You trust that person more.

Ramón, however, had difficulty with his therapist because of cultural differences, as well as because of his own views (that are not reflective of all Latino men's ideas regarding infidelity):

> One guy's wife left him, and she said, "Give her some time, maybe she'll change. And if she changes, go back with her." But if she was already with another man, why would you want to go back with her? We don't accept that in Mexico, not here either. I used to call my partner *Gorda*,[6] but Carmen [the therapist] told me it was a lack of respect, so I stopped it. We argued about it, Carmen and I. I told her that in Mexico that was a sign of affection, but she didn't agree. She's from Central America; she doesn't know.

Blas was the only participant who specifically mentioned the negative effect of stereotyping by his therapists, Carmen and Bill:

> I don't think either Carmen or Bill understand my culture well, because I felt that they think that Mexican men are very different from either of them. That they're all machos, all drunks, they apply those stereotypes of Mexican men to all of us. It's like they hear the word *Mexican man*, and a big movie screen goes up: drunk, womanizer, all that, like they don't have any other picture. They don't know that there are all kinds of men in Mexico, like in all the world, a bit of everything. I didn't take it as offensive, but I felt uncomfortable because it was like they were saying it like an attack or a put down, like despising us. That's what I felt.... The counselors knew Mexican culture, but just one part, even though they would say, "Not everyone is like that," but they seemed to always focus on the negative side. I would have liked them to know the culture in more depth.

The information about the interface of ethnicity and therapy was very important to the first author, a Canadian who has lived in Mexico for many years and worked with Latinos for over 30 years. The last comment by Blas was one of the most revealing, and one that we constantly quote in conferences and classes. Interethnic bias and stereotyping can be overt or subtle, and awareness of it is crucial for effective treatment. Our approach is often to leave the stereotyping to the men in the group and then to point it out, challenge it, and throw it open for discussion.

- The participants were more concerned about language fluency and cultural knowledge than about the ethnicity of their therapists. Cultural stereotyping was specifically mentioned as painful to them and as putting an end to group disclosure.

Thoughts and Feelings About Group Therapy

Self-Disclosure

The great majority of the participants reported that they began the group with a negative attitude. Their feelings about the group experience varied from furious and resistant to ashamed, uncomfortable, and afraid of being exposed. Only 2 men came into the group with a positive attitude, wanting help.[7] Other men took from 2 to 20 weeks to develop the feeling that they could participate without anxiety. Clinicians working in this field are already well aware of the resistance to group attendance that can be expected in a court-ordered population. Dealing with their anger, denial, and resistance is an inherent part of the first stage of treatment. The fact that most of the men had had no prior experience of therapy, including Alcoholics Anonymous (AA), further explains their skepticism. Rogelio summed up his discomfort:

> When I started, when I got there, like most of the men I've noticed, thinking that I didn't need to be there. I was saying to myself, *I know how to live, I don't need this program. Why did I get put here? They made a mistake.* But after a while I started to understand things. I realized I was wrong. It took me about three months to get there, honestly. I had so much anger inside. In the beginning, I felt really uncomfortable. I didn't want to tell the truth, like I should have. They asked me what happened, and I covered up some because I was ashamed.

Juan, too, described his problem with shame:

> I was a very shy person, very ashamed to speak. So I just stayed quiet. But after a while my companions there, in the group, told me we were all there to help each other, and they told me that nothing I said would leave there, that it was confidential. Really, it was very hard for me because I'm a very shy person.

Recall that Juan was a victim of child sexual abuse and severe physical abuse. Clinicians may not be aware, because a client has withheld information at intake, of the reasons for a client's reticence or lack of participation. Although court guidelines mandate that all members participate, how the therapist goes about eliciting this participation, and on what schedule, can make all the difference in a client's progress and level of disclosure.

Raúl, like people of many cultures, was brought up to keep family problems in the family:

> All the therapist wanted to hear was that we accepted the blame, and to make us talk about all our family problems. I was an enemy of all that. Because I have never confided in anyone about my relationship, neither problems nor positive things. That's personal. I don't have to talk to anyone about what's going on between my wife and myself.

Ramón was afraid of disclosing:

> I felt very tense, nervous. Anxious. I didn't know how to speak in front of the class. I was afraid to speak. Sometimes, when the others talked about what happened to them when they were children, sometimes I felt like crying. That happened to me too, when I was saying what my father used to do to me. I wanted to cry, but then I stopped talking about it to the teacher. I saw other men cry in the group, and I thought, *I would have got up and left before the tears came out.*

As a matter of course in the groups we facilitate, the men are given permission and even encouraged to shed tears in the group if they feel the need, or at some other time if they prefer. We openly discuss the cultural prohibition against men crying, which is certainly not limited to Latino men, and the benefits of healthy expression of emotion. We also create a safe space where no client needs to be afraid that others in the group will laugh at him or disrespect him if he discloses his pain. In spite of all this, it is not common for our clients to cry in the group setting. When they do, silence descends and the men are quietly supportive.

- The participants took varying amounts of time to overcome their resistance to being mandated to treatment. Therapists should expect this resistance and learn to work with it, rather than against it, by not forcing participation and self-disclosure prematurely.

The Decision to Change

Eight of the 12 men spontaneously mentioned the importance of their personal decision in the change process. They described how they began to benefit from the program when they themselves reached the conclusion that they needed to be different and to take the necessary steps to achieve that goal. This became one of the central themes of their therapy and one that we expand upon at length in later chapters. Here we will touch on it by way of introduction. They affirmed that it was not the composition of the group, the strategy of the therapist, or the particular content of the sessions, but the sole fact of their decision to change. The intensity and consistency of wording with which this phrase was uttered suggested to us that such an ability to make firm, life-enhancing decisions is very congruent with the positive male gender role for Mexicans, although the literature does not mention it specifically. The timing of this decision was varied, but it coincided with the beginning of the clients' self-disclosure, after which they began to reap benefits from the program. Motivational interviewing is now being used in some IPV treatment (Taft, Murphy, Elliott, & Morrel, 2001). Similarly, we found that tapping into a client's motivation to change is key to the rest of the process. Again and again, we heard elements of the hero's journey in their words, something about making that decision that was attractive to them, a sense that setting a goal of a new and different masculinity, and persevering on this difficult road of personal change up to the point of witnessing the transformation of oneself and consequently of one's relationships, was deeply rewarding. Men spoke of feeling better about who they had become, of not feeling comfortable in their own skin as they were before, even though it was all they knew. To extend the metaphor, there seemed to be an element of the dragon shedding his scales in their life change, revealing the authentic, more vulnerable, but infinitely more human person that had remained hidden under a frightening and invincible shell for decades. They described a sense of pride in their accomplishments, a new freedom, a new sense of direction, contentment they had never known.[8]

Rogelio spoke of his process:

> I think it was a decision that I made. In fact, when I left the jail, I said, *OK, that's it. I have to stop drinking.* Then, during the course of the program I gradually realized that alcohol was the source of my problems. It has a lot to do with the problems we have. So, I said, *OK, to start with I'm going to quit drinking.* So I kept going to the program and the change began slowly, gradually. Then my change of lifestyle began to kick in automatically.

Ignacio emphasized the importance of personal choice in his change process:

> Maybe you just realize yourself and take responsibility and decide to change, if you want to change. Because a lot of us think that we're fine, we don't need this, but in reality they do. The need to change, that decision you take yourself. Not because of anyone else. It's the need to

be different. You have to decide for yourself. If you want to change, you will change. If you don't, you won't.

Leonardo volunteered,

> The first few times, things were just coming in one ear and going out the other. I wasn't interested. I began to pay more attention when two or three guys were talking about their case, and I listened, and I thought, *Why am I just sitting here? Wasting my time, wasting my money, without taking in anything María* [the therapist] *is saying, without taking in the testimonies of my friends here. What am I doing?* That's where I made the change.

Ramón, at only 22 years old, was glad that his therapist understood his culture, but that wasn't what determined whether or not he would accept the material.

> I change if I want to. Why look at other people to decide if I'm going to change or not?

- All the participants reached a point in their treatment where they themselves decided that they needed to change, and from that time on they began to draw benefits from their therapy. Motivating clients to change, then, is of prime importance.

Empowerment

As the interview participants progressed through their group treatment, they began to experience positive benefits from being there. They began to listen to others and learn from them, to pick up new skills from the content taught, and to make their own positive contribution to the total experience. Yalom's (1985) first factor of group therapy is the instillation of hope.

> The instillation and maintenance of hope is crucial in any psychotherapy. Not only is hope required to keep a patient in therapy so that other therapeutic factors may take effect, but faith in a treatment mode can in itself be therapeutic.... Group therapy not only draws from the general ameliorative effects of positive expectations but also benefits from a source of hope that is unique to the group format. Therapy groups invariably contain individuals who are at different points along a coping-collapse continuum. Each member thus has considerable contact with others—often individuals with similar problems—who have improved as a result of therapy. (pp. 4–5)

Clearly, hope had been given to the men who were open to the program and the group. The hope they felt for the future was present even though in many cases their former relationship could not be salvaged. They knew that the skills they had learned would stand them in good stead in future relationships. Perhaps most significantly for them, they now had hope that their children would grow up differently from them, because now they were in a position to be the kind of fathers they themselves never had.

Learning From the Group

All of the men described ways in which being in the group itself had helped them to decide on the direction of their change. Leonardo commented,

> My companions gave me some good advice about how to handle it, even though it was a small thing, because everything starts small. I liked it that they paid attention to me. They took the trouble to give me advice.... Once you see the positive side of being in a group and having to get your problems out in the open, to get an opinion from someone else, it seems very appropriate to me. You feel good doing it.

Ignacio realized how the group had helped him to be more honest:

> When I'm talking in front of everyone, they ask me things like, "Why did you do it?" or "Would it have stopped you if you had been calm?" Things like that. So you realize that people are interested, and sometimes you say things that you're afraid to say because they're asking you questions.

Feelings About Treatment

All of the men remarked on the positive experience that it was for them to receive the support of other men who understood them and their struggles. The issue of support is a critical one. They reported receiving more help from the group itself than from the material that was presented, as useful as it was. This is important for the therapist to remember. Being too focused on "getting through" the curriculum can block the realization that the group is the most helpful component of the therapy. Men of many ethnicities have made the same observation in other domestic violence groups that we have facilitated. The support, advice, example, successes, and even failures of other group members made the deepest impression on them.

Some of the positive feelings the men identified in their group experience were confidence, pride in self for gaining self-control, and feeling valued, respected, relieved, grateful, accepted, important, and supported. McKinley (1987) stated that group therapy offers the Latino client a corrective family experience, breaks through social isolation, especially the isolation of machismo mentioned by Casas et al. (1994), and helps them to learn needed assertiveness skills. The participants affirmed that it was easier to work on change when they had positive feelings, versus struggling with their own resistance or reacting to perceived put-downs by the therapist. Similarly, Murphy and Baxter (1997) found that an effective IPV facilitator creates a safe, empathic, respectful environment, where men can be honest without fear of reprisal or humiliation.

In spite of the importance of therapist empathy, in court ordered groups in the United States, reporting of reoffense is often mandatory, depending on local regulations. Therapists must make the limits of confidentiality clear to clients from the outset, remind them frequently in the group, and not hesitate to make a report when the safety of the partner and children is in question. Naturally, with such constraints in place, most men will not disclose incidents of violence or failures to stay within the limits of their probation.

The participants demonstrated that their group experience had empowered them to be different husbands and fathers, to share their new knowledge with family and friends, and to make a difference in their environment. This response on their part supports Fromm's theory (1973) that describes violent behavior as the blocking of creative energy, needing to be expressed in positive ways. Once these men have learned to control their aggressive impulses, they seem anxious to create positive outlets for the energy that has been freed up. We were struck by their enthusiasm for sharing what they had learned with others, starting with extended family members. Some of the participants expressed a desire to share their experience of lifestyle change with other violent men in the Latino community through the auspices of some agency or organization. The potential to utilize such peer mentors is an untapped resource in the Latino community, and one that would be well worth exploring and facilitating.

Learning Through Content Taught

All the participants mentioned topics discussed in therapy that they found exceptionally helpful. Eleven of the men were unable to identify a single topic that they found useless, unhelpful, or offensive. The 1 participant who recalled a topic he found offensive took exception to the decision of the group and the therapist that the man in the relationship should always give his entire paycheck to his partner.[9]

Many men mentioned the usefulness of the check-in method, where the therapist dedicates time at the beginning of session to find out how the week went for the clients. This gives the group an opportunity to practice empathy and to brainstorm and evaluate different ways to resolve the clients' difficulties, reinforcing material learned. The check-ins are an important means for the development of group cohesion, which is one of the main components of effective group therapy (Yalom, 1985). The topics mentioned as extremely helpful varied depending on the participant, but among them they identified all the major components of standard IPV treatment.

The content areas that men found helpful may be divided under the major headings of anger management, cognitive restructuring of negative attitudes, improved relationship skills, conflict resolution and problem solving, and identification of the types of IPV with the power and control wheel (Pence & Paymar, 1993). Even though the Duluth program was the accepted format for intervention at the time of the interviews, as stated, it was evident that all the group facilitators had used cognitive-behavioral and psychodynamic interventions as well. Other areas emerged from the interviews that the participants found very helpful, such as the discussion of equality or teaching on parenting. These, and other topics that they hoped could be explicitly included in treatment programs for Latinos, are explored in depth in a later chapter.

The interview participants expressed the belief that all the information and skills that were offered them were appropriate and that none should be left out of a program for Latino men. They expressed the opinion that men who are violent act the same everywhere, and couples have problems in every country. Their observations on this point are accurate, as Campbell (1992) pointed out. It seemed important to them to normalize their experience and not to believe that as Latinos they are somehow worse or more morally deficient than men in other cultures. It was gratifying to realize that even without specific cultural changes, the treatment programs being offered in Southern California were meaningful for Latino men mandated to IPV therapy groups. However, all of the participants mentioned a small subsection of the men in their groups who did not seem to benefit from treatment and who sometimes held others back from learning. Some researchers (Jacobson et al., 1995) have suggested that the more extreme Type I batterers (*Cobras*) may not be amenable to treatment and may not be appropriate for standard IPV groups; they may benefit more from incarceration. At present, research on effective treatments for different types of batterers in the general population is not yet sufficiently developed for any definitive statements to be made. Rogelio mentioned self-management skills:

> Like learning how to control yourself when you're having a conversation, to know when you're getting heated up, and know when to stop, because if you don't, off you go again. So I learned with the handout he gave us to know when I need to turn around and leave, get away.

Ignacio also commented,

> To take a time-out before hitting someone, or basically to run away. Instead of staying and just saying, *I'm going to do it, I'm going to do it, I'm going to do it, I'm going to do it.* So you stay there and there's more violence. I never knew about that, to be able to say, "I'm going to leave now." I used to say, "Why should I leave?" Such a simple thing. And I didn't know it.

Blas found cognitive techniques helpful:

> We learned a lot of things that really work if you do them. There are other ways to communicate that we didn't know about. There are three things that Carmen taught us: what you're doing and thinking, and how you are going to react. The way you're thinking affects what you decide to do. Like if you think negative, you act negative. I found this very helpful.

Leonardo spoke of the relationship skills he had gained. Along the way, his previously rigid gender role beliefs were modified:

> The topic we spent most time on and gave most emphasis to was to know how to live with your—partner—in a much more positive way....I learned, thinking in a more positive way, that the kitchen is not just for women! Yes, I learned that there.

José agreed:

> Communicating with your wife, and your family, because violence comes from not communicating. We had a lot of classes on communication.

> When a man graduates from our 52-week program, we always invite him to share with the group what he found most helpful to him in the curriculum.

> Sometimes men will comment on a simple empathy exercise, where they take the part of their partner or their child and describe what happened from their point of view. Some men have revealed the deep shift that took place in them during the role-play when, for the first time, they put themselves in the position of the person they had hurt.

Contributing to the Group

Being in the group eventually brought out skills and values that the participants had never been conscious of before and gave them a chance to practice them in the group setting. Raúl developed the capacity for introspection:

> The whole time I've been in the program I've been doing something I had never done in my life—to reflect and take stock of my own life. Put the good and the bad in the balance.

Hilario volunteered,

> Some of the guys told me the therapy I give before group is better than the class.

> It is our belief that an important aspect of the men's therapy takes place before session in the parking lot and during the 10-minute break. Sometimes group rebellion against an unacceptable intervention will become evident after the break and must be handled. Or men will encourage a companion to bring up an issue that he was unwilling to mention earlier. Oh, to be a fly on the wall while our clients discuss their real problems and their reactions to the group! The research project that will never be...

Gregorio encouraged other men:

> I used to feel good saying to them, "Yes you will change. Get involved in the program and you will change. Because if you don't try, then no. If you hold on to not changing, you won't."

Ceferino reported that group was like training:

> If I had been with a male therapist all the time, I wouldn't have had the same opportunity to practice being respectful to a woman as I did. It was constant practice. I'm learning how to treat another person, even if I don't like it sometimes. I know it's a better way to live.

Leonardo empathized with *machista* members and tried to help them:

> We had about three men in the group who came in like that at first [*he imitates their puffed-up, hostile, in-your-face posture*]. Later I used to talk to them, "Listen man, it's one thing to recognize that you made a mistake and it's an entirely different thing to let the woman order you around. We're not here to be intimidated. No, they're teaching us how to be better, not trying to intimidate us. No one expects you to leave here and go home, and everything will be the opposite of how you were before."

Ramón encouraged other men to take responsibility for themselves:

> I say, "It's OK, let her [my partner] shout." The guys tell me I'm crazy, very Catholic.[10] And I tell them, "No, it's not that I'm very Catholic, but when someone has a problem, they need to focus on that." If not, why are they going to the group? They're just wasting their time.

GROUP BEHAVIORS

Helpful Aspects of the Group

Most of the men (10 out of 12) mentioned helpful and supportive aspects of the group. Lucio enjoyed going to group each week:

> Each experience helps you to understand what happened to someone else, and so if he was at the point of doing something, and he thought, *Oh, that happened to this other guy, it may happen to me*. Or, *I could do that*. So it got to the point where I realized the value of sharing and really listening in the group.

Gregorio mentioned group leverage and the wisdom of leaving *machista* behaviors for the group to deal with:

> If the guy believed it was just the therapist trying to dominate him, then he'd get angry. Especially if he was *machista*. But when the whole group agreed, it was a lot harder to argue with.

Blas described the repentance of other members:

> They always supported me and gave me courage to go ahead. Here, they admit it because what they did really causes them a lot of pain. I saw that in most of the guys. We realize it was our fault—that we did wrong. We don't know why. There's no reason to be violent to a woman. A woman is the most beautiful thing in the world.

Ignacio talked about group disclosure increasing over time:

> If you want to lie you can, if you want to tell the truth you do it.... But
> it does come out. You can relax once you get it out. The group gets
> closer, more united.

Negative Group Behaviors

All of the men identified group behaviors that were resistant or negative.
Rogelio described the difficulty men had accepting new concepts:

> It's hard for us to accept that the woman has to be equal to the man. To
> have the same rights. There were guys in the group who were always
> contradicting it, who just couldn't accept it. But later they did. I think
> it took a minimum of two months for guys to come around.

Gregorio, a member of AA, spoke about alcoholic group members:

> Most of the men drank, they weren't in any program, and you know,
> when someone drinks, they're very ignorant, like they see every-
> thing backwards. Everything negative, nothing positive. All negative
> stuff.... They don't know what they're doing to themselves and their
> family.

Juan commented on some members' attitudes:

> I see some guys who don't seem to learn. They don't talk, and when the
> counselor asks them what they learned, they answer things that have
> no connection to what she's saying.

Ramón complained about some of his peers:

> Some of the guys just go through the motions, just go and talk but it's
> all lies. They just pretend to be paying attention. Sometimes Carmen
> [the therapist] asks them something and they say, "Oh sorry, I didn't
> hear you." And some of them will turn their backs on you when you're
> giving them some advice. When that happens I just stop talking to
> them.

Leonardo returned to the theme of machismo connected with resistance:

> Several, really many, of the men would say, *They're* [the therapists]
> *crazy*. But María explained it in a way that made it easy to accept.
> They feel afraid that they are going to be under the woman's foot.

When the men in our groups immigrate to the United States, their attitude toward women as inferior to men, ingrained in them as normal in their subculture, is called into question by the very fact of the cultural difference, and more so by their being mandated to therapy. This is threatening to their sense of themselves and must be dealt with cautiously and patiently. Most of what we know about working with *machistas* in the group comes from the experience and comments of the men we interviewed, as well as from the hundreds of men we have worked with over the years. They are the true experts in what works and what blocks progress.

They think there's no middle ground, either machos or wimps. That's the fear they have.

Respeto in the Group

Only 1 of the men said that he did not feel respected by his (female) therapist. The other 9 men who responded to this question experienced a respectful environment most of the time, both from therapists and peers. They identified *respeto* as central to their experience in therapy. Indeed, who could benefit from a therapeutic environment where he or she did not feel respected?

Lucio described being respected by peers:

We all respected each other. We know we're all here because we had problems, so *respeto* comes from that. You did what you did, and now you're paying for it. So we have to respect each other. Like letting someone talk, and get out what he has inside. Listening to what happened.

Juan explained,

Respeto means giving the same importance to every member, not to one person that she prefers because he talks more, or the one who talks less, or the one who's like that. She's respectful whether you talk or not.

Ceferino commented,

Respeto for me means, if I'm talking, the other person listens. It means communication, listen to each other, and let the other person talk....When there's a woman there's more *respeto*. That's the first thing we learned, was how to respect a woman.

THERAPIST INTERVENTIONS

Effective Teaching Style: Clarity and Structure

Although pedagogical methods were not mentioned in the IPV literature, 11 of the participants spontaneously commented on the efficacy of their therapist's teaching method. Given the low level of education of many of the group members, their input was invaluable for future program development. Our findings support McKinley's (1987) work on Latino group members of low socioeconomic status. She found that they lack a wide vocabulary and are more comfortable with concrete as opposed to abstract thinking. They have little experience with the use of language as a vehicle for the communication of personal differences. Furthermore, many are hampered by few years of formal education.

Optimizing creative and straightforward ways to impart important information should be a goal of every therapist working with this population. Some of the teaching methods the interview participants praised were the willingness of the therapist to correct members who were interrupting or being disruptive; the ability to maintain an orderly and respectful group; the frequent use of role-plays to clarify and reinforce material and skills; the use of the board to visually explain concepts whether through written words or diagrams; the practice of hearing each man's opinion on the topic under discussion; the therapist's openness to group suggestions; the practice of repeating concepts until every member had understood; the practice of defining all difficult words (therapists may not realize how limited some of the members' vocabulary actually is); and the use of nonconfrontational technique when dealing with rigid and angry *machistas*.

Juan, who was unable to pass out of first grade until the sixth attempt due to multiple trauma, appreciated his therapist's methods:

> She uses the board for everything that we talk about. So if we're talking about something on the power and control wheel, like last week we talked about male privilege. And everyone has to participate, like by saying what being *machista* means for you in your case. But she taught us to raise our hand if we want to speak, or ask a question.

Raúl commented on his therapist's creativity:

> So when that topic [sex] and other difficult ones came up, what we tried to do were role plays, to sit in front of each other and do a drama in front of the group. That got people interested to see how we really behave and compare it to your own behavior. It's different from just telling someone how they are or what they should do; that is really a way to make people think and examine themselves.

José summarized his therapist's skills:

> She always clarifies words that you aren't sure of. Sometimes you don't really know what a word means and she tries to explain and correct all that. When I understand the word we're discussing I raise my hand to answer. I like the way the teacher explains things.

Effective Therapeutic Style: *Simpatía* and Empathy

All of the participants remarked favorably on their therapist's way of being and working with the group. Murphy and Baxter's (1997) research on effective clinical strategies with IPV offenders found that a supportive stance is most effective. Bordin (1994) emphasized the prime importance of establishing a working alliance for effective therapy. Tseng and McDermott (1981) emphasized that showing empathy, providing hope, taking a firm and positive approach, and utilizing the client's personal and cultural strengths are universal precepts that facilitate healing across the boundaries of culture. The effective group leader acts as a positive role model for all members, assisting clients to feel valued and understood, and sharing the clients' worldview without being critical or judgmental (Corey, 1990; Yalom, 1985).

The most effective therapists described by the men demonstrated an open and accepting personality. Men who had been in their groups appeared to have internalized the greatest amount of the material. These therapists were kind, friendly (*simpático*), and not afraid to exercise an appropriate level of self-disclosure (*personalismo*). They were respectful to group members and open to suggestions. They exuded an air of self-confidence and mastery of the material, and they had the patience to take clients where they were and walk with them on their path. The most effective therapists combined an appropriate teaching style with an empathic, firm, and tolerant therapeutic style. They sent a clear message that the clients were respected for who they were, and not branded as wife-beaters.

Some of the most salient personal qualities of therapists that interview participants mentioned were fairness; self-confidence; personal concern; clarity and directness; being reserved and able to keep an appropriate distance; being respectful, courteous, friendly, understanding, kind, flexible, a good communicator, peaceful, and calm.

Therapeutic skills that the participants appreciated were the use of humor; good listening skills; allowing men the freedom to take or leave the material; the ability to self-disclose, experienced as *simpatía* and *personalismo*; the ability to stay with the client until he accepted responsibility; taking the men and their concerns and ideas seriously; the ability to utilize whatever good desires the clients had; and willingness to wait until trust had developed before insisting that the men tell the story of the violent incident.

The effective therapists had the ability to offer clients a new vision of gender roles without attacking, rejecting, or putting down clients or their culture. They had an appreciation of the struggles Latino men have with acculturation. They showed respect for the rhythm of change of clients without attempting to prematurely force them into compliance. They did not neglect to positively reinforce clients' treatment gains, recognizing and verbalizing the progress they were making. In short, the "good" therapist had the ability to see the men in the treatment group as human beings—as clients, not criminals. Leonardo described his therapist's approach:

> In the case of the *machistas* in the group, María has a very good strategy. She explains to the whole group, not specifically to that person, but as she explains to the whole group, she tries to give him a little bit at a time. I remember once she gave a man an extra three or four sessions before he was able to start hearing what she was saying. She would never confront or make them feel bad. She had a very good technique.

Lucio spoke nostalgically about his first therapist:

> Martha used to tell us what her experiences were. We had more trust in her. It was easier to tell her about ourselves. Because we cared about what had happened to her too. Or at least I did. There was more companionship in the group, with Martha.

Juan commented,

> María's quiet, she's never shouted at me or corrected me like that. If a counselor did that you'd lose respect for them. If she's trying to be abusive to me, why would I put up with that? I wouldn't. But she talks clearly and tells you if there's something she doesn't like. "If I don't like the way you behave here, I'm going to let you know. If I don't like it, I'll take you out of the group."

Leonardo said more about learning new ways of thinking:

> So someone else comes along and says, "No you're wrong, it's not like that. Let's look at it another way. You could do this." It's like you just reject it at that moment, but if you look at the other side, you think, *Wow, I like what this person's saying better than the way that I am and the way I behave.* I learned this way of thinking from María. María

explained it in a way that made it easy to accept. She tried to help us understand what she was saying in every way.

> We are forever indebted to María for teaching us, among many other things, the use of the phrase "Let's look at it another way. You could do this." Just offering options and choices to the men in our groups opens up new possibilities for them, without the sense that they are being coerced or that their core values are being attacked.

Raúl had a much better experience the second time he completed the program:

> María had a very nice personality, like peaceful and calm, and I felt that I could communicate with her. I began to trust her. The simplest way to do it is how she did it. "If you want to tell us what you're feeling, and if you want to tell us what happened, go ahead. If you feel bad and want to get to know us better before you tell us what happened, that's fine. There's no pressure here. You come here to participate, go ahead and pay attention to how the group goes so that you can participate, and that's it. It's all up to you." If there hadn't been that kind of respect from the beginning, if I hadn't felt that respect—that's where the trust began, and the desire to participate.

José mused on what was helpful about his therapist:

> You go where you think you can grow and develop, with good words, where you feel accepted. But if you go to hear words that make you come away the same or even worse, no. That's not OK. Some people are very bad-tempered, but I think there, in those classes, all the teachers should have a good personality. There's no point otherwise.

Ineffective Teaching Style: Authoritarian and Unfocused

Six of the participants mentioned methods that they did not find helpful: the therapist straying from the topic and not clearly finishing one subject before going on to the next; the excess of repetition engendered by frequent therapist changes, leading to inability to grasp all the material the court requires; the use of blatant feminist views to confront machismo, which alienated the group; and insufficient explanation of new words. The men with the least education had obviously labored to absorb the material. Therapists may be unaware of the lack of experience with classroom learning of many of the men. Thus, the men's feedback is invaluable for the improvement of teaching technique.

Juan, who had difficulty learning, reported,

> I think if we're going to talk about a subject we should focus on it and
> flesh it out, and finish it. Not bounce all over the place. Because there
> we go over a bunch of topics.

Ceferino commented on his therapist's ineffective technique:

> She would criticize us a lot, we debated machismo a lot. I think she
> could have used a better strategy to make us think and debate instead
> of the way she did it. Because the way it is, the men just see her as a
> feminist. And it shouldn't be like that. It's better if we can focus on that
> we are equal.

Feminismo turns out to be a pretty bad word in this circle! If we want to be
effective as therapists, whatever our sociological and philosophical beliefs,
we will get further with the men in the group if the focus is on justice,
nondiscrimination, and equality. The men in our study reported feeling
attacked when the topic of feminism came up. Although it does not hurt
to spend some time explaining feminism to the group, the very breadth of
the term lends itself to misinterpretation. We have chosen to take their lead
and focus on the current worldwide goal of gender equality, which they
find less threatening, although by no means easy to accept. Their beliefs are
often held with deep conviction and considerable stubbornness. Lecturing
them on the evils of chauvinism or overtly displaying disgust, amazement,
or frustration is counterproductive. Our patience and perseverance in
showing the men the benefits of equality over the course of their treatment
is what will eventually gain their trust and facilitate change.

José had difficulty with basic vocabulary:

> She chooses the topic, and you have to be there trying to understand
> what she's saying until she's finished. But if you don't know a word,
> there's no way.

Our findings on pedagogical technique support Herrera and Sánchez's (1976) assertion that Latinos unaccustomed to group therapy prefer groups that are highly structured and behaviorally focused. A few of
the participants mentioned the problem of illiteracy or functional illiteracy in a large percentage of group members, and the negative effect
this had on their ability to grasp the material and discuss it in group. It
seems that creative approaches need to be taken to ensure that all men
learn the material as well as possible. One of the participants with a
sixth-grade education but poor verbal skills completed the entire year
without understanding the meaning of the word *equality*. Such important

omissions would not go unnoticed if therapists were more aware of the truly low level of education of a subgroup of their clients.

Again, the cultural script of traditional gender roles and differences created an obstacle to their ability to grasp the concept of equality. They simply had no experience of it, and the idea was foreign and suspect, not to mention threatening to their beliefs about male prerogatives. This is a good example of how a culturally competent therapist needs to be aware of clients' backgrounds and work slowly and gently, in a stepwise fashion, at the task of presenting and "selling" the idea of gender equality. It is probably worth repeating once again here that among Latino men there is a great deal of variability regarding traditional gender roles (Mirandé, 1997), and so our comments about our participants' gender role beliefs cannot in any way be generalized to all Latino men.

It is obviously not enough to ask clients if they have understood what is being taught, because they may be ashamed to admit their failure to grasp basic material. Rather, pains should be taken to specifically define even words that a therapist might assume everyone understands, and to be very aware when one is introducing a concept that may be culturally foreign to the men in our groups who have less education.

Ineffective Therapeutic Style: Confrontation and Blaming

Yalom and Lieberman (1971) found that an authoritarian and aggressive stance is highly correlated to clients' conditions worsening. Henry et al. (1990) found that clients feel unsafe and rejected in an environment where premature confrontation abounds. Some of the men reported attitudes and behaviors of their therapist that hurt, confused, or angered them. The main issue for the participants was the therapist's blaming them for all the problems in the relationship and refusing to even hear what they wanted to say about their partner's negative behavior. The adherence of the female therapist to what participants described as "feminist" principles, as a strategy to initiate change, had the opposite effect and generated anger, because they interpreted feminism as female superiority rather than gender equality—and we have already mentioned the extreme difficulty many men have accepting even the concept of gender equality. They also felt attacked when therapists criticized their traditional gender roles and inferred that they were trying to force their children to live the same way. Predictably, true to *machista* behavior, when the therapist behaved in this manner, the men in the group tended to become more domineering and confrontational themselves, or to withdraw into resentful silence.

> Therapists who have used a confrontational style in the past would do well to rethink the efficacy of their approach. Alienating clients will only block their progress and perpetuate gender struggles in the group, creating a parallel process for what is already happening in the home. This complex dance of modeling empathy requires both patience and skill. Of course, in every therapy there is a time for confrontation. However, it should not be the first line of treatment and should always be used with restraint and prudence.

Many of the men (8 out of 12) mentioned aspects of their therapists that alienated them. Some of the examples of a therapeutic stance that they and others found hurtful, distressing, confusing, and frustrating were being disrespectful and closed to their beliefs and ideas; always taking the part of the woman and being unwilling to even hear what clients had to say about their side when they had difficulties; giving the men low evaluations for the court when they spoke their mind; blaming the men for all the problems in the relationship; accusing men of lying in front of the group; neglecting to point out clients' positive qualities; female therapists working out their own anger toward men with the group; being insensitive and judgmental about traditional gender role beliefs; and refusing to answer simple personal questions without any explanation. Lucio commented on the distance his therapist created, and in the process illustrated how therapy can be a corrective emotional experience, recapitulating the family, or in his case recapitulating the loss of family and its replacement with stepfamily:

> I thought it was strange. We'd ask her a question and she wouldn't answer it directly. A couple of times, she wouldn't answer, or she'd answer something else. So I lost trust in her. Like you say, "Oh well." But at the same time, you don't feel the same trust towards that person. You still have to talk because that's why you go, but it's not the same level of trust. Maybe it was part of the change from our previous therapist, like from a sister to a half-sister. I don't know. Like from a mother to a stepmother.

Raúl, a man with a forceful personality whose first experience of IPV therapy was with a Mexican male therapist, commented,

> The part I never could understand about him was his therapy. Because instead of having some sort of structure for speaking, to help us participate, it was more like being closed up in this circle and just giving them what they wanted. Not what I felt, but what they wanted to hear. When we used to come out of the group, that was what we used to

say to each other. "Just give him what he wants." So I think that the rest also felt that it wasn't about getting out what you had inside, or even to learn new things, but just to tell him what he wanted to hear, like, "Everything is good in my family, we're getting along, we have no problems now. Everything's perfect." You couldn't talk about your problems and if you did, it became a two-edged sword, because he would use it against you and terminate you, which is what happened to me. Sincerely, he didn't help me at all.

Fortunately, Raúl's second experience of therapy was with María, who was much more successful in treating him. This is an example of how it *does* matter what program is used, and the way in which a therapist approaches the clients and the material.

Blas, who demonstrated borderline features in his interview and was hypersensitive to criticism, had strong feelings about his therapist's style, especially as it reinforced his potent feelings of shame and self-recrimination:

The therapist always took my wife's part. She would say, "I came here to help you, not her." She always says it's the man's fault—she used to say that a lot. I felt, not so much upset, as uncomfortable, like things are upside down and I can't understand it. I was confused. Like I used to say, "The things I'm saying in here are happening to me, and what you're saying doesn't fit my situation, my experience." She used to always attack me about the past. Sometimes I felt that she was blaming me and I knew that it was true, and I myself was blaming myself, and I continue to.

Ceferino, another victim of abuse from both parents, and thus sensitive to criticism, withdrew when feeling attacked:

There's times when she's talking, and someone says something against it, and if it's against what she says, she attacks us. I don't disagree, I just keep quiet. She doesn't let us express ourselves. I don't want to argue, I don't want to disagree, I prefer to listen. One time I was trying to say something about my partner and she cut me off. I don't know why. After that I didn't want to talk, I said *No, no.*

José was offended by his Mexican male therapist's comments, which he perceived as intolerant and thoughtless:

Once he scolded me because I let my daughter help in the kitchen when she was seventeen or so. So he [male therapist] says, "You're sending her straight into the kitchen so she'll never have a profession, so she'll just spend her life in the kitchen." I said, "That's her thing if she likes the kitchen; she's still going to school. What's wrong with the kitchen? We all eat."

Ramón's resentment was evident when he said,

Carmen [the therapist] has two sons, her husband left her. So I think she says, "Oh this is the way it is, this is what men are like." I think she's angry with men. Like I said, she doesn't want to hear my side, always my partner's, so I just don't talk to her. I tell her everything's great, because if I told her we argue....Sometimes I tell her I took a time-out, and she asks why, and I say, "Because I don't want any more problems, and I can't talk to my partner, she likes to shout a lot." Then she tells me I'm afraid of my wife. But I'm not afraid of her! When we leave the group we're all talking about how she doesn't understand Mexican men, we can't talk to her. I think she's like that because she's a woman, that a man would be able to see both sides.

Although Ramón's opinion that a man would be a more effective group facilitator was not shared by any other participant, his comments poignantly illustrate just how distressing it is for a partner abusive man to be in an IPV therapy group with a female facilitator who lacks the therapeutic skills we have been discussing.

ORGANIZATIONAL FACTORS

The Setting

All of the participants mentioned qualities of the agency where they had attended treatment that they liked and appreciated, such as continuity of therapists, or if there had to be a change, a gradual transition rather than a sudden shift. They were grateful where free female victims' groups were offered, and they reported that these groups had helped their relationship to heal. The one agency that offered information about financial resources in the community also received praise. Leong and his associates (1995) found that low-income Latinos and other ethnic groups greatly benefit from referral to such services, and that the referral itself increases trust in the agency, which is then perceived as an ally in a foreign culture.

However, half of the agencies did not offer women's groups free of charge, and three out of four did not provide a resource list. Agencies could be more helpful to Latino clients and their families if they were able to secure funding for women's groups[11] and if a current resource list were routinely made available. In this way, the agency may contribute to stress reduction in these families. One man reported that he had seven different therapists in his first year in the program, clearly a serious problem if therapeutic progress is expected. Several men complained of being treated like criminals by agency staff. A few men mentioned the problem of illiteracy or functional illiteracy, and the failure of the program material or approach to accommodate their level of education. Raúl's commentary on the staff's attitude captures his experience well:

> At first you see the secretary, like the assistant of the person in charge. From the minute you arrive, she makes you feel like a criminal, like dirt, like a wife-beater, she sees you as the worst. I don't know what her experience has been, but I found out later that many of the men had the same kind of treatment from her.

The interview participants were very enthusiastic about what they had learned and how it had changed their lives. They wished they had known before so they could have spared their partners, their families, and of course themselves the pain they have been through. In the next chapter we will detail the outcomes they described.

NOTES

1. We are very cognizant of the potential for violence that springs from the belief that "family honor" is to be preserved at all costs (Vandello & Cohen, 2003). In this present context, we are focusing on its potential for good and for respecting the woman as the heart of the family. All too often, however, "honor" is used as a reason to rape, injure, and murder women, as well as men, in many cultures.
2. Like every characteristic, loyalty has its shadow side. This is evident when men share their bitterness over their wives' "betrayal" of family loyalty by calling the police on them, thus breaking the family secret and exposing them to shame and to legal consequences.
3. One of the outcomes of this research has been the education of churches about what their members want and need to hear about IPV.
4. A list of resources regarding Latino spirituality is included in appendix A for therapists who work with Latino men.
5. At the time of the interviews, the only treatment program approved for use in San Diego County, in any language, was the Duluth model "Education Groups for Men who Batter." Since then, several different treatment programs have been approved for use by therapists in the region, including the Welland/Wexler program, *Sin Golpes,* in use since 2001 under the title *Violencia Doméstica 2000.*
6. *Gordo* means fat in Spanish, and is often used as a term of affection in Mexico.
7. Two out of 12 with a positive attitude from the outset is unusually high, given our clinical experience. Our interview participants were volunteers who wanted to talk about their experience.

8. This finding applies to the men who did not suffer significant trauma in childhood. For the victims of severe abuse, the journey was evidently far from over, and remained fraught with pain.
9. Most IPV facilitators would leave decisions regarding money management to the couple, after discussing economic abuse with the client and teaching negotiation skills.
10. The connotation of "very Catholic" is "goody-goody."
11. In the state of California, Victim Witness funds are available to pay for therapy for victims of IPV and their children, as long as there is a case number, which is always true when a perpetrator has been mandated to therapy. Often therapists are not aware of this and do not facilitate these referrals.

CHAPTER 7

Making Decisions About Personal Change and Healing: Outcomes of Treatment

The whole time I've been in the program I've been doing something I had never done in my life—reflecting and taking stock of my own life. Putting the good and the bad in the balance.

—Raúl

In chapter 6, we quoted some of the participants' comments on deciding to change. In this chapter, we explore the actual changes that they reported, in attitudes and behavior, as a result of that decision. Again, the importance of making their own personal decision cannot be overstated. Addressing the clinical implications of working with Latino men who have a strong male gender identity, Casas et al. (1994) pointed out that these men avoid all situations in which they perceive themselves as helpless or weak. Masculine self-esteem in the case of these men is tied to the ability to cope and problem solve independently. Such clients are likely to view therapy as a humiliating admission or accusation of weakness and dependence, which is only compounded by the therapeutic focus on expression of feelings. Casas and his associates suggested that the therapist be aware of the wounded self-esteem of such clients, their lack of motivation, and their mistrust of therapy. They recommended redefining a truly strong person as one who admits to difficulties and obtains temporary assistance for his own and his family's best interests.

Incorporating the client's need to take responsibility for himself as a man of strength, and taking our cue from the participants' decision to change, we were inspired to make the initial session in our treatment program an exploration into personal transformation. We called it *Seeking a Different Path: Quetzalcóatl,*[1] *the Hero's Journey* (Leeming, 1990; León-Portilla, 1963; Townsend, 1992).

For the Mesoamericans, Quetzalcóatl was the god of the wind, venerated long before the Aztecs, by the ancients of Teotihuacan. He was renowned as the priest-king of legends, as the plumed serpent, an image of the wind that raised a huge cloud of dust from the earth. Quetzalcóatl was the god who offered to descend into the underworld to bring back precious bones, so that men and women could be created. Along with the other gods, he sacrificed his own blood and sprinkled it on the bones so they would have life. Because of this, the Aztecs believed that the sun required blood sacrifice to continue in existence and give life to humanity. As priest-king of the great city of Tula, Quetzalcóatl fell into temptation and became drunk, along with his courtiers, thus neglecting his duty to offer sacrifice to the sun at dawn. Realizing his failure to fulfill his responsibility and filled with shame, he lay down in a coffin for 4 days, lamenting to the elders, "It is enough! Let everything cease! Bury all the wisdom we have discovered, the joy, the riches, all that we have accomplished and made." He left the city and, sobbing, arrived at the edge of the divine sea. There, after adorning himself with glorious quetzal feathers, he set fire to himself. All the birds of heaven flocked to the place where Quetzalcóatl sacrificed his life. When his ashes ceased to glow, he was taken up to heaven and was transformed into the Morning Star.

In this session we explore pilgrimage and migration as sacrificial journeys and connect them to the men's own process of migration and personal maturation as individuals and in relationship, utilizing the theme of Quetzalcóatl's fall from grace, his repentance, and the subsequent redemption of his tribe. His story becomes a powerful metaphor for their yearlong journey to transform themselves from the men, husbands, and fathers they have been in the past to "a different way of being a man."[2] It directs them to the goals they must set for themselves during their treatment. The fact that members in the pilot group have asked us many times over the years to repeat this session when several new members have joined the group is a testimony to the effectiveness of this approach. Our goal was to shorten the time and ease the difficulty that several of our participants described in making the decision to change, by touching on it explicitly, yet obliquely, through storytelling. The discussion about the sacrificial journey that most of our clients have endured to come to the United States is also deeply affirming to them, because right from the start their positive masculine qualities of strength, courage, decisiveness, creativity in problem solving, perseverance, and ingenuity are disclosed, amplified, and shared with others who fully understand and appreciate the challenges they have faced. Instead of feeling stigmatized and stereotyped, the men feel valued and respected, which is a good place to begin their therapeutic journey.

TREATMENT OUTCOMES

The participants were proud of the changes in their attitudes and behavior that had resulted from the program, such as better communication skills and the ability to manage their anger. They also identified becoming more flexible in their gender roles as a vital element of their new approach to their family. Gender equality was a new idea for them, but they reported that they had eventually accepted it and were integrating it into their current relationship. Overcoming addiction to alcohol, and its attendant personal and relationship problems, was another major accomplishment, and one that cannot be overemphasized.

They spoke gratefully of the new parenting skills that they had acquired as part of their treatment. Learning to be nurturing fathers was one of the most valuable gains they received from their programs, although therapists placed varying emphasis on the topic. The idea that they could be the ones to break the cycle of violence for their children and grandchildren was intensely motivating. The men also commented on what they believe needs to be done in the arena of public education for Latinos in the United States.

One of the drawbacks of this research is that we have no corroborating evidence to verify whether the participants' progress was as stellar as it appeared. Nevertheless, by the time 2 hours of one-on-one time had passed with each of the 12 participants, our clinical sense was that they had indeed made remarkable progress. Insight is difficult to fake, and they had nothing to gain but $25 and our gratitude from sharing their stories. Future research will corroborate or nullify our results. However, our hunch is that clinicians who work with such men will probably recognize their best clients in the voices of our participants.

In support of much research that points to the relationship with the therapist as the greatest factor in therapeutic change, the men who reported the strongest therapeutic alliance, with the therapist as well as with the group, appeared to have internalized the material at a deeper level and to have experienced genuine changes in their attitudes. However, even the men who reported a less than satisfying relationship with their therapist demonstrated significant change, which their partners had noticed and commented on. There seems to be little question that the participants gained a great deal of support, many skills, and much hope from the group process. These changes are typical of what we have observed in our groups for Latino IPV offenders, changes that we *have* been able to verify by confidentially interviewing their partners over the telephone during and after treatment.[3]

Changes in Attitude and Behavior

All the participants took responsibility for their violence and for the hardship they had caused their families, especially the men who were alcoholics. They changed for themselves and for their families, wanting to be better people. Several of the men stated that they wanted to be perfect, or if not that, the very best they could be. Another refrain was "putting into practice" what they had learned. They mentioned the newfound self-control they now enjoyed, and the sense of mastery it gave them. Participants were grateful that they had learned how to walk away from a fight and no longer felt obligated to prove anything to anyone.

> It is encouraging to work with a group of Latino men in IPV treatment. We have had much success with our program, finding that men respond to the interventions we use, based on what we learned had been effective with our research participants. We have also been able to catch ourselves when we were about to make the same mistakes some of their therapists made, or to recognize our errors after the fact and correct them.

Men reported giving up vengefulness and vindictiveness with their partners, and trying to create a new relationship with them. They were communicating better and experiencing a whole new intimacy and fulfillment in their relationships. Or, if that were no longer possible, they now felt hopeful that they had better relationship skills and would be able to live a very different kind of life with someone else in the future.

> One of the goals of group therapy, of any therapy, is to give hope. Even the man with the worst possible case, where he has lost his marriage and custody of his children, can learn to use respectful relationship skills at work and in a potential new relationship. He may have brought great losses upon himself, but his future is not necessarily bleak.

Although some of the men were fearful that they might slip, they were determined never to live with violence again. Lucio described his experience in the group and the strides he had made. He also pointed out that not all the men had reached the point of deciding to change:

> Some of the guys don't take it seriously. Many of us don't want to admit what we did. Personally, I admit what I did, and I'm not proud of it. I know I did wrong. I asked her forgiveness, I asked God to forgive me, and I asked my son to forgive me. And she has forgiven me. But I have heard a lot of the guys who don't tell the truth; they just go because they have to. When we come outside [during the break] we talk, and I say, "You know, in this group you need to talk, because if you don't no one can help you." I think they're ashamed, afraid, they feel embarrassed. Shame because Mexican men are famous for thinking that we're real men, real machos, that nothing touches us, that we should never cry. But those are just words. Even so, those words take root in people, so they think things like, *OK, well I don't need to tell my problems to anyone. I can solve my own problems.* But really ninety-five percent of us, ninety-nine percent of us, can't solve our problems by ourselves. We need help. And so that we can get that help, to really understand, we need to open up our hearts. But many people don't do it. Many guys don't take it seriously. Especially the younger guys. There were one or two guys who had finished about forty weeks and it seemed like they hadn't got anything out of the class.

Part of this quotation is included in the first session of our program, about Latino men not needing help outside themselves. Lucio says it so clearly and succinctly, nothing further needs to be added. We placed it there, at the beginning, so men might allow the idea of participation in the group to penetrate some of their armor.

Half of the participants described some of their own negative behaviors in the group prior to their decision to change. These included lying about the details of the IPV incident in the beginning, usually out of shame; acting in an angry and negative manner toward the therapist; denying that they needed to be in the group; demonstrating resistance to the therapist, especially if she was female; and clamming up for long periods after a perceived or real attack by the therapist.

The 2 men who took the longest to reach the decision to change (almost 5 months) were the men who had suffered the greatest trauma and abuse from both of their parents, and who had difficulty with the criticism of their therapist, the same woman for both of them. There is an interesting parallel here to the abusive personality, the man who is painfully sensitive to any hint of criticism or rejection, as described by Dutton (2006a). These men interpret criticism as a global attack on their sense of self, and would frequently become violent under such circumstances, if the "attacker" were their partner. However, because violence to one's therapist is not an option for the great majority of IPV clients, they may instead withdraw and nurse their wounds.

> We have already commented on the importance of screening for trauma. Beyond that, therapists will benefit from paying close attention to the reactions of men in the group when they perceive an attack. We have found that approaching the hypersensitive client briefly with an attitude of listening and openness, after group when possible, is an effective strategy for breaking down resistance. Simultaneously, the clients will know from our entire demeanor that the therapist is "in charge." This can be established without the need to engage in power struggles. The therapist's "power" can never be in question. If it is, the antisocial element in the group will exploit it as weakness and use the group as a place to "torture" the facilitator. Although in our clinical experience this is more likely to happen in an English-language group of mixed ethnicity, that does not rule out the possibility that it could happen in a group of Latino men.

In their clinical research, Murphy and Baxter (1997) have also found that direct confrontation of machismo, or controlling and hostile behavior on the part of the therapist, is an obstacle to treatment. These observations may appear self-evident to the reader, especially after listening to the voices of our participants. However, some IPV programs have advocated such a stance, or perhaps more accurately, what appears to be such a stance to the client, in their treatment programs. Henry and his associates (1990) have found that clients make progress when therapists disconfirm the clients' expectation of rejection by the therapist. In the experience of the men mentioned above, their expectation of rejection was confirmed, and they shut down.

Change of Attitudes and Behaviors Toward Others

All of the participants identified many ways in which they had changed internally and behaviorally. They reported feeling more confident, more able to form effective relationships and get along with others. They were empowered by the skills they had learned and the new way that they viewed themselves. Rogelio radiated genuine joy as he related the change he had experienced:

> The most useful thing I learned was how to love myself. Sometimes there are no words to explain something, you know? It's like time

passes, and the computer [*points to head*] just changes by itself. It's not like we talked about it, it's something that just happens. It's like you put one thing in place firmly and the next thing just happens naturally. It's like when you learn to control yourself and then you begin to think positively. To set goals for yourself, all that. And it feels great to reach that goal. It's like, I feel really proud of myself, because I've gone this long without drinking, not because I want them to think I'm so great, but because it feels so good to be able to conquer myself.

The increase in self-esteem that comes with mastery is a wonderful experience for clients and a powerful antidote to the shame that has paralyzed them in the past and that leads to violent behaviors. Therapists who take note of and comment publicly on clients' progress can play an important role in helping these men to value themselves. This also creates a culture of affirmation in the group, a place where safety and positive interactions among clients can thrive.

Raúl described the gains he has made:

More than anything I'm grateful for what I learned. If what happened had not happened, being in the group, maybe I would still have the same mentality, violent and negative, maybe creating even more hatred in myself than what I already had and felt. It has been something very positive for me. It's never too late. I'm taking the time to examine what I expect from life, what I want. And to try to find what I'm looking for, or at least to start. I know I can't just say I want a woman like this or that, and I get her, or create her, and let's go. No, it's hard. You have to work at it.

Ceferino considers himself a new man:

I'm not an aggressive person anymore. I know how to stay calm, how to take a time-out so I don't offend other people. So now, when someone begins to insult me, I know how to leave, without saying anything. I don't have to argue. Some people want to get to hitting each other, but I'm not into fighting and arguing like that anymore. I have this program and it's helped me, and thank God I have my social worker who sent me there, and it's very good. I began to see that you can't live with violence. That it's not OK.

Ramón too is different:

Before, I didn't care about controlling myself. I don't know if it's because if I get in a fight she'll call the police and I'll go to jail, or because of the class. I don't know, but I'm not like that anymore.

Healing From Past Trauma

Because the abuse that men perpetrate is often patterned on the abuse they suffered as children (Dutton, 2003, 2006a; Straus et al., 1980), Harway and Evans (1996) and many others have suggested that retraining is inadequate as a means to change batterers. Batterers need healing and recovery, like any other victim, before they can stop using the coping patterns affected by their own victimization. The compassionate and effective therapist understands that perpetration of partner abuse is a symptom of a human being living a maladaptive pattern of behavior, as a result of negative life experiences within a violent society.

It was evident from our extended interviews that several of the men had unresolved symptoms of trauma that had not been dealt with in the group. Although they had learned how to cope with hyperarousal in more adaptive ways due to anger management training, such as relaxation training and cognitive-behavioral self-talk strategies, they still had vestiges of trauma-based responses that group therapy had not healed. Referrals to mental health clinics were offered to the men who broke down during the interviews, usually over severe childhood physical and/ or sexual abuse.

In the United States, non-Hispanic Black, American Indian or Alaskan Native, and Pacific Islander children have higher rates of child maltreatment than do non-Hispanic White and Hispanic children, whose rates of child abuse are almost identical (Child Trends Data Bank, 2007). However, child abuse is a serious problem in all ethnic groups, in spite of the statistical differences. Furthermore, Romero, Wyatt, Loeb, Carmona, and Solis (1999) found that 33% of a community sample of Latina women had been sexually abused in some way as children, mostly by a young male whom they knew. In Mexico, although the statistics are not methodologically comparable, rates of child physical and sexual abuse are also troublingly high (Inmujer, 2007). In 90% of cases, the parent who abused them was a victim of child abuse himself or herself.

As we have noted elsewhere, it is important for the overall effectiveness of IPV treatment and to prevent future relapse that victims of

When working with this difficult population, it is important to balance the recognition of many of our clients' status as past victims with their current status as perpetrators. This can be done without ever insinuating that their past experience excuses their present behavior. Nevertheless, not to recognize it and empathize with it is to risk never building rapport with these men, and losing the opportunity to make a profound difference in their lives and in the lives of their families.

trauma be identified and referred to individual therapy. The best-case scenario is when clients have been referred by social services and their individual therapy is part of the court-ordered treatment plan. In these cases, it is a covered service and is not a financial hardship to the family. Otherwise, for reasons both financial and of limited time, many men do not receive the trauma treatment that they really need.

CONTRIBUTIONS TO THE GROUP EXPERIENCE

The participants reported personal and group progress after reaching the decision watershed. They learned to be honest with themselves and others; they learned to communicate with other men; they took responsibility for their behavior and were relieved from anxiety; they felt and expressed compassion for other men in the group; they encouraged new members who were as negative as they had been at the outset; they learned to speak to others respectfully, especially their female therapist; and they guided resistant *machista* men toward change. In summary, not only did they learn how to relate to and treat women; they also learned to relate to men in a more honest and open manner. Being in treatment and reaching the goals they set enhanced their self-esteem. Gregorio noticed that his contribution to the group was valued:

> That was something that made me really feel good in the group. I even want to continue to go, because when I spoke—sometimes someone else would speak and no one would listen to him, they'd keep on talking in the corners—but when it was my turn to speak, they listened. I liked that. I think because when I spoke I said positive things.

> If you are the therapist and men are "talking in corners" when someone else has the floor, you are not doing your job! The clients expect their therapist to take charge and to enforce a respectful atmosphere at all times. Disrespectful behavior can be averted once the group consistently realizes that such socially unacceptable behavior will never be tolerated. Of course, this rule must be respectfully enforced or it loses its power.

Ceferino wanted to extend the reach of what he had learned to other members of his family plagued with uncaring and violence:

> Yes, I want to take this program to my family, to teach them that you can't live with violence. Most of the time I feel really good when I come out, because I feel like I learned one more thing about how to make the next relationship better.

Leonardo felt heard by his peers and made an effort to do the same for them:

> My companions gave me some good advice about how to handle it, even though it was a small thing, because everything starts small. I liked it that they paid attention to me. They took the trouble to give me advice. Once you see the positive side of being in a group and having to get your problems out in the open, to get an opinion from someone else, it seems very appropriate to me. You feel good doing it.

Ramón was aware of the difference in his feelings depending on his participation in the group:

> The most interesting thing is when I speak up, then I come home happy. When I don't say anything, I come home just the same. When I've discussed something that's on my mind, my companions help me. Sometimes my partner notices how happy I am when I come in.

> An effective intervention is to comment on and make conscious the positive feelings in the group when such sharing takes place. This amplifies the permission that men feel to talk and to collaborate with one another.

They understood that an important part of their personal change came in making a contribution to other men. Leonardo took the lead:

> So I said to him, "If you don't talk we can't help you. That's what we're here for; we're members of the same group." First he said one word, then he began to tell all his problems, and he began to cry. Everyone was listening and people got really surprised and quiet. The other guys helped him to figure out how to solve his problem. And after a while you could see he was really relieved and he started to laugh with the others.

Juan was finally able to talk about the childhood sexual abuse that he had concealed for a lifetime, suggesting a high level of trust in the group:

> It's a very difficult problem, we're talking about a rape. Things that happened in my life. I have talked about it this year. It's helped me to get it out. One other person in the group said he had an experience like that too. Most of the men were just beaten. Beaten a lot by their father, and their mother. I feel that all of us have value there. Yes, I see that there. Most of the guys say, "This is really helping me." Many of the men do change.

Juan was fortunate to have an empathic and talented therapist; that was evident from the level of discourse and disclosure in this group. Not all groups enjoy such a level of trust. It is the role of the therapist to create a safe place where men can be honest with each other, even if they reserve the telling of sexual abuse for their individual therapist, as most clients do.

Leonardo described the how the veterans in the group assisted new members:

I learned from both the group and the counselor. I learned a lot from both of them. There was a lot of communication. A lot of understanding. There are other men who are more advanced, but they still had that same upbringing. Men who were further along in the group helped the newer members.

Ramón made friends with men in his group:

Some guys were understanding, some weren't. There are about four of us there that support each other. We help each other in the group. Outside the group, we talk on the phone, we stay in touch.

Gregorio was invested in the process of change for others and took pleasure in seeing it happen over time:

For me it was interesting because the more new people came in, and told their experiences…it was more important to me to hear their experiences, and to hear them believe that they aren't going to change. And then they change and it feels good. I used to feel good saying to them, "Yes you will change. Get involved in the program and you will change. Because if you don't try, then no; if you hold on to not changing, you won't."

Juan understood that he could learn for a different relationship and began to experience hope for the future:

At first I didn't want to go, but later when I began to hear what was being said, then I thought, *This is something useful for the future. Even if the relationship is over, now I'm better prepared for another relationship.*

Rogelio, whose extended family lives in the same area, has taken it upon himself to educate them in respect and nonviolence:

I talk a lot with my brothers and sisters, I'm teaching them, like how to talk and how to listen to someone. I would encourage them to talk

about their problems and then find a way to help them. I really feel like
I have a lot of valuable information to share. Absolutely...I am proud
of myself, of what I am doing. I'm keeping my resolutions and changing my life. So I feel proud of myself as a person.

Rogelio is a powerful example of the man who has experienced change and
feels the need to share it. To our knowledge, the IPV field does not do enough
to extend our therapeutic work to include the positive influence these men
could have on the community if they were given the forum to do so.

Raúl also described his hope for the future and his pride in his
efforts:

I've learned a lot. I hope I didn't give up everything for nothing. In the
beginning I had no idea what to do. Now what I'm trying to do is to
set a goal for myself and establish a foundation.

OVERCOMING SUBSTANCE ABUSE
AND DEPENDENCE

*Most of the men (10 out of 12) had overcome addictions due to man-
dated substance abuse treatment.* They had been mandated to Alcoholics Anonymous (AA) treatment by the court, and in most cases, to
DUI classes as well. Five were sent at the same time as the IPV incident,
because they were under the influence at the time of the arrest, or known
to be using drugs during that period. The men who had already overcome
alcoholism and the men who were more recently in recovery were very
grateful to AA and to the United States for enforcing the law and making
them obtain treatment.

Some of the men who were still in the IPV program at the time of
the interview had not become fully abstinent. Even so, they were satisfied

AA has its detractors, as well as those who are firm believers. Although it
is not our intention to enthusiastically endorse or disapprove of the 12-
step program, it was evident that for many of the men it had saved them
from a lifetime of alcoholism and imminent self-destruction. The group
format, the structured belief system, the spiritual orientation, and the support offered seemed to be a good fit for many of them. Some had been
to other mandated programs, when AA had failed to produce results on
previous occasions.

that they had learned enough in AA not to abuse alcohol or to use it as an escape. The participants were able to articulate quite clearly what they had learned at AA, even those who were not verbally adept. The men who were most involved in AA reported great gains from their treatment and from the experience of sharing their difficulty with others. They never want to go back to alcoholism as a way of life.

The importance of assessing Latino men mandated to IPV groups for alcoholism cannot be overstated, because most recidivism takes place when alcohol intake is not controlled. Alcohol addiction specialists and IPV therapists are becoming more aware of the need to evaluate their clients for both behaviors and to make appropriate referrals. In previous chapters, we have clarified the severity of the alcohol problems that characterize many partner abusive men in the Latino population. Some IPV courts are very cooperative in mandating substance abuse treatment if the therapist recommends it, and the benefits to the family are incalculable. Latino men need help in overcoming their addictions, and IPV treatment is often the avenue that leads to this goal, as well as the goal of ending the violence in the family. Rogelio was grateful that he was sent to AA:

> The court sent me to AA as well. And I went, three times a week for twelve months. I had to go. But it was really helpful. After a while you start thinking positively. Like we say in the program, "If you do good things, the consequences will be good. And if you do bad things, the consequences will be bad." There was a time when I felt like I had a lot of energy; I'd come back from AA after hearing all the good things people there said.

Although Lucio was not under the influence of alcohol at the time of the violent incident, he had a substantial history of alcohol and drug abuse:

> What they want in the DUI class is to make sure that we realize that if we keep drinking and have an accident, who's going to suffer? The consequences of the stupid things we do. The consequences of what alcohol, what drugs do to you. It helped me, because after that, I haven't driven drunk for eight or nine years. I don't drink anymore. If you don't want to drink anymore, you can do it. Like they say in AA, "One day at a time."

Gregorio finally looked within and became a fervent advocate of sobriety:

> I've had two DUI arrests here. That's how I got into AA and quit drinking. The first time I was in a program for three months. The second time the program was for eighteen months, including AA. But I didn't go back to drinking because I really took in the program.

I understood what it was, and I taught myself to love myself. Because
before, I didn't love myself. Before, when I used to drink and all that,
I never blamed myself. It was always someone else. Always. I would
never say I was wrong. That was one of my defects. It was AA that
helped me to change that. That program helped me to know myself.

Leonardo did not consider himself an alcoholic, but he obeyed the court
order and received a great deal from the program:

The court ordered me to attend AA also, for thirty days. I completed
it in one month. I went every single day and I took it to the judge. He
said, "This is really good." But when I went to therapy with María,
she said, "You know, Leonardo, since your case included alcohol,
I want you to continue going to AA." I said, "OK." She told me to
go once a week. So I continued there for the whole year.... When you
come into the AA group, for me personally, it's really like therapy.
Like an intense therapy, like what we receive for domestic violence.
But it's a therapy that many of us follow. There are the steps that you
need to follow. It was a one hundred percent positive experience for
me. I would recommend it to people and I have taken people there,
when I see that they're on their way down.

Hilario, who had one of the most conflicted relationships reported by the
participants, used his wife's insults as leverage to quit drinking:

My ex-wife gave me the key to quitting. She said some really bad words
to me. She called me a fucking son of a bitch, with a rotten soul, a piece
of shit—really bad words, that really hurt me. When she said all that
to me, I said to myself, *No, how can I let her have this kind of power
over me?* And that was when I said, *OK, no more drinking. If I keep
drinking, I will become like what she called me.* That's why I said she
gave me the key. I said, "No I'm not going to give you the pleasure, and
you're never going to see that." And I said, *That's it. I will not drink
anymore. I'm going to show her that I'm not what she says I am.* So
I said, *No more liquor, no more beer, nothing.*

THE NEED FOR PUBLIC EDUCATION

Knowing the Legal Consequences of IPV

*The participants identified an enormous need for more public education
of Latino men and families. Eight of the 12 participants said they were
unaware of the full legal consequences of IPV in California prior to the
incident.* Many of the men knew they could be arrested but envisioned a
small fine and a few days in jail, not a full year of treatment that could

impinge on their ability to get or keep an evening job, with monthly or bimonthly daytime court dates, court fines, community service hours, and therapy that would cost them a minimum of $1,000.

They felt that educating Latino men about the legal consequences of IPV on themselves and their families could have an important impact. Rogelio commented,

> How much did I know? I'd say nothing. I knew it wasn't OK to be violent, but I didn't know the consequences. I thought you went to jail and that was it. But I didn't know I'd be paying and that I'd have to attend all those groups.

Ceferino wanted more public education:

> I found out when I went to group. I used to see something on television, that the man is stronger than the woman—don't hit her. They talk about consequences for child abuse, but not for domestic violence. I think it would be good for people to know. They might think before they hit her. But it would be better on the radio, because many people don't watch television. Or both.

José responded,

> I didn't know anything. I knew I could be arrested but I didn't know I'd have to go through all that embarrassment, because everything you have to do is shameful. Well, as a Mexican you think that it's shameful, but really it's for your benefit.

Knowing About IPV Prevention and Treatment

Although the participants were grateful in retrospect that they had been sent to treatment, they spoke of the importance of educating the Latino public about the evils of IPV before the fact, and about the physical and psychological damage it can inflict on individual women and whole families. They believed the public should also be informed of the detrimental effects on children of witnessing domestic violence, and that such information should be widely disseminated.

Eight of the 12 men felt that the Latino public needs more education about domestic violence. Ignacio, true to his personality style, was somewhat pessimistic as to the value of public announcements:

> It would be good to announce that on the radio and the television. Many people would pay attention, many people wouldn't. Many people would just continue what they do.

Lucio was very insistent that children should be taught domestic violence prevention in the schools:

> I think if the son learns that domestic violence is wrong at school and then he sees his father doing it, he'll tell his father, "Look, Dad, what you're doing is wrong." And many times a father will listen to his son more than to other people who are adults. Because to the adults he just says, "This is my business. Don't pry into my life and my family affairs." So the child would learn that domestic violence is wrong, and at the same time he learns that you should respect women.

Here Lucio gives some violent fathers more credit than they deserve. Most therapists have heard countless stories of children and adolescents who have intervened with their violent fathers and have been beaten or otherwise abused because of it. Nevertheless, there may be cases where a son talking to his father later, when he is calm and/or sober, might have some effect.

José is the announcer himself:

> Now, if I see some friends who have a problem with domestic violence, I tell them, I tell them to go outside, or if they're drinking, a bit of everything. I've talked to many, many people like that. I'm good at giving advice. Of course it's up to them to take it or not! It's good to share.

Dissemination of Knowledge About IPV in Mexico and Latin America

The participants expressed disillusionment in the ability of the Mexican government to make laws against IPV that would be similar to American legislation. Even more so, they were cynical about the Mexican government's ability to enforce such laws, especially regarding treatment. They cited their beliefs about the corruption on every level of the Mexican police and judiciary. In spite of the daunting obstacle that this presents, the participants believed that such laws and treatment programs are long overdue in their homeland, and that something must be done.[4]

In February of 2007, the Mexican National Congress passed a comprehensive federal law, Ley para una Vida Libre de Violencia para las Mujeres (2007) [Law in favor of a Life Free of Violence for Women], which is to be implemented by each state. Included in this law is psychological treatment for both violent men and female victims of IPV. It will take time for the states to establish firm procedures for enforcing this much-awaited new law, but prospects for change in IPV in Mexico have improved dramatically with its approval.

Although all of the men felt that education about IPV and treatment for it are urgently needed in Mexico, only 5 were optimistic that such an undertaking would be effective. Seven of the men voiced pessimism, due to the tenacity of machismo, the lack of legal support, and the corruption of the police and judiciary. Rogelio observed,

> In Mexico, how shall I say this, you don't feel so responsible. For example, if it's the government, if they said they were going to do the program by court order, I'd just pay some money and then I wouldn't have to go. It's very different. You'd absolutely have the chance, the way everything works from the bottom up, to be able to get out of it.

Hilario recognized the need and also predicted the difficulty of enforcement:

> That's what they need in Mexico, these classes to educate people. Therapy for batterers. But look, Mexican people are very narrow-minded, very closed to anything new. For the same reason, the lack of education. But I think it would help. But they would have to make them go like they do here.

Lucio was cynical about any such program's success in his native land:

> In Mexico there are no laws; the law doesn't help. People wouldn't go. And because there's no law, it would just lead to more corruption of others. Like, "You know, just put down that I came to group, here's the money, and that's it." That's what's bad about corruption. In Mexico at least, you can fix everything that way.

Ceferino commented,

> It wouldn't work. Machismo is too deeply rooted. Here people are ordered to the group. And if you don't go, you go to jail. Who would leave machismo voluntarily?

Indeed, who would leave machismo voluntarily? The need for IPV treatment to be court-mandated is plainly obvious for partner abusive men of any ethnicity, because the most common characteristic of the violent man is that he believes he is not responsible for his behavior. Regardless of the level of machismo endorsed by the client or of his ethnicity, he is unlikely to be in the group unless he has been ordered to be there. In more than 10 years of group therapy with hundreds of men of every ethnicity, we have had only one who voluntarily completed the year of treatment, and that was so that his wife would consider staying with him. Nations and states must find a way to enforce such regulations, creatively if need be, so that men will obtain the treatment they need. It is not enough to encourage women to leave violent situations, because the statistics show that they frequently stay. A therapeutic response to violent men *must* be accompanied by a strong and effective legal response. We can only hope that over time the new law in Mexico and other similar laws in Latin America will change the status quo as regards enforcement of treatment for partner abusive men.

On the other hand, Juan was optimistic:

> I think Mexicans are more open. If there were people who could go to groups in Mexico, it would help a lot. Because there is a lot of violence in Mexico. Some people would even go voluntarily, to make their marriages better. The counselors could put up flyers in businesses and announce it in churches that there are free classes, well, not free, but if they were free people might go. I think if maybe the classes weren't free but if they just charged a little, like for the price of printing the material, the program would have good results in Mexico. Especially in Tijuana. In Tijuana there is a huge amount of violence. A lot of abused women. I think only the men who are really *machistas* would be the ones who wouldn't want to go to classes like that. They'd say, "I don't need that."

The irony of Juan's comments is not lost on us. The *machista* man is the one who needs treatment the most and is the least likely to go on his own. Not only that, who will pay the therapist for his or her long hours of work if the treatment is free or at a nominal cost? It makes sense that governments should step up to that plate, but how likely is that to happen, even with new laws? We are in a quandary but must not give up. There are solutions to this complex problem, and failure to act is not an option.

Because San Diego County, where this study was conducted, is positioned on the border with Mexico, we believe that therapists working in the field of IPV in this region have a special ability and responsibility to share what we have learned with our fellow professionals in Tijuana, our border sister city.

Several such initiatives are under way, between police departments, legal experts, and therapists who work in treatment and prevention.[5] Working together, without the need for reinventing the wheel, we can create a safer environment for women and children and attend to the psychological needs of violent men and their families.

To summarize, the following major policy implications emerging from this study stand out: the need to educate Latino families about the legal, social, and economic consequences of IPV, through radio and television public service announcements, as well as through community and religious organizations; the need to educate the Latino public regarding the importance of preventing IPV, by offering them the skills they need to respect people of both genders, manage affect, and improve communication; the need to emphasize the intimate connection between alcohol abuse and IPV, and to offer treatment solutions in the community; the need to teach Latino families about the potential consequences of witnessing domestic violence on their children, including on their future behavior.

As José, a man with a sixth-grade education and a history of trauma and alcoholism, said, "I'm from there too. I was like that, and I changed. If I can do it, so can they."

In chapter 8, we continue to explore the results of the men's treatment as it relates to gender roles, equality, and parenting, and we listen as they describe the culturally specific content of therapy sessions they believe should be included in sessions for Latino men.

NOTES

1. Quetzalcóatl is a hero god in the Aztec pantheon, but actually much older in Mesoamerican mythology. We selected his story because his name is well known to Latinos from Mexico and Central America, and also because of the universality of the message of the story: god-hero, savior of his people, and personal sacrifice leading to transformation.
2. Leonardo made this remark while praising his therapist, María. It struck a deep chord with us, as it effectively and succinctly sums up the ultimate goal of IPV treatment, even though stopping the violence is always the primary goal.
3. It is unfortunate that we were unable to obtain sufficient funding to conduct the formal, empirical outcome study we had planned. We hope that such funding will become available to researchers in the field of Latino IPV, as there is a serious need for more research.
4. Men from Central America and the Caribbean have expressed the same desire for more action to be taken in their countries of origin. We are aware, as they may not have been, of the many initiatives in most of Latin America being taken to prevent and combat IPV. Just as it has taken decades for laws and treatment to become standard in the United States and Canada, and there is still an immense amount of work to be done, change in Latin America is slow but is under way.
5. Special mention is made of the Family Justice Center in San Diego, the Domestic Violence Council of San Diego, the San Diego Police Department and Sheriffs Department, the Men's Leadership Forum of San Diego, the Tijuana Domestic Violence Unit, DIF of Tijuana, Universidad CETYS, Colegio de la Frontera Norte, Universidad Iberoamericana, Universidad Autónoma de Baja California, Mujeres Fronterizas, and Mujeres por un Mundo Mejor, all of whom are working together in different ways to serve the needs of those involved.

CHAPTER 8

Personal Transformation: Redefining Self as Person, Husband, and Father

I liked that my therapist taught me another way to be a man.

—Leonardo

When you change to being equal in the relationship, you aren't alone anymore.

—Raúl

By the time the participants had reached the end of their treatment, they had made some very radical changes in their view of themselves as people, as men, as partners, and as fathers. In this chapter we listen as they describe some of the lifelong perceptions and attitudes that changed over the course of their therapy—the beliefs they had held and acted on previously, without ever questioning them. It will be evident to the reader that these attitudinal changes are the true goal of IPV treatment. Not all men will attain this level of insight, because not all will develop the same level of motivation. However, based on what we heard in chapter 6 about therapeutic style and technique, the arrival of clients at this level is not entirely up to them. The attitude of the therapist and his or her grasp of how to present complex cultural issues can have a profound impact on men's response to these topics.

CHANGES IN GENDER ROLE PERCEPTIONS

The participants came to realize that "there is no reason to be violent to a woman." They expressed their determination to never go back to being the *machistas* they once were, because they recognized that their change in gender roles had been very positive for themselves, as well as for their partners. Brought up to be in charge, the participants reported that they had relinquished that role to some degree and had learned to share decision making with their partners. They came to understand that mutual respect and communication are the basis for a good relationship, and that the traditional model of noncommunication that they experienced as children was much less rewarding. They had begun to see their partner as a free adult, not as a child or a possession. Having learned to trust her as an adult, they became more willing to give up suspicion and jealousy.

Several of the participants mentioned that they now realize that they do not own their wife or partner. The men who previously did not allow their partners to work came to see the value of recognizing their partner's right to employment outside the home. They also came to understand that the employment of both partners is frequently a necessity in the United States, as it is increasingly in urban areas of Latin America. The man who showed the least change in gender role beliefs was the oldest man with the least education. It was clear from his interview that he felt he had really lost the battle, and that he no longer received the respect that he felt he deserved as a man. However, all the other participants, in varying degrees, appeared to have genuinely accepted and internalized new ideas about gender roles.

Most of the men (11 out of 12) identified the changes in their perception of gender roles as central to their "new look" after treatment. It bears repeating here that the modeling our participants received was of rigid, traditional gender roles of the patriarchal variety, and that not all Latino men share these attitudes. Furthermore, as we stated in chapter 2, if cultural influences were the major factor in the perpetration of IPV, we could expect to see a 100% rate of IPV in generally patriarchal cultures, yet this is by no means the case.

There will always be a certain number of men in IPV groups who will not totally grasp and put into practice being a "new kind of man." This level of change is the best case scenario. Stopping the physical, sexual, and emotional violence, however, is the primary goal of treatment. The loftier goal of changing men's gender beliefs and cultural attitudes is much more difficult to achieve and is not realistically attainable for all of our clients. However, we consider it a completely worthy goal to strive for with all the men in our groups, with all the therapeutic skill at our disposal. The rest is up to them.

Transformation of their gender role beliefs was one of the greatest gains the men identified in their year of therapy. This stands to reason, given that they also perceived rigid male gender roles, specifically machismo, as the greatest and most challenging obstacle to be overcome. Juan had this to say about equality and relationship change:

> The most important thing I've learned there is something I didn't know, that we are all equal. Like now that I'm separated from my wife—if in that time I had had these classes—I wasted very precious time. And now with the lady I live with now, we've had problems; she is under a lot of stress because of her children. She has many children in Mexico and it's a lot of stress. We argue, but that's when I realize that I've learned self-control in the program.

As we have already pointed out, the economics of immigration also play a role in the struggles and achievements of Latino partner abusive men. Leonardo worked hard to provide for his family, as Latino men do in their country of origin as well as in their adopted country. Yet he began to realize it was not enough for him as a father to just earn money for his family:

> The topic we spent most time on and gave most emphasis to was to know how to live with your partner. In a much more positive way...I learned, thinking in a more positive way, I learned that the kitchen is not just for women [*chuckles*]. Yes, I learned that there....I also learned that the obligations that parents have are not just the obligation of the wife. And my responsibility is not just to bring money home. There are many other responsibilities we have as parents. We should be close to our children, close to them. We talked about our responsibilities as fathers about seventy five percent of the time in the program. I think it was useful, very useful....I really liked several of the topics my therapist taught. I liked that she taught me another way to be a man.

Rogelio explained:

> To show a woman you love her you can't be hitting her. You have to learn that we have the same rights. You have to learn that we need to get along.

Juan regretted his former *machista* attitude that led to his destructive behavior:

> I think if I had been to even a couple of sessions before all this happened it would never have happened. Because if your wife leaves you,

you shouldn't expect her to live alone. She's going to look for someone; she doesn't want to be alone.... With my [new] partner now we
talk a lot. I learned that in the group. Before I used to come home from
work and shut myself up in my room. I never used to sit with my wife
and talk to her. Never. But with her I do. We talk about our jobs, how
we are.

Ceferino discusses his new perception and resultant behavior change:

Last week we [myself and ex-partner] had a court date and I went up
to where she was and said hello to her partner. He's from Cuba. We
treated each other like adults. The program has really helped me. I'm
sure that before I would have reacted very differently, with a fight, or
something like that. I understand now that I'm not her owner, and she
can do what she wants.

Leonardo and his wife have reached a new level of intimacy:

It's different because we talk more as a couple about our problems,
we go out to dinner together sometimes. What has changed, like I said
before, the communication that we have now is much more valuable
than what we had before. It's like we're more united, it's easier, we're
more intimate, there's more trust so we can have a dialogue, deal
with a problem, and find a solution. I've seen this change over the
past year.

When asked if his wife had changed over the course of his year in therapy,
José had this to say:

My wife is a good person like she was before. I was the one who was
off track. I realize that I was the problem. I know it was my fault.

There is a great deal of individual difference in clients' perceptions of
their partners during any group session. Some men feel the way José did,
although this is less common. Most men report mutual conflict of the "common couple violence" variety (Johnson, 1995), even when they have arrived
at taking responsibility for their own violence and abuse. Some men report
behaviors by their partners that are truly problematic, suggesting mental illness or personality disorders, that we have verified in our telephone
contacts, or because they, too, have been referred to treatment by Child
Protective Services. The latter is more frequent when drugs are involved.
In any case, in order to show progress and graduate from the program, all
men in treatment must arrive at recognizing that violence is a choice they
do not have to make.

Raúl worked hard to change his attitude toward women. Like many of the men in our groups (Latino as well as non-Latino), the issue of controlling someone else is central:

> Now the way that I think is not that I have a child in my house, but that I have a partner. It was very hard to make the change, but it happened simply when I realized that most of the things I was doing were wrong, in the sense that it is impossible and negative to try and control the woman who's your partner.... You don't want to be very *machista* or very passive. It's a divided thing, something you do together.

Ramón described his attitude shift from irrational jealousy and ownership to deeper trust and respect. Note than even though he despised his father for his behavior toward his mother, he was reproducing his father's jealousy and controlling conduct in his own relationship:

> I was jealous. I thought I should act like my father—my mother never left the house. So here with my partner, she would tell me she was going to the store with her girlfriends and I'd say, "No way, you're just going to hang out with some guys. Just wait and see what happens to you." Now I think, *Well, if she's an adult she knows what she's doing.* At first I used to think, *Where could she have gone? Who is she with?* Now I think, *OK if that's what she's doing, she's old enough to decide for herself, let her do what she wants.* But I trust her. And she tells me, "You know what, if I'm going to cheat on you, I'll tell you about it straight up." We need to have a lot of trust in each other, but there's no use fighting with each other like that.

APPRECIATION OF GENDER EQUALITY

All 10 of the interview participants who responded to the question on equality reported that the concept of gender equality was new to them when they came into the program. The men who had less than a seventh-grade education had had no previous idea of equality or human rights. Even the men who were more educated had never previously connected the idea of equality with women specifically. This may seem hard to believe, until one realizes that the idea of equality in American society is highly stressed, whether it is practiced or not. But in many countries in Latin America, there has been much less emphasis on the concept. This is certainly the case among those who are of low socioeconomic status, who themselves have not enjoyed equal rights or opportunities as men in their societies of origin. The participants reported that over time they came to understand that women have the same rights that men do. They had felt and shown resistance to the idea in the group initially, because it challenged all their beliefs, but they eventually came to recognize the value of the concept. For most of the participants, the inequality of women was a given with which they had always lived.

Lucio opined that "from seventy-five to ninety-five percent of Mexican men" would be open to the idea, unless they were already "old and set in their ways." The topic of equality led to a discussion of discrimination against women with some interview participants, which we have already discussed and will elaborate on further. They were very grateful to the program for relieving them of the ideas about women with which they had grown up. They reported satisfaction that they had been able to grasp this concept, because it epitomizes the opposing view to machismo, which was so ingrained in their subculture.

The ability of the men to accept the concept of equality has important clinical implications. It speaks to a level of mental flexibility that is encouraging and perhaps surprising, and may give new impetus to therapists who feel pessimistic about teaching the concept. It is also important to take note of the participants' feedback. Many of them reported great resistance to the idea of gender equality, and they stated that it took time for men in the groups to arrive at acceptance. This suggests the need to approach the topic sensitively and with tolerance, not coercing, but inviting the men to rethink their position.

The placement of this concept in treatment programs should be carefully considered. In the Pence and Paymar (1993) model, it is the first lesson. It was this fact that led the first author to select the topic of cultural components for Latino men for her doctoral research. After finding that men were unfamiliar with the concept of gender equality but that they appreciated it once it had been explained in depth, we decided to include selections from the Mexican Commission for Human Right's Web site in our handouts. These quotations deal explicitly with the issue of family violence and women's rights and are written from the perspective of Latin Americans and for Latin Americans. We felt that this would help men to be more open to the idea, if it were perceived as a value in their culture of origin and not merely a concept imposed on them by American culture. We introduce this topic in the extensive section on human rights, around the middle of the year, so that men will not be taken aback or threatened by a premature discussion of such a loaded subject.

Introducing the concept of gender equality is always a moment of joy and excitement. We have come to see it as a challenge that opens so many avenues of freedom, fulfillment, communication, and peace to our clients that by now we are efficient salespeople when it comes to this idea. To be effective in "selling" this concept, the therapist has to have thought through the real advantages that come from evening out and equalizing the male–female relationship for our clients. Our conviction and the stories we share among ourselves in the group help to break down even the most stubborn resistance. The response is, of course, not 100%, but based on client feedback and comments from their partners, it appears to be successful.

Hilario commented,

There has to be equality between a man and a woman. I don't want to be the one who gives the orders; there has to be an understanding between the two. Communication, talking, agreeing on things together. That's what I never had with her.

Ceferino discussed how his views have changed, and importantly, he points out that the idea of equality is gaining considerable ground in Mexico as well. This is also true of the rest of Latin America:

I see that now in Mexico women are raising their voices, demanding their rights—it's really good because machismo has to move out of the way so there can be equality. It's not good for the man to be in charge of everything, because sometimes the woman wants to do something, to help out, but the man says, "No, I have to pay the electricity, I'll do it after work." He feels like he has to do everything. And he wants the woman to be in the house, while she could be out working. She can learn to drive; she can do the same things that a man does. But when I was with my partner I didn't think like that.

Ignacio came to realize that men and women are both people with the same individual and sexual rights:

The woman is raped in reality, because you're saying, *She's my wife, I provide for her, and I have the right. She has to accept.* But they teach us there that a woman is not a toy, not a doll. She's a person the same as you are.

Leonardo commented on sharing power and decision making as a couple. As we pointed out in chapter 3, research has shown that there is considerable diversity in the level of shared decision making in Latino couples:

> I don't think the man should be in charge of making all the decisions, not all of them. Because they should share if they are a couple. Responsibilities should be shared between them. Because you get a better solution when you work on a problem as a team. It's much better than if I take all the responsibility, and things get messed up for some reason, I'd feel bad if my wife said, "I told you, why didn't you tell me or consult with me?" Then a problem begins. And so that doesn't happen, it's much better to share decisions.

Raúl reflected on one of the greatest motivators for change today among violent and controlling men, Latino or otherwise—being left alone because of the way your treat your partner:

> I think equality is one of the most important foundations for a good relationship. Before I used to think that I was always right. I was one of the *machista* men who thought that the man had to be in charge of everything…but over time you see how things work out. When you change to being equal, even, in the relationship, you aren't alone anymore. As time goes by. You learn this. Many times you don't need to attend these courses, many times the situation itself, when you lose your partner and begin to reflect on all you've done, makes you think.

Blas came to recognize how he had destroyed his relationship and tried to make amends, even though he and his wife no longer lived together:

> I admit the huge mistake I made, I accept it as it is, I am guilty.…My eyes were completely opened there. That's why now I say, *Why did I hurt the person I love the most?* I got back with her and tried to make a better life. And I told her, "The treatment that I never gave you, I'm going to give you now." And I've come to think that if I ever have a woman with me, I will treat her like a queen. "What I never gave you, I'll give you now." She was happy when she heard that, and I was being gentle to her, and I was giving her so much attention.…Now I can talk to her and communicate, eat with her, do many things, without getting violent. Without attacking her or being attacked.

One of the great challenges for men in IPV groups is discovering that their partners frequently do not accept, believe, or welcome the changes they have made. This topic comes up often in the group. We help the men to empathize with the difficulty that human beings (i.e., their partners) have in immediately trusting someone who suddenly shows up wanting to try out a new relationship skill, when the past has been marred by abuse, violence, and an accumulation of broken promises. Men have to learn to be patient and to recognize their partner's difficulty. About half the time, by the time men finish the program, they are no longer with their partners. By the end of the year, many are divorced or separated, and often there is a custody arrangement in place. The men who are still with their partners are the ones who perhaps have done less harm, or who have been able, through their sincere efforts, to win back her trust. Sometimes the woman does not see the changes she would like, but the situation has become tolerable enough for her to stay, usually for the sake of the children or financial stability, sometimes on account of religious beliefs. These are, from the therapist's standpoint, the less desirable outcomes.

IMPORTANCE OF FAMILY AND NEW PARENTING SKILLS

Eleven of the 12 participants identified the new parenting skills that they learned in the group as one of the most important components of their treatment. Their only complaint was that there was not enough emphasis on parenting. The men had come to see their responsibilities as fathers in a new light. Before, they had been ignorant of their children's emotional needs. Afterward, they wanted to be the best fathers they could possibly be.

The participants were grateful that the program had shown them new ways to be a father. They reported living for their families in a different manner, appreciating them and their love, and trying to make up for some of their past errors. The men who were no longer with their children because of restraining orders or loss of custody reported great sadness at the virtual loss of their children. Several of the men who were with their families recounted that they had sat down with their children at some point over the course of their treatment and apologized for what they had done to their mothers. They reassured them it would not happen again. This seemed to have been a very powerful therapeutic tool for the men, to facilitate their own and their children's healing and the rebuilding of trust. That, along with the level of childhood trauma experienced by the men, inspired us to include a session on asking and giving forgiveness in the unit we compiled on spirituality and prevention of IPV, using the work of Enright (2001). Parenting emerged as such an important theme that we will discuss it further in the next chapter.

The participants reported important improvements in their attitude toward themselves and others, especially their partners and children, and were able to discuss the specific skills they had learned with enthusiasm.

Learning to Be a Father

The men lamented that they lacked parenting skills in most cases. Most were unaware that children had emotional needs that a father could attend to; they had believed that was the mother's job. Some of the participants used verbal discipline prior to treatment; others used verbal abuse. None of the men mentioned the use of physical abuse on their children, except for 1 man who had hit his daughter 12 years before. It is possible that none of the participants had been physically abusive in the recent past. Alternatively, their silence in this area may have been due to the informed consent explanation at the outset of the interview, detailing our mandate to report child abuse. Men in these programs quickly learn to be careful when they speak, and child abuse on their part is not a topic they are likely to bring up. However, generally 30–60% of men who abuse their partners in the United States are known to also be violent to their children (Edleson, 1999).

All the men expressed sadness that they had not known how to communicate with or play with their children, in large part due to lack of experience, based on the abusive environment of their own families of origin. Learning how to be a nurturing father was one of the most salient outcomes of the study, and the one that had given them the greatest satisfaction. They expressed that the experience of group therapy had opened their eyes to new vistas of fatherhood that they might never have perceived had they not emigrated to this country and been mandated to treatment. The participants knew something about what was expected of them in their nuclear family, in this case positive manhood and fatherhood, but they seemed unable to deliver it, as we have noted before. The toxic mixture of childhood abuse, lack of education in parenting, and alcohol abuse eroded their capacity as fathers, just as it had with their ability to be loving partners.

Their gratitude for the new parenting skills they had acquired in treatment appears in several different contexts. Lucio stressed the importance of his role as father several times:

> Yes, it's true that your son wants to be like you. He tries on your shoes. And he does what you do, so you are the main example. So for me personally, I'm trying my best to get as much as I can out of the classes so that I can give my son the best possible education. Respect for others, women, teachers, adults....Like I said in the beginning, I don't want my son to be like me. I want him to be better.

Lucio also commented on how to reach Latino men, something that he considered of prime importance:

> I think they can be motivated through their children. Like giving them advice to teach their children, so that their children won't be like them,

you understand? Because all men want their children to be better than them. All men think that all the time. Mothers too. I want my son to know more, to behave better, so you could say, "You know, tell this to your son, teach him this."...My behavior needed to change, for my family. I wanted to have the satisfaction of being a better husband to my wife. And to learn, so that what's happening to me won't happen to my son.

Blas wept as he explained how inestimably important it is for him to be a good father:

I grew up without my mother and my father. And I never want that to happen to my children. And I must have told my wife that one thousand times. "I don't want my children to grow up without their father and mother." But now it's not within my power. Because their mother isn't with them....But for most Mexican men, they'll never understand, until what happened to me happens to them. To understand that in reality, his family is the most important thing in the world to him. To understand that he must love his wife and children and put them first. Then yes, his eyes will begin to open.

> Sessions when parenting is the topic have the potential to be very healing for the men in our groups. They are often opportunities to talk about their childhood experiences of pain, abuse, and neglect and to help them decide to work to obtain and practice the skills they need to ensure that they do not mindlessly reproduce those negative patterns with their own children. Parenting skills are also so closely related to relationship skills that men can learn in these sessions much of what they need to practice with their partners as well.

Ceferino has a large part of his new, positive self-concept invested in his new role as a loving and effective father to his children. His comments are truly poignant when we reflect on the severe abuse and neglect he suffered as a child:

What I do is now I give them the very best of myself—love and affection. I pay attention to them. I don't want them to think I am a bad father. That maybe I'm not bad, that I may be good. I want to be good to them and I love them very much. I want them to live in a healthy environment, to grow up in a different world from the one I lived in. I want the best for them in every way. I'm not rich, but whatever I have in my pocket I give them. I try to give my family now, my children, what my own family never gave me.

Raúl doesn't want his son to repeat his mistakes or to have to go through the painful separations he suffered:

> So now, what I'm trying to do, even today, is to teach my son to avoid violence. He's had some problems with it at school. That was some time ago, and the problems began to be worse at the time that I began to see them again, because I didn't see them for a long time. For three or four years. That was because it was a very difficult battle. First there was the restraining order. No matter where I went to look for them, at school, at home, it was the same. "There is a restraining order. Don't come here because I'll call the police." "Daddy, I want to see you but don't come, because they'll call the police." It was always that. That was very hard. After some time they lifted the restraining order, and later, it was because I was so heavily into drinking, and I stopped trying. . . . I don't see my ex-wife when I go to get them. I don't know if she's with someone else. I don't want to ask my children and be investigating all that. I don't want to substitute one thing for another. I go to see them because I love them, because I want to be with them and make them feel good.

Leonardo commented on how he has changed as a father:

> Now, if they need something or something happens to them, they have the trust to come to me and tell me. I've changed as a father one hundred percent. I'm not saying I'm that perfect, but in comparison to how I was before, I'd say one hundred percent different. We try to be perfect but we'll never achieve that. Before, as a father I'd come home from work—"There's the money, do what you want with it"—like I didn't care about anything. I've tried to analyze it; I think it was just ignorance. I thought by working and bringing home money that was enough, but it really isn't. It's ignorance, not knowing that children need more than money.

José described a new kind of paternal authority, with less domination and more respect and humility:

> Sometimes I tell them that I won't do it [be violent] again, that I need to change how I act, but also that I need them to listen to me, to pay attention when we talk to them. I've told them that what I did was wrong. But even so they have to listen to me. If not me, then who? It's very good that they teach you how to talk to your child. And to your wife, and to tell her, "Help me." Because often the woman is protecting the child. We talked about that a lot. It's very important.

Juan describes the father he would like to be now that he has learned so much:

One of the ways we try to help the men in our groups to overcome the lack of coordination in their parenting, and the feeling that their partner takes the children's side against them, is to invite them to share the hand-outs and homework assignments with their partners, without, of course, coercing them to do so, because their partner is not court-ordered as they are. In this way, the mother can learn the same skills the father is learning and they can both become better parents. Occasionally, a man will ask us to make a copy of the parenting section of the program so that his partner, from whom he is now divorced or separated, can learn to be a better parent too.

To be a good father, who talks with his children, who asks them questions and communicates with them. To help them with their homework, Or if they're sick. I didn't do those things. If they were sick, I'd say, "You take them," to the woman. "You're the mother, you take them."

Of course, Juan never thought of helping his children with such things because his parents were so cruel to him and ignored even his obvious needs. With so little personal experience of empathy, how could he show that to his children?

Ignacio's understanding of his children's emotional needs has developed considerably from his treatment:

I used verbal discipline a lot. I used to shout at them a lot. Now that's totally changed. I think a father who shouts at his children can hurt them tremendously. I notice the difference in my youngest daughter from the changes I've made since I began the classes. I hardly ever shout at her, but sometimes I say something like, "I told you not to do that!" And her attitude changes, because she's not used to me talking to her like that anymore. She interprets it as anger. And she gets angry too. So it hurts me. I see that I hurt her the way I shouted at her or spoke to her. I never thought of that before, but now I realize.

SHARING THE INFORMATION
THEY HAVE RECEIVED

Many of the men (9 out of 12) described how their perception of the role of family has changed since treatment. This attitude change included a desire to share the information they had learned with extended family as well as with their partner and children. Rogelio remarked,

> After all the bad example I gave them, I feel like now it's important to say, "No, my child, be someone in life, become a professional, get educated for your life. Life isn't easy, we have to prepare for it." Things to do, things to know, all that. I talk a lot with my brothers and sisters, I'm teaching them, like how to talk and how to listen to someone. I would encourage them to talk about their problems and then find a way to help them. I really feel like I have a lot of valuable information to share. Absolutely...I am proud of myself, of what I am doing. I'm keeping my resolutions and changing my life. So I feel proud of myself as a person.

Ceferino had made tremendous changes in his life, after such an abusive childhood. He shared what he had experienced with the group:

> I feel proud because I know I can do things better for my family and for many other people. One man asked me what I was like in the past, and I told him I used to do drugs and drink a lot. I used to come home and I wanted to have my dinner served to me, as soon as I walked in, no matter what time, midnight or whatever. And I said it was wrong, it was a negative way to live, and that if they did the same thing, it was almost sure that the same thing that has happened to me would happen to them. They took my wife and my family away from me. I was separated from them, and I'm not allowed to have my children overnight yet. And all that was very painful for me and I don't want it to happen to any of them.

Ramón, another victim of a brutal and alcoholic father, had this to say:

> You learn from the experiences of everyone in the group, also when you talk about those things, like what my dad did to me. It makes you think about how to treat your own children. It has helped me. I wouldn't say that I have changed a lot, but I have changed some. I never want to treat my children like my dad treated me.

CULTURALLY SPECIFIC TOPICS IDENTIFIED AS HELPFUL TREATMENT COMPONENTS

The interview participants identified six major areas of emphasis that are culturally specific and that they felt should be included in IPV treatment programs for Latino men. Although half of these categories are generally included to some degree in standard treatment in the United States, the participants believed the following areas merit special attention for Latino men, and should be dealt with specifically according to Latino culture, because they viewed these topics as essential to enhancing treatment for Latino men:

- An emphasis on parenting education
- Extensive discussion of rigid male gender roles, especially machismo
- Acknowledgment of discrimination, against immigrants and women
- Discussion of the difficulties that spring from immigration, with a special emphasis on changing gender roles
- Open discussion of sexual abuse in relationships
- Inclusion of spirituality as it relates to the prevention of domestic violence

Some of their therapists had touched on some or all of these topics, but often they "just came up" and were not a planned part of the curriculum. The participants expressed the desire to have these topics be included as a regular part of treatment.[1]

Emphasis on Parenting Education

The literature and our own clinical experience had prepared us to expect fatherhood to be an important issue for the participants. But we were not prepared for the level of passion, of vital importance, that this theme had for them. The men we interviewed and most of the men in our pilot study were hard-pressed to be good fathers, when they themselves had rarely or never received positive examples or affection from their own fathers. In our study we found that half of the men surveyed, and a higher ratio of interview participants, were victims of child abuse and/or had witnessed IPV as children.

The participants were deeply motivated by the idea of being able to break the cycle of violence in their families. *Eight of the 8 men who brought up this point, because it was not included in the interview schedule, emphasized the importance of educating Latino men to be better parents.* The men who received a great deal of parent education in the group considered it a central theme and entirely relevant. The ones who did not wished they had received more, because they felt their inadequacy as fathers deeply. We have already quoted several of the men on this topic in chapter 7 and add a few more of their comments here.

Ceferino insisted on more parent education:

> I think the domestic violence program should teach us more about the family. I know it's about domestic violence, but why not? About how to treat children. All that. It's really important.

José was grateful that he had learned to relate to his children in new and better ways:

> Learning to communicate has helped me too. I play more with everyone, my children, everyone. I'm going to try to be the best, I really want to finish my class, and I want to be, not the best, but more or less—talk better, maybe not perfectly, but I want to grow and be better. It makes me feel good.

The participants also stressed the importance of teaching men about the negative effects of witnessing IPV. All 7 of the men who responded to this interview question (5 did not, due to lack of time) were very motivated to change by the pain they had caused their children and by the understanding that violence is learned behavior (Dutton, 2000). They believed that knowledge of the effects of witnessing domestic violence could serve as an important deterrent to Latino men. Rogelio, who stopped strangling his wife when he heard his 5-year-old daughter scream, "Daddy, stop!" commented,

> More than anything else we learned that children learn to do what their parents do. So if the father and mother are hitting each other, they're going to learn that too.

Ceferino had firsthand experience, as did many of the interview and survey participants:

> The children are traumatized by it. It's a very powerful trauma for them. And like me, they learn it, they think they are always going to live like that. And they will grow up just like their father and mother. The same. If they see violence in their own home, they learn how to do it.

Ignacio, our most pessimistic participant, hoped the topic would act as a deterrent:

> Children get scared and they get traumatized. I think it's useful to talk about that in the group, because many of us don't know how to act. That could motivate a man not to hit the mother of his children, but who knows?

Ramón didn't want to subject his stepchildren to the same terror he had experienced as a child:

> They were asleep. They didn't hear either. If they had seen, they would have cried, they would have been scared, like me. What happened

to me would have happened to them. As a child you feel really bad. Because when they grow up they would say, "He's not my father and he used to hit her."

Ramón's belief that the children did not see or hear the violence is a common one. Research indicates, however, that in many cases, children are aware of the violence, which they frequently hear even if they are not in the room. There is also the issue of an atmosphere of constant tension and fear in the home that affects children's mood, cognitive performance, and development of relationship skills.

Raúl discussed what he had learned about conflict resolution:

If you need to discuss something, send the children to bed or whatever, and sit down and talk. And if the children see you arguing, show them that you know how to solve a problem. Not with shouting and threatening and beating. Teach them how to resolve a conflict.

One of the greatest examples the group facilitators can offer to the men in their groups is to resolve conflicts between themselves appropriately when they come up in the group. This is especially effective when the facilitators are male and female. It is important to be aware of the gender dynamics between you, because the men are watching to see if the male facilitator is dominating the woman, or worse from their standpoint, if the female facilitator is dominating the man!

Extensive Discussion of Rigid Male Gender Roles, Especially Machismo

The participants told us that the timing and approach to modification of gender roles, as well as pressure from the group rather than the therapist, are key to effecting change. Equality was seen as an essential value to inculcate in the group, but therapists should expect to encounter a great deal of initial resistance. Eleven of the 12 men mentioned the importance of placing special and continuous emphasis on the transformation of rigid gender roles and that the influence of machismo could be counteracted by focusing on human rights and equality. Some of the quotations in previous chapters illustrate the sensitivity of the topic of machismo, and the doggedness with which many men in the groups held on to it as if to their very identity, which it frequently is (Casas et al, 1994; Gutmann, 1996; Mirandé, 1997). If the old identity is to be relinquished, a new one must be available to take its place. As Leonardo said, "I like that she taught me another way to be a man." Therapists need skill and training to be able to accomplish their task successfully and foster true change, rather than a mere acquiescence for court evaluation purposes—men telling you what they know you want to hear. Raúl expressed it succinctly:

> The bottom line was, get rid of the machismo, be the man, and be fair. And let's see how things work out in your relationship.

Blas described his need to be taught skills he had never learned:

> I thought that that was the way to show her that I was a man. I thought the way I touched her was good. But, on the contrary, I didn't realize—everything I did, everything was wrong. No one ever taught me. I never saw a good example of how to treat a woman. If I had seen it, I would have done it, but I never did.

Lucio commented on the difficulty of changing:

> Some men say think things like, "OK, well I don't need to tell my problems to anyone. I can solve my own problems." But really ninety-five percent of us, ninety-nine percent of us can't solve our problems by ourselves. We need help.

Gregorio, raised in a *machista* rural enclave, recounted his ignorance of other gender roles, of different ways to express masculinity:

> Then I didn't realize, now thank God I know, that the woman is a companion, not an object that belongs to you. I learned that in the programs I've been in. When I came to the United States I had those same ideas, machismo, all that. That the woman belonged to you, that she was an object, not that she was a companion, a person.

Blas, frequently given to black-and-white thinking, expressed his opinion that all IPV among Mexicans is due to machismo:

> In all cases, not in some, in all cases. Machismo is the culture of the Mexican man. I'm Mexican, and I'm changing because people helped

---

Although the available evidence demonstrates that it is incorrect that *all* Mexican men and *all* Latino men are *machistas*, Blas's controversial comment is important, and as such makes an excellent starting point for a lively group discussion. Put the timer on!

me to open my eyes. Because I'm looking at what happened and I'm accepting that I did wrong.

Acknowledgment of Discrimination Against Immigrants and Women

Most of the participants were aware that many other Latino immigrants in their IPV groups had experienced the negative effects of discrimination. Discrimination or the threat of discrimination has been shown to be an added stressor in the life of ethnic minorities in this country (Falicov, 1996). Lucio described his struggles to come to terms with the treatment he has received:

> Sometimes I think the discrimination has affected my self-esteem. Like I ask myself, *Is it true?* Just for a moment, then it passes. People don't have that kind of power over me.

Not all therapists opened up the topic of discrimination to the group, nor did they make the connection between the men's experiences and discrimination against women. This topic is not discussed in standard IPV groups. However, in their work on IPV and men of color, Carrillo and Tello (1998) and contributors hypothesized that institutional racism and oppression affect the lives of men of color to such a degree that their use of violence against their partners and children could be partially explained by their history of discrimination in the United States and subsequent displacement of anger and helplessness onto their female partners. We are currently unaware of any empirical research on this hypothesis, which to us seems reasonable to some degree. However, we cannot discount the very high rates of IPV in all the countries and cultures of origin of the perpetrators of IPV of varying ethnic groups.

The issue of discrimination is a touchy one for a therapist, not because it has not been present in the lives of men of color in IPV groups, but because one of the primary goals of IPV treatment is for violent men to take responsibility for their violence so that they can learn to overcome it and replace it with more adaptive strategies. Our approach is to discuss it and to allow men to vent their legitimate feelings and stories, but not to allow the conversation to degenerate into a place where men refuse to accept that IPV is a choice made by the individual, whatever his background, that can be changed by that individual if he is motivated.

We asked the participants whether their own experience of discrimination in this country might serve as a springboard to understanding and empathizing with the oppression of women, including by themselves. Lucio commented,

> We never talked about that. That would be really good. A man can work just like a woman can. But a man gets more respect in Mexican society than a woman. Women get pushed aside. They don't give her the value she deserves.... We did talk about sometimes you feel bad because they treat you bad at work because you're Mexican, and you come home and take it out on your family. That's really wrong.

Gregorio's group had discussed the issue as it relates to discrimination among different Latino ethnic groups:

> Yes, we talked about it several times. I think it was useful because we had some men who came from other countries who talked about discrimination in Mexico, like Salvadorans. They said they were looked down on in Mexico. It needs to be discussed. It shouldn't exist. There would be more unity among people.

Blas appeared to have never realized that gender discrimination existed prior to his group experience:

> I think once we talked about discrimination against women in the group, and it made me think a lot. *Why do we do that to them? It doesn't make sense. They have the same feelings that any one of us has.* After that I tried to give her more support, more respect. I was thinking, *She feels the same things that I feel.*

It was surprising and disconcerting to us to hear Blas's comment about women feeling the same things he feels. Indeed! Such a lack of empathy is not unusual among the men in our groups, to varying degrees. It is obviously of vital importance to help them develop this essential skill if they are to have meaningful relationships with anyone in their lives, including their children. This deficit speaks to the parenting they themselves received, as well as to the insecure and fearful attachment styles found to be predominant among violent Latino men in Welland et al.'s research (unpublished).

Leonardo had experienced his mother's partiality to her daughters and spoke about discrimination from the hurt he felt as a child:

> We did talk about it one time. How it's similar for an Anglo to put down a Mexican and for a Mexican to put down a woman, to insult

her. The example is really very similar. I think in Latino groups we should always discuss the topic of discrimination. That will help the guys. As fathers also, we need to learn not to prefer one of our children over the others. I have seen many parents putting down one of their children—they love one more than the other. It's the same thing in a different way; it has the same effect.

Discussion of Difficulties Stemming From Immigration

The participants were generally glad that they had emigrated to the United States, but they did emphasize changing gender roles and the specific challenges this situation created for them personally and in their relationship. The literature on immigration suggests that the process of immigration itself and ongoing struggles to acculturate contribute to stress in Latino families (Falicov, 1996). All of the participants stated that immigration had been a tremendously positive experience for them. They came here primarily to be able to have a better life and to give their children the education and the future they would not have had in Mexico.

However, immigration also presents challenges and dilemmas, not the least of which is being arrested and mandated to a yearlong program for what in many of their countries would still go unnoticed or unpunished. Behavior that was tolerated in their country of origin can land them in jail in the United States.[2]

Although we are unaware of any research that specifically targets changes in gender roles threatening Latino men and acting as a risk factor for IPV, in chapter 3 we have cited theoretical literature where such stress is hypothesized. Many participants reported difficulties stemming from immigration and the process of acculturation. Of these, several reported difficulties specifically with their partner and the way that she had changed, and they reported that such problems were common among members of their groups. Ignacio spoke about what he has observed:

> I don't think that all Mexican women change. But I've heard a lot of men in the class say, "Ever since I brought my wife here, my wife totally changed. She was no longer the woman I knew when we lived in Mexico. As soon as she got her papers, she wasn't worth a damn." I've heard a lot about how women change, like one guy says, "When my wife lived in Tijuana she was really good. As soon as she got her papers, she changed completely. Her way of behaving, of thinking— like, she used to do whatever I said, we had no problems, now that she's here, I don't know what to do."

Leonardo mentioned that other men in his group had problems with changing gender roles but that he and his wife had not. He also pointed out that men change as well as a result of acculturation:

> Many of the men talked about it. They said their wives were changing after coming here. Many guys say that women, or men too, come here, and they're different people. But that hasn't been the case for us. But I think we need to talk about that in the group. It's important—it would be a good topic.

Latina women who have been raised in the United States are more likely to share the same gender role expectations of any woman in American culture. This makes for tension when the Latino man is unprepared for the difference in levels of submission and service.[3]

Ramón, whose partner is Mexican American, lamented the difference in role expectations, as did others who had difficulty negotiating marriage with Latinas raised in the United States, which becomes effectively an intercultural marriage. Ramón is equating his wife's lack of dedication to the home to being Mexican American, rather than Mexican, which is of course untrue. However, it is his experience and thus a valid area to explore with him. Ramón commented,

> When someone says that they go to work, and then they have to come home and clean up the house and there's nothing cooked, and he has to do it, that's not OK. You know what? It'd be better if I looked for another woman who will do all that for me. You go to work happier if you know there will be food ready when you come home....She doesn't have a sense of responsibility. Nothing matters to her. She just blows everything off. She says she doesn't give a crap. In Mexico if your partner doesn't cook or anything, why would you give her money? Here they expect us to give her money when she doesn't do anything. It's very different here.

Blas, too, was married to a Mexican American woman and was baffled by her criticism of the way women were treated in his family. We are already familiar with Blas's previous lack of empathy and insight:

> She speaks Spanish, and she has all the habits of Mexican culture, almost, but her ideas were different. She used to always attack me about how Mexican men treated women. She'd say—even though I had nothing to do with it, she was attacking me. And I'd say, "What have I done? I didn't do anything!" "Yes, but look at your brother— see how he talks to his wife?" When she attacked me like that, I realized she didn't want me to be that way, but even so I was doing what she didn't like. I couldn't understand it.

Open Discussion of Sexual Abuse in Relationships

What little we know from statistics indicates that sexual abuse in marriage is no more common among Latinos in the United States than in the general population. It may even be lower (Tjaden & Thoennes, 2000). This does not mean, however, that it is a nonissue. *Seven of the 12 men stated that the topic of sexual abuse, usually interpreted as forced intercourse, was not discussed clearly or sufficiently in the group.* The reason that they gave for this lack of coverage of the topic was that their therapists were female. The 2 men who had a male therapist for the whole year stated that the topic was explained satisfactorily. The participants acknowledged that although it is difficult to talk about sexual abuse in their relationships in the presence of a female therapist, such coercion happens so frequently that it must be understood and discussed openly. Here is what Ceferino had to say about the importance of this topic and how it was not handled in his group:

> We've never talked about sex and domestic violence. But it's a reality. I even did it; she didn't want sex and I used to force her. I think we need to talk about that. Men just don't get it by themselves. There are lots of ways to talk about sex with the men in the group, even if it's a female counselor. Even though she needs to keep her distance . . . it's too important to leave it out.

Recalling how poor the rapport was between Ceferino's therapist, Carmen, and her group, it is not surprising that she did not dare to expose herself to more discomfort by running a session on sexual abuse. "Keeping her distance" is an art for the female therapist, who is often by herself in a room with 12 fairly young men to discuss the topic of sex gone awry. If one appears too chatty and informal, or worse, coarse and vulgar, the men feel uncomfortable, even scandalized, and lose respect. Men new to the group may misinterpret the therapist as loose, or interested in them sexually. On the other hand, if one is too vague, the necessary information is not imparted. An unabashed, respectful tone and educational demeanor seem to work well. Young women may find this session especially challenging, as it is in any men's IPV group. We have found that expecting a respectful response to the content and accepting nothing less is effective. Veterans of the group can usually be counted on to support the therapist by monitoring the level of respect of the men, as she explores this difficult topic with clients. This is one area where true fluency in the language is an advantage, because new members may try to make jokes and comments that they think the non-Latina therapist will not understand.

Leonardo wished he had learned more and was concerned that the men in his group had not received sufficient explanation of what sexual abuse entails.

> We didn't talk about it much. We mostly talked about physical abuse. We gave it minimal attention. It wasn't enough. María was going to talk about it more because she said we didn't have a clear idea of what sexual abuse is. She was just going to begin it because we had five new men, but I finished the program.

Gregorio was dissatisfied with how sexual abuse was handled in his group:

> They spoke about sexual abuse a little, but not all the guys understood it. Because many of them didn't take it seriously. They didn't open up about it. Only very rarely.

We have also experienced how the great majority of our clients fail to mention sexual coercion in group discussions, even when they are describing to the group the different forms of abuse they have perpetrated on their wives during the course of their relationship. The men who do mention it tend to have been drug users or gang members. We can only hypothesize that these men are more desensitized to behavior that is generally perceived as shameful than their less criminal companions and feel less embarrassment when bringing up the topic. Over the years, we have developed a matter-of-fact, educational style when discussing sexual abuse that seems to minimize the embarrassment of the men when such a taboo topic is brought up in public by a woman. We make sure that all the men understand what coercion is, but we do not exact public confessions out of anyone. Because ours is not a sexual offenders' group and marital rape is never the presenting problem per the courts, we consider it sufficient that the topic has been covered thoroughly and thoughtfully, and that men know themselves if they have committed this most damaging type of abuse. We cite instances (appropriately altered) that our female clients have told us about in individual therapy, or news reports, that clarify and personalize sexual abuse for the men. We talk about how hard it is for a woman to get over, much less forgive, this particular trauma. Occasionally, a man will express surprise that what he had been doing was abusive and violated the human rights of his partner. We also never hesitate to let men know what the criminal penalty is in California for marital rape. This never fails to focus their attention.

Inclusion of Spirituality Related to the Prevention of IPV

Falicov (1996) theorized that the Catholic or Christian religion provides Mexicans with universal principles of behavior that are reassuring and make meaning for them. Edgerton and Karno (1971) found that first-generation Mexican immigrants gave great importance to their spiritual beliefs and to church attendance, and Bach-y-Rita (1982) discussed the anchorlike effect that their faith can have on Mexican immigrants who feel cast adrift in the pluralism of American society. Our extensive volunteer experience with migrant workers from Mexico and Central America, as well as with the Latino clinical population, strongly supports these comments. A recent study by the Pew Hispanic Center (2007) also details the importance of religion and spirituality in the lives of Latinos living in the United States.

As we mentioned in chapter 1, a large majority of both the survey respondents and the interview participants felt strongly about their religion. Eleven of the interview participants believed that their religion is against IPV. All of the 10 men who responded to the question regarding inclusion of the issue of spirituality in the IPV group were in favor of it. They felt it would give them an opportunity to integrate what was being learned in the group with what their church believed and taught, one supporting and reinforcing the other. There was no sense in their comments that discussing religious beliefs regarding IPV would be divisive, or that they would be uncomfortable with the topic. They felt that the subject could be handled in such a way as to avoid controversy and find common ground. They expressed an interest in knowing what other men in the group believed, while displaying no desire to convert group members to their way of thinking. They did, however, comment that men who were involved in their religion would be a good resource for others who wanted to get their lives back on track, spiritually as well as behaviorally. They saw the topics as related because churches teach the same basic values that they learned in the group—self-control, communication, caring for others, and respect. José commented,

> We talked a little about our religious beliefs, just a little, not much. You could include them in the group because they're very similar. Like I said, going to church is like going to class.

Rogelio was seeking meaningful spiritual connections to help him to consolidate his change:

> I would have liked us to talk about some religion. Because when you're going to make a change you need to hold onto something. You have

to have a solid foundation, whatever it is. Something that really helps you. Whether it's the program or something else. But it would be helpful to bring in some religion, to talk about the spiritual side....They don't talk about that there. Our therapist never talked about religion. I felt like he wasn't very open to that, that he wasn't very respectful about that. I think it would be very useful to talk about religion in the group, to talk about what we believe as human beings.

Rogelio is not alone in feeling that his therapist was not very open or respectful to the issue of religion and spirituality. We often hear Latino clients and patients commenting on how alienating it is for them to have a therapist who in some way mocks or puts down their religious beliefs, or just makes it clear that this topic is off bounds. Spiritual beliefs, even unpracticed ones, are a core ingredient of the self and cultural identity of many Latinos (as for many groups), and respect for such essential aspects of their life is vital to building and maintaining rapport.

Leonardo commented,

We talked about our religious beliefs and domestic violence in the group. I think it was useful for the whole group. How to connect one thing to the other, how to unite them. There were two or three men in the group who preferred not to talk about it, about religion in the group. I'm not sure why they didn't want to. But I think it's important. It would help them to get a little fear, at least for those who don't practice any religion. They have nothing. But I think it would help to mention it.

Although it would never be our goal to help clients "get a little fear," we do not hesitate to bring up the issue of religion and spirituality.

Gregorio, an avid member of Alcoholics Anonymous, lamented the lack of spirituality of some of the men in his group:

We discussed religion a few times in the group. I think it helped most of us, although some probably not because they don't believe, they think they're God. But without spirituality how can we be better people?

Raúl was in favor of integrating therapeutic and spiritual information and practice, so that men in the groups can get all the support that is available to them:

> We talked about it a little. I think it helps. Many of the men tell us that they are going to the kind of weekend [Marriage Encounter] that I told you, and they share what they've done and what they're doing. I think we should talk about it because there's a lot of help and support out there. It's like a mix, where you do a little bit here and a little bit there, it's like a mix that makes you wake up and react.

In the next chapter, we discuss all the cultural adaptations that we included in our treatment program to reflect what we had learned from the research participants, and how our 4-year pilot program helped us to refine the content and process to maximize its acceptability and applicability.

NOTES

1. Their feedback, as well as the literature on cultural values for Latinos, formed the basis of the treatment program (*Sin Golpes*, Welland & Wexler, 2007a, 2007b) we created to meet their needs.
2. As stated, increasingly in Latin American, IPV can land them in jail in their countries of origin as well. But it is not usual for men in our groups to have been jailed in Latin American for IPV in the past. In our survey (n = 159) we found that 99% of respondents had never been arrested for IPV in Mexico. However, most of the men we studied had married once they were in the United States. Only 4% admitted to being violent to their partners in Mexico before immigration.
3. Latino men in our practice sometimes state that they are going home to their country of origin to look for a partner, because they are aware that Latinas or other American women are not a good fit for their gender role expectations, as voiced by Ramón.

CHAPTER 9

Partner Abusive Latino Men on a Journey to Redefine Their Masculinity for the Twenty-First Century

I think men can be motivated through their children. Like giving them advice to teach their children, so that their children won't be like them, you understand? Because all men want their children to be better than them, all men think that all the time. Mothers too. I want him to know more, to behave better, so you could say, "You know, tell this to your son, teach him this."

—Lucio

The Latino man who avoids contact with his true Self, who sees the world from a position of irresponsibility (Ramírez Hernándcz, 1999), is unwilling to challenge the destructive social influences in his culture. It is easier to be irresponsible, for he does not know how to change himself or his society; he does not even think it is possible. This man distances himself from his problems and avoids the pain and fear they cause him. However, Ramírez Hernández believes, based on his years of therapeutic work with partner abusive men, when the violent man sees that some men are nonviolent and have healthy relationships that bring them happiness and peace, he will begin to desire this kind of relationship.

Abalos (2002) spoke eloquently of the need for a creative drama of loving mutuality for Latino men and Latina women that will foster families able to meet the challenges of the twenty-first century. "Latino men know that women are no longer blindly loyal to them, and that times have changed. Latino men and Latina women feel in their bones that this way of life is dying, but they are not sure what to do" (p. 164). In his sociological study of Latino male gender roles, Mirandé (1997) found that men who scored very high on his measure of machismo were significantly less likely to evaluate their marriages as happy or very happy. Gutmann (1996), in his anthropological study of working-class men in Mexico City, found that, in general, attitudes toward IPV were shifting in the direction of disapproval, and that partner abusive men were the object of opprobrium. The men in his study also described the difficulty they had negotiating ongoing changes in gender roles that left them feeling jealous, disempowered, and unable to cope with the new demands being placed on them. Clearly, Latino masculinity both in the United States and in Latin America is under fire, as social change and growing freedoms for women throw the old system into imbalance and call into question beliefs and behaviors that many of the grandfathers, and grandmothers, of these men took for granted as unchangeable.

CULTURAL ADAPTATION OF TREATMENT FOR LATINO PARTNER ABUSIVE MEN

In chapter 8, we explored the topics that the participants in our study felt were essential if Latino men are to benefit from treatment to the fullest possible extent. The violent Latino men both in the survey and in the interviews presented overall a very similar pattern in terms of history, demographics, and behavior to the violent men in the general population of the United States who have been the object of much research. These include such maladaptive coping skills as poor impulse control, inadequate relationship and communication skills, and a high degree of alcohol abuse and/or dependence, as well as histories of trauma through child abuse and/or witnessing IPV. Because their problems in this regard were so similar, and the participants could not identify any topics presented to them in unadapted programs translated into Spanish that they felt were irrelevant to their lives, we decided to use as the basis of our program for Latino men a nationally known and esteemed program, Domestic Violence 2000, originally developed for the U.S. Navy and now widely in use throughout the United States and Canada.[1] Dr. Wexler's work is a skill-based cognitive-behavioral and anger management approach, which significantly includes a self psychology and attachment emphasis based on respect for the client. His program also contains psychoeducational sessions on such topics as masculinity and parenting. We considered it to be an excellent vehicle to train and educate the Latino men in our groups.

We added 12 sessions and appendixes to it specifically for Latino men and made adaptations throughout when necessary, all based on what we had learned in our research as well as in the scant literature.

We were fortunate to have the assistance over the 4 years of the pilot study of several therapists who also used the program at their respective agencies, and most of all, the help of the many men who passed through our IPV groups. We always made it clear that their comments on the material or on the process of therapy were welcome and that their feedback would be taken into serious consideration. Frequently, they would offer a better word or phrase or take issue with an expression that had another possible (usually sexual) meaning. The material improved with their input. The clients commented on the effectiveness of certain interventions and suggested ways to improve them. Sometimes they offered their own artwork as a way to improve the visual appeal or to deliver material more effectively. It was their work in progress, their program. Like anything one takes ownership of, they were invested in it and wanted to see it, and themselves, succeed.

ADAPTATIONS TO THE PROGRAM

The areas of particular importance or challenge that the participants believed should be included in a program adapted to Latino culture included the importance of learning to be good fathers; rigid masculine gender roles, especially machismo versus the concept of equality; the experience of discrimination as it relates to their lives in the United States and how this can be connected to discrimination against women; couple conflict related to changes in gender roles in their culture and after immigration; the use of force in sexual relations with their partners; and the use of spirituality/religious beliefs as they might apply to relapse prevention.

Implementation of Cultural Additions and Adaptations

We made ample use in the adapted treatment program of direct quotations from the men who participated in our research, both about their personal experience of IPV and about their experiences as children growing up in violent environments, as we do in this book. When a new member joins the group we explain to him that throughout his workbook he will find text boxes with quotations. We briefly explain that these are real words from real clients like himself, interviewed when they had completed their year of IPV treatment. We explain that the names are fictitious, but their experiences and comments are not. We also use these quotations as reading assignments, where clients read the comments of the participants and then respond to questions in their workbooks on that topic. An example is one of the sessions on masculinity, where several of the quotations cited in chapter 5 are followed by questions about their response to the men's attitudes and experiences. *What do you think about the idea that the man should be in charge at home? When you were young, did you receive any training about how to establish a relationship with a woman? What do you think about Rogelio's comment about the man who helped his wife? Do you think people still believe that a woman should obey her husband? What do you think of this? What is the difference between a woman as an object and a woman as a companion?* Clients are asked to think about the responses, write down a few lines, and share with the group the following week. The discussion this generates can easily last a whole session, unless the therapist is pressed for time. The quotations from the participants, because they are simple and real, open clients up to genuine commentaries and reflections as they grapple with the material.

Cultural Stories

We also use cultural stories that encapsulate important themes, to make the sessions more meaningful. Stories are, of course, the ideal way to teach, because they engage the listener on several levels, with the senses and the imagination as well as logic and reason. The symbolism incarnated in the mythological being is seared into the mind in a manner quite different from lists of cognitive-behavioral exercises. By bringing up Quetzalcóatl in the first session, we set a tone of acceptance and reverence for Latino culture, as well as initiating the men into the universal idea of the hero's journey. The men's enthusiastic response and level of retention bears witness to the effectiveness of the story. It is a fitting beginning to a group that is not designed to be boring, overintellectual, or worse, unintelligible. We make use of quotations from ancient Aztec teachings, such as Nahuatl poetry (Leander, 1972) and the following explanation of the good father from the Indian informants of Fray Sahagún, quoted in the *Codex Matritense del Real Palacio*:[2]

- The father, root and origin of the lineage of men.
- His heart is good, he is careful of things; he is compassionate, he is concerned, he is the foresight, he is support, he protects with his hands.
- He raises children, he educates, he instructs, he admonishes, he teaches them to live.
- He places before them a large mirror, a mirror pierced on both sides, he is a large torch that does not smoke.

When working with court-ordered clients, we feel a special responsibility to make the work of therapy engaging. Men are eager to graduate after their year of treatment, but they also often express sadness that the group, which has become like family, has to come to an end for them.

Teaching Method

Learning from our participants, we conduct frequent, brief reviews of the basic categories of abuse, and the skills that clients are learning, for two reasons. First, our groups are open, which means that a new member might be enrolled at any part of the curriculum. Apart from the basic orientation he receives at intake, he also needs to learn what abuse is, how to control himself in a crisis, and how to change his self-talk, and he needs all this information as soon as possible. We have found that other clients' midterm oral exams, where they cover all this material and more with the group, is a perfect opportunity for new clients to learn these fundamental skills, because in a group of 12 men, midterm exams come up with some frequency. Second, we are aware that many of our clients have few years of formal education. They are not used to memorizing material, and they often find it difficult to express themselves in an articulate manner about the material. The court-ordered client must demonstrate to the therapist's satisfaction that he has mastered the essentials of IPV treatment, because his learning status is conveyed to the court on a bimonthly basis, as well as at graduation. Reviews, the midterm, and the final exam, as well as the weekly homework assignments, are all ways to ensure that the client is learning and, ideally, internalizing the information and the skills he has been taught in the group.

Appendixes

The program includes a relapse prevention unit, which is covered by clients before and at the time of graduation from the group. Apart from the exercises in the Wexler program, which constitute a personalized review of the many skills learned during the year of treatment, as well as goals for obtaining future support, we added a special intervention for the Christmas and New Year's holiday season. This is traditionally a period of high risk for several reasons. Apart from increased contact with potentially conflictive or emotionally challenging relatives, it is also a time when alcohol intake at frequent parties and family gatherings tends to increase for many populations, including Latinos. Office parties and the like can be threatening to men who experience irrational jealousy, as they may see their partner in what they perceive as a dangerous situation. We learned about the need for this from several of our clients' partners, who told us in confidence that Christmas parties were one of the most difficult situations for them to negotiate with their insecure, jealous husband. The session serves as an inoculation against high-risk behavior, by pondering and discussing potential stressors beforehand and making decisions about how to handle them in advance. There is also a spiritual component, which encourages men to engage in some individual or group practice that will help them to obtain greater inner peace and increase harmony with their partners and children. Men have reported enjoying their holidays more as a result, and we have received fewer complaints from partners about misbehavior around the holidays.

Masculinity/Machismo and Human Rights

> Someday you shall tie yourself to a skirt and blouse.[3]
> What will she drink? What will she eat?
> Is she going to live off of the air?
> You are the support, the remedy;
> You are the eagle, the tiger.
> ———Aztec teaching to men regarding the responsibilities
> of the husband (as cited in León-Portilla, 1963)

In view of the evidence from the literature and our study that the influence of male gender roles has great salience for the Latino partner abusive men, we added an entire eight-session section called Human Rights and Masculinity to the program. Into this section we incorporated teachings from the Mexican Commission for Human Rights, which describes part of its mission "to spread messages that are aimed at changing cultural patterns that reproduce violence and abuse." We quote their documents on human rights, IPV, and women's rights extensively, as well as those on sexual abuse in particular. We considered that clients might find it more acceptable to study these essential topics when written by a Latin American source than if it were a translation of an American source. Our intention was also to clarify for the men that the discussion of human rights, gender equality, and opposition to violence in the family is becoming more and more universal. These concerns are not foreign to their cultures; they are an increasingly important feature of many legislative, social, and therapeutic movements in their countries of origin. Our clients, who are usually unaware of the strides that have been made, are often surprised to know that the struggle for protection of women from IPV is only 30 years old in the United States. Perhaps more significantly, this seems to relieve their concern that as Latinos they are viewed as being somehow more violent than American men. It also opens their eyes to the newness of the global response to IPV.

We like to engage them in the process of being a part of this wave of recognition and change. Our approach to the topic of masculinity and changing gender roles is designed to be tolerant, nonstereotyping, and gradual. We let the veterans in the group lead the way in discussions, and we bring up topics by quoting real men from our study, with the quandaries and challenges they found themselves in as they navigated the difficult waters of something as fundamental as gender role transformation. Given that our gender role beliefs are a deeply entrenched aspect of our personal identity, it is important that we introduce this topic in a highly sensitive manner. We try not to engage in power struggles with the more *machista* men in our groups, knowing that this will be unproductive.

Our approach when a client with particularly rigid gender roles challenges the material is to allow the veterans of the group to handle his complaints, doubts, and fears over "losing his position" in his family. Although we do not allow clients to engage in generalized woman bashing, we do listen if a client has a specific complaint about his female partner, and as a group, try to help him to perceive the advantages of thinking and acting in a new and different way, as well as solving the immediate problem with his partner. This is most effective if the client comes to realize that the old way isn't working for him. We are also willing to acknowledge that some of our clients' relationships are very unhealthy on both sides of the equation. Although this is not the case most of the time, we do hear cases where the partner has a drug or alcohol problem, or appears to have an Axis I or Axis II disorder. Men in the group sometimes warn their companions that their partner's ongoing behavior puts them at risk for reoffense. In our groups, we have to deal with the realities that men bring in to session. Otherwise we risk behaving like Blas's therapist Carmen, who undoubtedly believed her approach was appropriate at the time:

> When she's defending the woman she always says it's the man's fault; she used to say that a lot. I felt, not so much upset, as uncomfortable—like things are upside down and I can't understand it. I was confused. Like I used to say, "The things I'm saying in here are happening to me, and what you're saying doesn't fit my situation, my experience."

As we described in chapter 6, there are moments when as a therapist, it is tempting to verbalize or demonstrate contempt for a client's beliefs, especially if they are related to *machista* gender roles. However, we try to never deviate from a respectful approach, perhaps asking how they came to think that way, as if investigating the phenomenon and sincerely trying to understand it. Invariably, the veterans in the group will comment on how they used to hold similar beliefs, but that their opinions have changed over time. Moments like this are excellent avenues for helping clients develop empathy, because often we might ask how the woman or child might feel if perceived or treated in the way that is being advocated by the *machista* man. Because jealousy is often an issue, these conversations can also segue into discussions about insecurity in relationships and how to handle it more effectively both cognitively and behaviorally. Sometimes the opportunity arises to delve more deeply into the origin of the insecurity, opening the door for the discussion of a client's childhood. Although the program does not dwell for long on such topics because of time constraints, referrals to individual therapy often follow from such disclosures.

As well as allowing other men in the group to intervene with their own experiences, we often use metaphors and examples to pave the way to new and different ways of approaching masculinity. Like any thinking and feeling human being, assuming that our clients are not antisocial and completely devoid of the desire to change, we find that men become convinced over time, with much patience, of the advantages of being a "different kind" of man. Once they can see that their lives are improved by these changes, they are less threatened and even become sold on the idea. They can begin to put it into practice without the gnawing fear that their authority or power will be eroded and destroyed. Rather, it will be transformed into a new closeness and intimacy with their partners and children that they have never experienced before. Or, in the event that that relationship is beyond repair, as stated before, their next relationship will be healthier and more mutual.

Sexual Abuse in Relationships

We included the topic of sexual abuse in relationships in its own special session, based on the information our participants gave us about its frequency. Although statistics do not show that there is more sexual abuse among Latina women in the United States than in the general population, our clinical experience in working with Latina victims of IPV teaches us that this issue is a pressing one, and not unusual among victims of physical abuse. We have already mentioned the troubling prevalence of sexual violence among Peruvian women in chapter 1, as reported by WHO in 2005. Many of our Latina clients do not define forced sex in marriage as sexual abuse, just as their male partners do not. They too may believe that marital rights include sex as an obligation of the wife, and that force is acceptable, if unpleasant, if the man is not "getting his due." They also fear that they will lose him to another woman if they refuse frequent sexual relations. We know of many cases where men use this as a threat to their fidelity, as if temporary sexual abstinence, even for a good reason, were an intolerable imposition on their sexual needs and drives.

We have found that it makes the men in our groups uncomfortable to enter into detailed accounts of potential types of sexual abuse, as some programs do. The expression of shock on their faces when using material from one of these programs in the past was enough to convince us that less detail is culturally desirable. In our program, we define sexual abuse from the outset as any undesired sexual contact, which covers everything. We invite them to come up with examples of their own, and of course, we use quotations from our participants to initiate the discussion, such as this one from Ignacio:

> Maybe the man wants to have sex anytime, without taking into account that the other person doesn't want to, or is tired, or for whatever reason. I think it's important to talk about it because I think many of us abuse our partners in this way. They think, *I'm married, you're mine,* and they don't wait for explanations, they just go ahead. But maybe we haven't got much information about this, about what that really is. The woman is raped in reality, because you're saying, *She's my wife, I provide for her, and I have the right. She has to accept.* But they teach us there that a woman is not a toy, not a doll. She's a person the same as you are.

We do not exact confessions from the men in our groups, as we outlined in the last chapter. But we do want to ascertain that they have fully understood the emotional and legal ramifications of sexual abuse in their relationship. We think it is important to take into account the frequent ignorance on their part that forced sex is "not OK." Many are not pretending they don't know this, as they may have been brought up to genuinely believe that sex in marriage is their right whenever they want it. When a therapist is sensitive to this, the topic is easier to approach, without demonstrations of shock and distaste that can alienate and shame the group. Again, a matter-of-fact psychoeducational approach works well. When the men are open and listening, it is vital to introduce empathy for the abused woman into this discussion, as well as the enormous difficulty a woman has in overcoming her anger and hurt when sexual force is employed against her.

Discrimination

Basing ourselves on the literature regarding the emotional difficulties that people of non-Anglo ethnicity experience in the United States because of the experience of discrimination, we chose to explore this concept in our interviews. It is not a major focus of our program, because our intention is not to turn therapy sessions into places where complaints against the system are prominent, or where men are encouraged to see themselves as victims. Our ultimate goal is to help men to take responsibility for themselves, develop a deeper estimation of themselves and respect for others, and learn coping skills that will lead to greater resilience and effectiveness at home and at work, without the use of violence.

Nevertheless, the session on discrimination has the advantage of exploring and validating their experience as people of color and deepening their sense of belonging in the group. We are also aware of the many levels of discrimination a person may face, whether in the United States or in their home country, such as social class, religion, employment status, sexual orientation, and so forth, as well as ethnic group.

We begin the session with quotes from the participants and then move to define discrimination, ethnicity, and gender. We cite civil and religious statements on the rights of immigrants and discuss the difficulties immigrants may have, as well as their inalienable rights as human beings. The main intention of this session is to move the focus to discriminatory attitudes and behaviors in ourselves, including questions designed to make clients aware when they are discriminating against women. We found that many of our clients have never reflected on or even noticed discrimination against women consciously; Blas, for example:

> I think once we talked about discrimination against women in the group, and it made me think a lot. *Why do we do that to them? It doesn't make sense. They have the same feelings that any one of us has.* After that I tried to give her more support, more respect. I was thinking, *She feels the same things that I feel.*

The following are some of the questions the men reflect on and discuss in the group: *How did you feel when you were discriminated against? How would you feel if that happened to your children or your wife? How do you think a woman feels when she is discriminated against solely because of her gender? Do you think our discussion will make you stop and think the next time you are about to discriminate against your partner, just because she is female? How would you feel if some other man discriminated against your daughter, just because she is female?* Men respond thoughtfully to these questions, and for some, like Blas, it is really the first time they have reflected on it in an explicit way.

Immigration and Marital Conflict

Because adjusting to a new culture is a challenge for all immigrants, we deal with the topic in a special section of our treatment program. The session begins, as usual, with some of the powerful citations of our participants about changes and conflicts in couple relations due to immigration. Because Ignacio's explanation is humorous (in the original, in any case), it makes a fitting introduction to a delicate and often painful topic that challenges the men in our groups in the very heart of their identity:

> I don't think that all Mexican women change. But I've heard a lot of men in the class say, "Ever since I brought my wife here, my wife totally changed. She was no longer the woman I knew when we lived in Mexico. As soon as she got her papers, she wasn't worth a damn."

We briefly define migration, gender roles, acculturation, assimilation, marginalization, and biculturalism (Berry, Poortinga, Segall, & Dasen, 2002) so that the men understand the various ways that one can adjust to a new culture. We explore their beliefs, thoughts, doubts, and emotions related to the experience of immigration and all the changes that it brings, especially with their partner and children. This topic is of great interest to the men and elicits considerable discussion, as well as occasional disagreements. We often ask the men what they have gained by emigrating from their country of origin. We ask them if they would mind losing some of the freedoms or benefits that they have gained here. This serves as an entrée to asking them if they think their partners have gained anything, and whether they think that, if they were in their place, they would want to let go of the advances that women have achieved in this society and are working hard to achieve in virtually every other society on earth. This seems to broaden their perspective a little and get them thinking about the issue of change. A colleague with great expertise in cultural adaptation, Oliva Espín (1994), suggests asking if in their village they ever used a burro. What was useful and normal there may not be so here, where one gets around in a car—and vice versa.

Cognitive and emotional flexibility builds resilience. Thus our discussions on immigration bring out the courage and adaptability of our clients, and also challenge them to let go of some of their more rigid gender role expectations, beliefs that are tethering them to attitudes and behaviors that do not fit with their new status. From this, we can segue into global changes, where gender equality is rapidly becoming the goal in many nations, including Latin America. Because many therapists who facilitate Spanish groups are also immigrants and have perhaps shared similar battles to make sense of a foreign land and value system, their input can also be of great value to the men in the group.[4] We consider it of prime importance to support and understand the difficulty Latino men in our groups have in grasping and accepting the idea of gender equality and to avoid an approach that would trivialize the challenge it is for many of them. Perhaps the female therapist's example of respect and empathy for the clients can be a major factor in men accepting the principle of equality.

Parent Education

In chapter 8, we explored the passion the participants demonstrated for the topic of parenting and how completely central it had been as an outcome in their IPV group, if any focus had been placed on it. Based on their enthusiasm and insistence, we decided to make parent education an important and integral part of our IPV treatment program. Realizing the need to teach from several angles, and the men's need to internalize many new attitudes and skills over time, we decided to introduce parent education early in the program in one session devoted to the effects of IPV on children. Later in the program we devote four entire sessions to parent education, including specific techniques to discipline children without the use of force, based on positive reinforcement and respect for the child and the parents' needs. We then include more material dispersed throughout six more sessions later in the program, entitled The Child's Corner, that continues to teach and reinforce effective skills for our clients to develop as fathers. Men are encouraged to share these parenting materials with their partners if they are still together. Homework assignments include actually trying on new behaviors with their children and then problem solving with the group at the next session.

Men respond with deep interest to these sessions and bring many complex parenting issues to the table. These conversations and real-life problems are a fertile ground for the clients to develop empathy for their children and for their companions in the group, as well as to compare their new style with the usual harshness of their father's style. Some are afraid their children will not respect them if they are not gruff and distant. However, with time they experience the positive response of their children to a kinder and more empathic style, and this convinces them better than any lecture could. As Leonardo described,

> Now, if they need something or something happens to them, they have the trust to come to me and tell me. I've changed as a father one hundred percent. I'm not saying I'm that perfect, but in comparison to how I was before, I'd say one hundred percent different. We try to be perfect but we'll never achieve that. Before, as a father I'd come home from work—"There's the money, do what you want with it"—like I didn't care about anything. I've tried to analyze it; I think it was just ignorance. I thought by working and bringing home money that was enough, but it really isn't. It's ignorance, not knowing that children need more than money.

Because the skills for being a good father should theoretically generalize into being a good partner, we do not consider time spent on parenting as time withdrawn from the issue of IPV. We responded to the feedback of the participants and are training them to be nonviolent and respectful in their dealings with their children, something most of them never experienced in their childhood. In a new prevention project, we are currently using the strategy of "motivating men through their children" (see Lucio's comment at the outset of this chapter) to prevent IPV among Latino men in San Diego City schools, through a no-cost 12-week "parent education" class attended by Latino couples. There they learn, and practice as a couple, parenting strategies such as respect, communication, anger management, interventions to improve attachment, and training in human rights that can just as easily be practiced in their romantic relationship.[3] Our hope is that these skills will in fact generalize to their intimate relationship, and more so because they practice them together in a safe environment.

Spirituality and Violence Prevention

In previous chapters we established the importance of spiritual beliefs in the lives of the Latino men in our study. Based on what they told us about their desire to bring spirituality into the program, we decided to create a section called Spirituality and Violence Prevention. The topic of spirituality is also discussed at the outset of the program in the session called Seeking a Different Path: Quetzalcóatl, the Hero's Journey, which we have already described in chapter 7. The need for this session early in the program was suggested by the theme that emerged from the interviews, which we called Decision to Change, discussed in detail in past chapters. All of the participants described a moment, at different times in their programs, when they made the decision to change because they realized they needed and wanted to. They described it as a personal challenge, a movement toward maturity. We found similar ideas in Tello's work (Tello, 1998) about The Noble Man Searching for Balance, where the true characteristics of masculinity, as outlined by the Aztec elders at the time of the Spanish conquest, are listed as dignified, a protector, responsible, nurturing, spiritual, faithful, respectful, friendly, caring, sensitive, and trustworthy.

Thus, the first session is dedicated to Aztec spirituality, the hero's journey, and masculine identity, and to the universal quest for transformation that is the mark of the conscious life. Men in our groups respond to this session with enthusiasm and have expressed the desire to initiate their new companions into the journey by specifically requesting that the story be retold during the year.

When spiritual or religious issues come up in the group apart from the session material, we treat the speaker with respect and interest and elicit feedback and advice from other members. We learned from the participants not to stifle the religious and existential questions of men in the groups but to welcome them as part of the process of healing from violence, as Rogelio wished his therapist had done:

> I would have liked us to talk about some religion. Because when you're going to make a change you need to hold onto something. You have to have a solid foundation, whatever it is. Something that really helps you. Whether it's the program or something else. It would be helpful to bring in some religion. To talk about the spiritual side.

We are also careful to set clear limits, without any trace of hostility, when the occasional man demonstrates a tendency to wish to proselytize in the group. This activity is inappropriate for the group setting, as it is time consuming, off topic, and potentially uncomfortable for most, if not all, of the group members.

In the section on spirituality, we included a session that discusses the current official and community viewpoints of Judaism and Christianity on family violence. For the sake of simplicity and because the large majority of the men we work with self-identify as Christians of some denomination, we do not enter into the beliefs or statements of other religions such as Islam, Buddhism, or Hinduism. The material quotes from Sacred Scriptures as well as from teaching materials published by various groups that endorse a nonviolent and loving family as essential to the practice of the religion. We begin the discussion by acknowledging that synagogues and churches have not always defended or protected the rights of women and children, and that they have often been slow to respond to the urgent need to eradicate violence in the family. We point out that for most denominations this has changed in the past 30 or so years. Jewish congregations actively denounce IPV. In most (but not all) Christian denominations there is a growing awareness of the damage to the family and to the institution of marriage itself caused by IPV. In our material we quote statements from an Evangelical marriage preparation program and from Catholic authorities such as the Latin American Conference of Catholic Bishops and Pope John Paul II:

> Authentic conjugal love presupposes and requires that a man have a profound respect for the equal dignity of his wife: "You are not her master," writes St. Ambrose, "but her husband; she was not given to you to be your slave, but your wife....Reciprocate her attentiveness to you and be grateful to her for her love." With his wife a man should live "a very

special form of personal friendship." As for the Christian, he is called upon to develop a new attitude of love, manifesting towards his wife a charity that is both gentle and strong like that which Christ has for the Church. (*Familiaris consortio*; Pope John Paul II, 1981)

Men respond thoughtfully to this material. It removes the wiggle room some men still like to claim by quoting Scripture as a pretext for male dominance, machismo, and abuse. The quotations we used stress principles such as love, dignity, and respect, and as such fit very well with the message of the program overall. As José remarked, "Going to class is like going to church. You get rid of your bad thoughts."

The second session devoted to spirituality was also suggested by the participants, when several of them remarked that they wanted to learn about local resources from their companions in the group. Raúl commented,

> Many of the men tell us that they are going to the kind of weekend [Marriage Encounter] that I told you, and they share what they've done and what they're doing. I think we should talk about it because there's a lot of help and support out there. It's like a mix, where you do a little bit here and a little bit there, it's like a mix that makes you wake up and react.

We assign the men to find out about resources from their church (we have been surprised by how many of our clients attend church regularly), so that they can share them with others. Giving men permission to talk about their faith in the context of their family life creates a different atmosphere in the group room. In our groups we have never experienced any difficulties with members trying to push their religion on others, perhaps because we explain the purpose of the session, and its limits, from the outset.

Our third session often extends into two sessions, because the topic is forgiveness, which is presented from two standpoints, forgiving others and asking forgiveness. Based on Enright's work on forgiveness (2001) and its place in psychological health, it is not a specifically Christian model. Clients explore the why of forgiveness, as well as steps in learning how to forgive and how to ask forgiveness of those we love. We decided to start off with forgiving rather than asking forgiveness because so many of our clients carry heavy loads of resentment, usually toward their fathers and sometimes their mothers as well, due to childhoods filled with abuse and neglect. We were initially surprised to learn that one of the things our clients find most difficult to forgive is that their partner called the police on them and had them arrested, unleashing a torrent of negative legal and financial consequences. This attitude can be found in clients even after many months of treatment, so we have now learned to take it in stride and explore it dispassionately with them. It takes quite a leap for men to realize that they are the ones who "caused" what happened when they were arrested for their violent behavior. Again, we find it most effective and productive of reflection when one of the veterans of the group points this out to the outraged, "victimized" client. This is not to say that we have never heard stories where the wife's violence appeared to match or exceed the husband's. But these are the exception, not the rule.

Next comes the issue of asking forgiveness sincerely from one's partner and children, when appropriate. Sometimes the man is unable to do so because of a restraining order forbidding all contact. Although we fully understand and support the need for such orders, in some cases they do prevent men from being able to take full responsibility for what they did to the victim and to come full circle as they complete their treatment by sincerely expressing their sorrow and asking for pardon. If they are unable to do so in person, we usually recommend that they send a message through a close relative conveying their repentance. The partner needs to hear it as much as the client needs to say it, even though she may not believe it is sincere. Of course, there will be occasions when it is not. We do not pretend to have a 100% success rate. However, we do offer these interventions to the many men who can benefit from them.

THE PILOT PROGRAM

We piloted the program with Latino men mandated to IPV groups over 4 years, encouraging the many men who cycled into the program to comment on the clarity of vocabulary and concepts throughout, as mentioned above. They were very willing to share their opinions and to make the program as user-friendly as it now is. The demographics of the men in the pilot program were very similar to the men we initially surveyed. By staying in contact with their partners over the years, we have been able to ascertain that the rate of recidivism is very low. In all cases, ongoing alcohol abuse has been connected to relapse into partner violence. A formal treatment outcome study to provide empirical evidence beyond the anecdotal evidence we already have is in the planning stages in the state of Arizona.

Williams and Becker (1994) found a higher attrition rate in mandated group attendance on the part of minority groups. They theorized that members of these groups receive treatment that may not be appropriate to the reality of their situation, and as a result, drop out. Over the first year of our pilot study (when the attrition rate was calculated), the opposite was found. Interestingly, the attrition rate for English groups with mixed ethnic attendance at the same agency in Southern California was 75%, that is, only 1 in 4 men completed the program, and 46% of these men dropped out in the first 3 months. In contrast, the attrition rate for the Spanish-language group using our program was only 26%, with most men dropping out in the first 3 months as well—thus 3 out of 4 men completed their therapy. This pattern of completion continued throughout the 4 years of the pilot.

WHERE DO WE GO FROM HERE?

The interest in culturally appropriate interventions and in prevention of IPV in the Latino community is on the rise in the United States and in Latin America. Together we can make a substantial difference in the incidence of IPV, and thus reduce the suffering of so many women and children. In the United States there are many initiatives and professionals who are dedicated to reducing IPV among Latinos. Julia Perilla, Etiony Aldarondo, Fernando Medcros, Raúl Caetano, Glenda Kaufman-Kantor, and Jana Jasinski are among the psychologists who have conducted research on the Latino population and IPV. The Alianza is a collaborative network dedicated to the elimination of IPV in the Latino community:

> The National Latino Alliance for the Elimination of Domestic Violence (Alianza) is part of a national effort to address the domestic violence needs and concerns of under-served populations. It represents a growing network of Latina and Latino advocates, practitioners, researchers, community activists, and survivors of domestic violence. Alianza's mission is to promote understanding, initiate and sustain dialogue, and generate solutions that move toward the elimination of domestic violence affecting Latino communities, with an understanding of the sacredness of all relations and communities. (Alianza, 2007)

Ricardo Carrillo, Felipe Antonio Ramírez Hernández, and Jerry Tello have written important books on the topic of Latino IPV and have contributed to our understanding of how to work clinically with Latino partner abusive men. Working closely with Arizona authorities, Ricardo Contreras of Yuma, Arizona, has created the AIN Counseling Center, where Latino partner abusive men can receive state-of-the-art treatment while research is simultaneously conducted on effective therapy and other aspects of IPV in the Latino population.

In Latin America, too, governmental and nongovernmental organizations are hard at work coming to terms with the problem in their countries and are working, sometimes nationally and other times internationally, to create solutions. Among the many organizations involved are the Pan American Health Organization, UNIFEM of the United Nations, and the World Health Organization, as well as innumerable nongovernmental organizations devoted to the victims of IPV and their children. In Mexico, nongovernmental organizations such as Hombres por la Equidad, Movimiento de Hombres por Relaciones Equitativas Sin Violencia, Corazonar: Abriendo Senderos hacia la Reconciliación, and Alternativas para la Equidad y la Diversidad are exploring ways to effectively help men to challenge their former views of masculinity and violence.

Students and young professionals in Latin America are increasingly interested in IPV and in how they can impact the suffering it causes for so many of their clients, patients, and colleagues. When we are teaching in Mexico and Peru, we are always inspired by their passion and receptivity to learning and adapting interventions and prevention programs to local needs. Men's groups are taking on the challenge of informing men in their countries of the need to change. Francisco Cervantes of Corazonar in Mexico City tells men that, increasingly, they will remain alone unless they are willing to change their attitudes and behaviors. Women are just not willing to put up with what their mothers, grandmothers, and ancestors had little choice of repudiating. Because of the complexity of IPV and the need to intervene politically, legally, therapeutically, and socially to attend to the needs of abused women and children and abusing men, as well as the violent society that nourishes this behavior, we do not have the luxury of acting alone or in a vacuum. We must work together to inculcate in every Latino man, especially the most at risk, that to be a real man he does not have to be violent. On the contrary, we can be instrumental in helping him and his sons to learn "a different way to be a man" and in doing so, to open the door to a new way of living with those he loves most.

NOTES

1. *Domestic Violence 2000*, by our esteemed colleague Dr. David Wexler of the Relationship Training Institute, San Diego. This program was recently updated and published in 2006 by Norton as STOP Domestic Violence.
2. Men respond positively to Aztec teachings, which expose them to pre-Colombian influences that, although they are unfamiliar, seem to resonate with the group. Furthermore, Aztec writing and poetry has exceptional beauty and cadence.
3. As a part of the Aztec wedding ceremony, the groom tied his clothes to the bride's.
4. The first author lived in India in her 20s and always recalls the cognitive leap that was required to imagine arranged marriage as the norm. Even after recognizing its merits and function, she could nevertheless never conceive of an arranged marriage for herself. This has helped her to be tolerant of others' values and beliefs and the immense difficulty sometimes involved in accepting a custom or belief different from one's own entrenched values, which somehow just seem "better."
5. This project, which is being evaluated for its effectiveness, is sponsored by the Club de Papás and is funded by the Parker Foundation and the California Endowment.

APPENDIX A

Lessons Learned

It occurred to us that it might be helpful to have to have a "lessons learned" appendix at the end of this book as a quick reference and summary for the working professional. Consequently we provide brief summaries of practical tips and pointers on various topics in the form of bullet points, for therapists who deal with Latino men in general and with the issue of IPV in particular.

Typologies of Partner Abusive Men (U.S. Research)

1. Generally violent/antisocial
2. Family only
3. Dysphoric/borderline
4. Low-level antisocial

Major Risk Factors for IPV Perpetration (U.S. Research)

- History of violence in childhood, with witnessing father-to-mother violence being the strongest predictor
- Low income/low academic achievement
- Use and abuse of alcohol

Other Risk Factors for IPV Perpetration (U.S. Research)

- Insecure or fearful attachment to the partner
- Lower age, usually under 30
- Low self-esteem
- High levels of marital conflict and low levels of marital satisfaction
- Generalized aggression
- Patriarchal gender roles, in subsection of more severely violent men

Major Results of the Survey Conducted as Part I of Our Research

- 89% of the men in Spanish-language IPV groups in San Diego County were of Mexican origin.
- Only 29% of respondents were under the age of 30, but 65% of the total sample were ages 35 or younger.
- 37% of respondents had a sixth-grade education or less, and 49% of respondents had an eighth-grade education or less. Only 18% of the men had completed high school or more.
- 45% of the men had witnessed moderate to severe IPV in their family of origin.
- 51% of respondents reported being abused by their parents.
- 70% of respondents lived under the federal poverty line, based on number of family members.
- 53% of the respondents had committed IPV before but had not been arrested.
- 37% of respondents had been arrested at least once for driving intoxicated.
- 44% reported being drunk during the IPV incident.
- 57% of the men's children were either present in the room or in the house at the time of the IPV incident.

Characteristics of the In-Depth Interview Participants

- 83% of the interview participants met criteria for alcohol abuse or dependence.
- 60% had witnessed IPV as children.
- 75% of the interviewees had been recipients of child abuse.
- 92% were exposed to frequent violence in their community as children.

In-Depth Interview Results

Ecosystemic Strengths of the Participants: Values That Could Have Been Protective Factors (but were not)

- Positive aspects of the male gender role (responsibility for family, protection)
- *Familismo*—strong attachment and loyalty to family
- *Respeto*—deferential behavior on the basis of social position
- Importance of spiritual values, in most cases Catholicism, in offering a framework for respectful and loving family life

Latino Research Participants' Justifications for their Violence (with corresponding theoretical explanations commonly found in the literature on IPV in the United States)

- Normalization of violence in the environment of origin [social learning theory]
- Negative aspects of traditional male gender roles, especially machismo [sociocultural/feminist theory]
- Psychological dysfunction related to early trauma, including child abuse, witnessing IPV, and fragile sense of self related to abandonment in childhood [clinical model, self psychology theory, attachment theory]
- Maladaptive coping skills, alcoholism, lack of relationship skills, and uncontrolled anger [cognitive-behavioral theory]
- Environmental stressors, such as financial and acculturation stress [ecosystemic theory]

Themes That Emerged From the Qualitative Interviews

- Violence in the Family of Origin: Normalizing the Experience: They learned to be violent by being frequently exposed to violence in their families and communities.
- Traditional Gender Roles as the Bedrock of Violence Toward Women:
  - Participants identified the negative male gender roles with which they were socialized and connected them to the attitude that makes IPV acceptable.
  - Participants described machismo as a special case of traditional male gender roles.
  - Many participants identified machismo as being involved in their IPV incident.

- Participants identified the traditional female gender roles that they were socialized to expect.
- Participants identified parenting problems related to male gender roles.
- Today's Perpetrator Is Often Yesterday's Victim: Child Abuse and Neglect in the Family of Origin
  - Participants described emotional and physical abuse perpetrated on them by their fathers.
  - Some spoke of emotional and physical abuse by their mothers as well.
  - Most participants witnessed IPV in their families of origin.
  - Some related childhood trauma and abandonment leading to a fragile sense of self.
- Maladaptive Coping Skills
  - Alcoholism
    - 50% of participants had alcoholic fathers.
    - Most had problems with alcohol, and one-third were under the influence at the time of the violent incident.
  - Lack of Relationship Skills
    - Arguing and poor communication
    - Jealousy
    - Extramarital affairs by partner
    - Partner was also violent, usually out of retaliation
    - Partners were verbally abusive to them
  - Uncontrolled Anger
    - Stemming from fear of loss
    - Sense of being disrespected, dishonored, betrayed, or ignored.
    - Jealousy over a real or perceived extramarital relationship their partner was having
    - Anger springing largely from gender role expectations their partner was "violating"
- Environmental Stressors
  - Financial Stress
    - Most participants mentioned the financial struggles of men in their groups and the difficulties they can provoke in the relationship.
  - Acculturation Stress
    - Most participants reported difficulties stemming from immigration and the process of acculturation, sometimes difficulties specifically with their partner and the way that she had changed.

- Discrimination
  - Most participants had not experienced discrimination themselves in the United States. All were aware that many other immigrants in Latino IPV groups had experienced the negative effects of discrimination.
- Group Experience
  - The participants believed that IPV treatment groups specifically for Latinos, in Spanish, were more acceptable and effective for them than heterogeneous (mixed ethnicity) groups in English.
  - The participants believed that audiovisual material used in groups for Latino men should be in Spanish and appropriate to their socioeconomic status.
  - The participants were more concerned about language fluency and cultural knowledge than about the ethnicity of their therapists.
  - Cultural stereotyping was specifically mentioned as painful to them, and as putting an end to group disclosure.
  - The participants took varying amounts of time to overcome their resistance to being mandated to treatment. Therapists should expect this resistance and learn to work with it, rather than against it, by not forcing participation and self-disclosure prematurely.
  - All the participants reached a point in their treatment where they themselves decided that they needed to change, and from that time on they began to draw benefits from their therapy. Motivating clients to change, then, is of prime importance.
  - *Respeto* from the group and therapist was a vital part of their positive experience.
  - The participants found all the program content useful and appropriate.

Characteristics of Cultural Competence for Therapists of Any Ethnicity (Sue & Sue, 2002)

- Respect for differences
- Awareness of one's own personal values and heritage
- Sensitivity to circumstances
- Awareness of one's own racist attitudes, beliefs, and feelings
- Specific knowledge of the ethnic group being served
- Understanding the ramifications of the clients' sociopolitical standing as a minority

- Awareness of institutional barriers to accessing services for minority clients

Postmodern Views on Cultural Competence and Co-constructing Meaning With Latino Clients (Taylor, Gambourg, Rivera, & Laureano, 2006)

- Cultural competence involves negotiating and co-constructing meaning with clients.
- When speaking Spanish, be aware of differences in meaning of words, from country to country and even within country.
- Therapists should be flexible and learn from their clients.
- Therapists should monitor themselves during the clinical conversation.
- Therapists should be aware that in Latin America, issues of social class are more predominant than issues of race, unlike with Latinos born in the United States, where race is an important issue.
- The potential for culture clash concerning the themes of gender and power can be mitigated by constant self-monitoring and self-awareness, as well as by an attitude of openness and tolerance.
- Therapists should not allow their own thoughts, feelings, and beliefs to interfere with issues of immigration and acculturation.

Participants' Views on Therapist Behaviors

- Usefulness of clear and structured teaching methods
- Unhelpfulness of an authoritarian, confrontational, and unfocused approach
- Clinical style of the therapist: self-confidence, calmness, *respeto*, *simpatía*, kindness, understanding
- Therapeutic skills: ability to self-disclose, to listen attentively, to use humor, and to be willing to wait for self-disclosure from clients

Treatment Outcomes Reported by Participants

- Improved communication skills
- Ability to manage anger
- Greater flexibility in gender roles; understanding and "trying on" gender equality
- Overcoming addiction to alcohol
- Learning to be nurturing fathers

Culturally Specific Topics to Include in Treatment

- An emphasis on parenting education
- Emphasis on discussion of rigid male gender roles, especially machismo

- Acknowledgment of discrimination against immigrants and women
- Discussion of changing gender roles stemming from immigration
- Open discussion of sexual abuse in relationships
- Inclusion of spirituality as it relates to the prevention of IPV

Policy Implications

- Educate Latino families about the legal, social, and economic consequences of IPV, through radio and television public service announcements, as well as through community and religious organizations.
- Educate the Latino public regarding the importance of preventing IPV, by offering them the skills they need to manage affect and improve communication.
- Emphasize the intimate connection between alcohol abuse and IPV and offer treatment solutions in the community.
- Teach Latino families about the potential consequences on their children of witnessing IPV, including on their future behavior.
- Therapists and law enforcement officials who are engaged in this work should share their knowledge and experience with their colleagues in the southern border region, as well as in other areas of Latin America, and come up with ways to work together and learn from each other.

Cultural Additions Made to the IPV Treatment Program *Sin Golpes*

Welland & Wexler (2007). *Sin Golpes, como transformar la respuesta violenta del hombre en la pareja y la familia.* Mexico City: Editorial Pax.

- Quotations about their personal experience of IPV from the men who participated in the research
- Quotations about their personal experience as children from the participants
- A thorough exploration of the influence of machismo in their relationship
- The use of cultural stories that encapsulate important themes
- A discussion of human rights and equality using documents from the Mexican Commission on Human Rights
- A discussion of Judeo-Christian religions as related to prevention of IPV, citing original sources, with an emphasis on participants' spiritual traditions
- Particular areas of emphasis that run throughout the program, especially parenting skills and how children are affected by IPV

- Frequent reviews of basic categories of abuse and reviews of the skills that clients are learning
- A special intervention for the holidays, as an inoculation against high-risk behavior
- Advocacy of provision of economic, social, and spiritual resource lists for group members

Areas of Special Emphasis in *Sin Golpes*

Machismo

- Tolerant, nonstereotyping, and gradual therapeutic approach
- Frequent use of direct quotes from men in research study and group discussions
- Addition of section "Human Rights and Masculinity," incorporating statements by Mexican Commission for Human Rights, regarding universal rights, family violence, and women's rights

Sexual Abuse in Relationships

- Acknowledgment of the frequency of this problem
- Group discussion of importance of respect and mutuality
- Addition of section on sexual abuse by Mexican Commission for Human Rights

Discrimination

- Exploration and validation of clients' experience; increase coping skills
- Definitions; civil and religious statements on the rights of immigrants
- Expand experience to include understanding of discrimination against women
- Increase empathy for experience of wife/partner

Immigration and Couple Conflict

- Acknowledgment of conflicts inherent in immigration, especially changes in gender role expectations for female partner, as well as male
- Use of direct quotations from men in research study
- Definitions of concepts related to acculturation and gender roles
- Open discussion of difficulties men face in negotiating what may be a major challenge to their very identity as men in an intimate relationship

Parent Education

- Most participants lacked a role model for being effective and loving father.
- Early session devoted to the effects of witnessing IPV on children.
- Later four-session parent education section with specific techniques to discipline children without the use of force.
- Further material dispersed throughout six more sessions that continues to teach and reinforce effective parenting skills for clients.
- Homework assignments include experimenting with new behaviors with their children and then problem solving with group.

Spirituality and Violence Prevention

- Decision to Change: personal challenge, movement toward maturity
- Hero's Journey: Aztec spirituality and masculine identity
- Current Monotheistic Religious Viewpoints on Family Violence
- Local Spiritual Resources: Getting connected to support
- Forgiving Others, for example, abusive parents
- Asking Forgiveness, especially of partner and children

Clinical Tips (to be kept in mind throughout treatment)[1]

1. *Respect:* The men in our groups deserve our respect, not for their action, but for their individual stories, which have led them to behave in a desperate and destructive manner. Although we must always stress personal responsibility, it is also essential to recognize our common humanity.
2. *Pacing and leading:* We use this mirroring technique developed by Milton Erickson, reflecting the experience of the client before offering a new perspective or intervention.
3. *Initial resistance:* Men frequently arrive in the group angry and resistant to treatment. We have learned to listen respectfully, and briefly, then move on, avoiding power struggles.
4. *Taking things seriously:* Men learn from the modeling of the therapist that violence against women is not humorous, without the need to sermonize.
5. *The 9 commandments:* These are core principles that are either posted on the wall of the therapy room or read at the beginning of the session, such as the need to take responsibility for our actions, the disapproval of violence, and the inability to control others.

6. *Cofacilitators of both genders:* Although this is not always possible, we do try to create an environment where clients can experience a man and woman collaborating appropriately, problem solving respectfully, and providing a corrective family experience to clients.

7. *Verbal attacks against women:* When clients attack women as a gender, this is confronted immediately. Individual remarks about one's partner's negative attributes are permitted and dealt with in the group; pejorative generalizations are disallowed.

8. *Verbal attacks against the system:* Because there is little, if anything, that the therapist can do about the malfunctions of the system (courts, Child Protective Services, etc.), when clients complain (as some do), we cut short these commentaries by encouraging men to focus on what they *can* change in their lives and in the session.

9. *Treatment failure:* When it is obvious that a member of the group is not progressing as expected, we issue him a warning early in treatment. If no further improvement is demonstrated, the member is asked to leave the program.

10. *Helplessness:* Although power and control are core issues for many offenders, it is helpful for clients to empathize with their personal experience of helplessness, while never absolving them of responsibility for their abusive actions.

11. *Self-disclosure of the therapist:* Normalizing the struggles that we have in our relationships, though in moderation, builds trust and can help clients to react with less explosiveness in their family.

12. *Limitations:* Not every communication technique that is taught will be effective in every situation. We explain to clients that, in the long run, respect and assertiveness are usually the best way to communicate.

Summary of Study (Proyecto Quetzalcóatl) Results on Psychological Characteristics of Latino Partner Abusive Men (Welland et al., in press)

(Note similarities to risk factors in U.S. population of IPV offenders.)

1. *Alcohol abuse:* 50% of the men in treatment for IPV admitted to being under the influence at the time of their arrest. Men in the Anglo population of IPV perpetrators are likely to be alcohol abusers in 50%–60% of cases (Tolman & Bennett, 1990). Alcohol problems were correlated to a history of neglect by the participants' father (.01) but not to trauma symptoms overall.

2. *Drug abuse:* The level of drug abuse across the treatment sample was not so high as to indicate significant problems with drugs in this population on average.
3. *Self-esteem:* Self-esteem was significantly lower in the treatment groups versus the controls. Lower self-esteem was also significantly correlated to insecure and fearful attachment and higher self-esteem was correlated to secure attachment. Our findings on attachment and self-esteem, though simple correlations, suggest that further research may detect the presence of low self-esteem in DV offenders *prior* to the abuse.
4. *Marital satisfaction:* Marital satisfaction was very significantly higher among men in the control group than either of the treatment groups.
5. *Trauma symptoms:* Trauma symptoms *were* correlated with injury by the father, with psychological aggression by the father, minor physical abuse by the father, and neglect by the father, but not the mother. These results lend support to the hypothesis that childhood trauma sets the stage for future DV in some men.
6. *Gender roles:* We found no significant differences in the gender roles of the IPV offenders versus the control group. Only on the factor labeled *Fostering Values and Unity* were men in the control group more likely to exhibit these behaviors with greater frequency. On the *Dominance in the Family* factor, both treatment and control groups scored at the "Almost Always" level, on such behaviors as decision making, establishing rules, controlling family members, providing for the family, and solving problems. This result is more in keeping with what we might have expected in terms of male dominance, yet the behavior of the violent men did not differ significantly from the controls, except that the controls tended to score *higher* on this factor.
7. *Attachment style:* Our data matched investigations conducted with the Anglo population of batterers. Men in the control group, who also evidenced higher marital satisfaction, demonstrated significantly higher levels of secure attachment to their partners. The treatment groups, on the other hand, had significantly higher levels of insecure (anxious-ambivalent) or of fearful (anxious-avoidant) attachment. Insecure attachment was correlated to low self-esteem, psychological aggression, and injury by the father. Fearful attachment was correlated to low self-esteem and injury by the father.
8. *Parent-to-child violence in the family of origin:* The treatment group had received significantly more psychological abuse from the mother than the control group. Psychological aggression

from mother was correlated to physical abuse from both mother and father, and neglect by mother was associated to injury by mother. The treatment groups experienced significantly more psychological abuse and injury by the father than the control group. Psychological abuse by father was also associated with physical abuse, injury, and neglect by the father.

Resources Regarding Latino Spirituality/Religious Beliefs

- Pew Hispanic Center and Pew Forum on Religion & Public Life. (2007). *Changing Faiths: Latinos and the Transformation of American Religion.* http://pewhispanic.org/reports/report. php?ReportID 75
- Espinosa, G., Elizondo, V., & Miranda, J. (2002). *Hispanic Churches in American Public Life: Summary of Findings. Center for the Study of Latino Religion.* http://www.nd.edu/~latino/ research/pubs/HispChurchesEnglishWEB.pdf
- Center for the Study of Latino Catholicism, University of San Diego. http://www.sandiego.edu/theo/Latino-Cath/
- Institute for Latino Studies, University of Notre Dame. http:// www.nd.edu/~latino/Resources on Religion and IPV
- Fortune, M. Faithtrust Institute. http://www.faithtrustinstitute. org/index.php?p Domestic_Violence&s 28
- *When I Call for Help* (2002).United States Conference of Catholic Bishops. http://www.usccb.org/laity/help.shtml

NOTES

1. Reproduced and summarized with the author's permission from *STOP Domestic Violence,* D. B. Wexler, PhD, 2006. These are reproduced in full in *Sin Golpes* in the introduction for the therapist, with the permission of the author and W. W. Norton & Co.

Results of Demographic and Risk Factor Survey of Latino Domestic Violence Group Members

Survey participants were drawn from the following agencies:

Escondido Youth Encounter, Escondido, CA	39
South Bay Community Services, Chula Vista, CA	48
Women's Resource Center, Oceanside, CA	20
YWCA of San Diego County, San Diego, CA	52
Total number of survey participants	159

1. Average age = 34 $SD = 8$
2. In what state of Mexico were you born?

Northern Mexico	19%
Central Mexico	40%
Mexico City	8%
Southern Mexico	18%
United States	4%
Sons of Mexican immigrants	
Cuba	2%
Central America	6%
(El Salvador, Guatemala, Honduras)	
Total first-generation Mexican participants	85%

3. In what state of Mexico was your father born?

Data shows some internal migration within Mexico, and a few men whose parents immigrated to the United States. The majority of fathers came from same place as the son.

4. In what state of Mexico was your mother born?

Data shows some internal migration within Mexico, and a few men whose parents immigrated to the United States. The majority of mothers came from the same place as the son.

5. Place you were born:
   a. A big city   41%   Urban 56%
   b. A small city 15%
   c. A town   32%   Rural 44%
   d. A village   12%

6. Place you were raised in:
   a. A big city   42%   Urban 60%
   b. A small city 18%
   c. A town   28%   Rural 40%
   d. A village   12%

7. How many years of education do you have?
   Average = 8 $SD = 4$

8. What is your religion?
   a. Catholic   80%
   b. Christian, but not Catholic 15%
   c. Other   1%
   d. No religion   3%

9. How important is your religion in your daily life?
   a. Very important   51%
   b. Important   38%
   c. Not very important   11%
   d. It does not matter to me at all   0%

10. What language did you speak in your home as a child?
    a. Spanish   92%
    b. Mixteco   2%
    c. Zapoteco   0.6%
    d. Nahuatl   0%
    e. Other (please specify)   0%
    f. English and Spanish   3%
    g. Spanish and Mixteco   2%

11. Did your father drink when you were a child or adolescent?
    a. Yes, frequently   28%
    b. Yes, sometimes   49%
    c. No   23%

12. Did your father hit, slap, punch, kick, or otherwise abuse your mother when you were a child or adolescent?
    a. Yes, frequently   14%
    b. Yes, sometimes 30%
    c. No   56%

13. Did your parents hit, slap, punch, kick, or otherwise abuse you when you were a child?
    a. Yes, frequently   9%
    b. Yes, sometimes 42%
    c. No   49%

14. What language do you mostly speak in your home now?
    a. Spanish   71%
    b. English   8%
    c. Mixteco   0.6%
    d. Zapoteco   0%
    e. Nahuatl   0%
    f. Other (not specified) 0.6%
    g. English and Spanish 19%

15. In your home as a child, what was the status of your mother?
    a. Equal to my father in power and authority 51%
    b. More power and authority than my father 10%
    c. Less power and authority than my father 28%
    d. No power and authority at all   10%

16. Your present marital status. Please check correct item.
    a. Married, living with wife   44%
    b. Separated   20%
    c. Divorced   5%
    d. Cohabiting   26%
    e. Remarried   0.6%
    f. Not in a relationship at present 5%

17. Do you have children? Yes 94% No 6%
If yes, how many? Average = 2.6 $SD = 2$

18. Do you have stepchildren? Yes 31% No 69%
If yes, how many? Average = 0.5 $SD = 1$

19. How long have you and your wife/partner lived together? Please specify.
Average in years = 10 $SD = 7$

20. How many years of education does your wife/partner have?
Average = 8 $SD = 3$

21. Have you hit, slapped, punched, kicked, or otherwise abused your partner before, but were not arrested for it?
    a. Yes, in this country   46%

      b.   Yes, in my country of origin   4%
      c.   Yes, in both countries   4%
      d.   No   46%

22.   Were you ever arrested for IPV in Mexico?
      a.   Yes   1%
      b.   No   99%

23.   How long have you lived in the United States?
      Average in years = 15 $SD = 7$

24.   What is your immigration status? Please check correct item.
      a.   U.S. citizen   12%
      b.   Legal permanent resident   64%
      c.   Temporary work permit   11%
      d.   Undocumented   13%

25.   How long has your wife/partner lived in the United States?
      Average in years = 14 $SD = 9$

26.   What kind of job do you have? (Please specify)
      a.   Agriculture   13%
      Construction   21%
      Factory/Maintenance   18%
      Food Service   15%
      Retail   4%
      Technical   6%
      b.   Unemployed   15%
      No reply   8%

27.   What is your personal annual income?
      a. $0–5,000   10%
      b. $5,001–10,000   27%
      c. $10,001–15,000   26%
      d. $15,001–20,000   19%
      e. $20,001–25,000   11%
      f.   More than $25,000   7%

28.   What kind of job does your wife have? (Please specify)
      a.   Child Care   0.6%
      Cleaning   11%
      Factory   4%
      Food Service   4%
      Retail   5%
      Technical/Professional   5%
      b.   Unemployed (employed in the home)   67%
      No reply   3%

29.   What is your wife's annual income?
      a. $0–5,000   43%
      b. $5,001–10,000   13%

c. $10,001–15,000   26%
d. $15,001–20,000   14%
e. $20,001–25,000   3%
f. More than $25,000   1%

30. What is the *total* income of your present family, including your working children's wages that they contribute to the family?
a. $0–5,000   7%
b. $5,001–10,000   17%
c. $10,001–15,000   28%
d. $15,001–20,000   18%
e. $20,001–25,000   15%
f. More than $25,000   15%

31. How many people live in your home?
a. 1–2   22%
b. 3–5   63%
c. 6–9   15%
d. 10–12   0%
e. More than 12 0%

32. Do your parents live with you?
a. Yes   3%
b. No   97%

33. Do your wife's parents live with you?
a. Yes   8%
b. No   92%

34. Do other adult relatives or roommates live with you?
a. Yes   18%
b. No   82%

35. Do your parents, siblings, and/or other close relatives live in the San Diego area?
a. Yes   65%
b. No   35%

36. Do you have compadres and other close friends who live in the San Diego area?
a. Yes   73%
b. No   27%

37. Do you feel sad and depressed?
a. No   37%
b. Yes, sometimes   58%
c. Yes, most of the time 4%

38. Do you feel anxious and worried?
a. No   36%
b. Yes, sometimes   59%
c. Yes, most of the time 5%

39. Do you argue or have disagreements with your wife/partner?
    a. No   43%
    b. Yes, sometimes   53%
    c. Yes, most of the time   3%
40. How well do you understand and speak English and/or Spanish?
    a. I can only understand and speak in Spanish.   23%
    b. I can understand and speak in English
       and Spanish about the same.   28%
    c. I can understand and speak more Spanish
       than English.   49%
41. Do you think you have adjusted well to living in the United
    States?
    a. No, not at all.   2%
    b. Yes, more or less.   39%
    c. Yes, I am comfortable living here.   59%
42. Do you have enough social support from family, friends, and
    the Latino community now that you live here?
    a. No, not at all.   12%
    b. Yes, more or less.   41%
    c. Yes, I am satisfied with my social contacts.   47%
43. How much did you drink before you began this program?
    Please check all that apply:
    a. 1–2 drinks occasionally at parties or with friends 44%
    b. 2–3 drinks per night after work   8%
    c. More than 3 drinks per night after work   7%
    d. 4–6 drinks per day/night on the weekend alone   11%
    e. 4–6 drinks per day/night on the weekend
       with friends   9%
    f. 7–12 drinks per day/night on the weekend alone   1%
    g. 7–12 drinks per day/night on the weekend
       with friends   3%
    h. More than 12 drinks per day/night on weekends   1%
    i. I did not drink before I began this program.   16%
44. Have you ever been arrested for a DUI (driving under the influ-
    ence of alcohol)?
    a. No   63%
    b. Yes, once   25%
    c. Yes, more than once   12%
45. Were you drunk at the time of the IPV incident towards your
    wife/partner for which you were arrested?
    a. Yes   42%
    b. No   58%

46. Did you do illegal drugs before you began this program?
    a. No   82%
    b. Yes 18%
Please check all that apply:
    a. Marijuana: Sometimes 8%   Often 2%
    b. Crystal methamphetamine: Sometimes 8%   Often 3%
    c. Cocaine: Sometimes 3%   Often 2%
    d. Heroin: Sometimes 1%   Often 1%
    e. Inhalants (glue, paint thinner):   Sometimes 0%   Often 0%
    f. Hallucinogens (peyote, LSD):   Sometimes 0%   Often 0%
    Polysubstance abuse = 6%
47. Have you ever been arrested for any other crime other than
    IPV, including possession of illegal drugs?
    a. Yes   14%
    b. No   86%
48. Did your partner have to be treated by a doctor because of the
    injuries she received during the IPV incident?
    a. Yes   5%
    b. No   95%
49. Did your partner have to go to the hospital because of the inju-
    ries she received during the IPV incident?
    a. Yes   4%
    b. No   96%
50. Were any of your children present during the violent incident?
    a. Yes, they were in the same room.   7%
    b. Yes, they were in the house.   50%
    c. No   43%

References

Abalos, D. F. (2002). *The Latino male: A radical redefinition*. Boulder, CO: Lynne Rienner Publishers.

Access Project. (2007). *Federal poverty guidelines*. Retrieved December 11, 2006, from http://www.atdn.org/access/poverty.html

Acosta, F. X. (1982). Group psychotherapy with Spanish-speaking patients. In R. M. Becerra, M. Karno, & J. I. Escobar (Eds.), *Mental health and Hispanic Americans* (pp. 183–197). New York: Grune & Stratton.

Aldarondo, E., Kaufman Kantor, G., & Jasinski, J. (2002). Risk marker analysis of wife assault in Latino families. *Violence Against Women, 8*(4), 429–454.

Aldarondo, E., & Sugarman, D. B. (1996). Risk marker analysis of the cessation and persistence of wife assault. *Journal of Consulting and Clinical Psychology, 64,* 1010–1019.

Alianza (National Latino Alliance for the Elimination of Domestic Violence). (2007). *Our mission*. Retrieved May 19, 2007, from http://www.dvalianza.org/about/mission.htm

Alvirez, D., & Bean, F. D. (1976). The Mexican American family. In C. H. Mindel & R. W. Habenstein (Eds.), *Ethnic families in America* (pp. 271–292). New York: Elsevier Scientific Publishing.

American Psychological Association. (1996). *Violence and the family: Report of the American Psychological Association Presidential Task Force on Violence and the Family.* Washington, DC: Author.

American Psychological Association. (2002). *Guidelines on multicultural education, training, research, practice, and organizational change for psychologists.* Washington, DC: Author. Retrieved August 27, 2007, from http://www.apa.org/pi/multiculturalguidelines/diversity.html

Asian and Pacific Islander Institute on Domestic Violence. *Fact sheet.* Retrieved March 31, 2007, from http://www.apiahf.org/apidvinstitute/ResearchAndPolicy/factsheet.htm

Atkinson, D. R., & Lowe, S. M. (1995). The role of ethnicity, cultural knowledge, and conventional techniques in counseling and psychotherapy. In J. G. Ponterotto, J. M. Casas, L. A. Suzuki, & C. M. Alexander (Eds.), *Handbook of multicultural counseling* (pp. 415–438). Thousand Oaks, CA: Sage Publications.

Avila, D. L., & Avila, A. L. (1980). The Mexican American. In N. A. Vace & J. P. Wittmer (Eds.), *Let me be me* (pp. 225–281). Muncie, IN: Accelerated Development.

Babcock, J. C., Green, C. E., & Robie, C. (2004). Does batterers' treatment work? A meta-analytic review of domestic violence treatment. *Clinical Psychology Review, 23*(8), 1023–1053.

Babcock, J. C., Waltz, J., Jacobson, N. S., & Gottman, J. M. (1993). Power and violence: The relation between communication patterns, power discrepancies, and domestic violence. *Journal of Consulting and Clinical Psychology, 61,* 40–50.

269

Baca-Zinn, M. (1982). Familism among Chicanos: A theoretical review. *Humboldt Journal of Social Relations, 10,* 224–237.

Bach-y-Rita, G. (1982). The Mexican American: Religious and cultural influences. In R. M. Becerra, M. Karno, & J. I. Escobar (Eds.), *Mental health and Hispanic Americans* (pp. 29–40). New York: Grune & Stratton.

Bandura, A. (1979). The social learning perspective: Mechanisms of aggression. In H. Toch (Ed.), *Psychology of crime and criminal justice* (pp. 298–336). New York: Holt, Rinehart, & Winston.

Baradello, C. (2006). *United States Hispanic distribution by country of origin.* Retrieved December 11, 2006, from http://www.techbasv.com/jzavala/webminars/w2006/Tech BAWebinar—CarlosBaradello.pdf

Barling, J., & Rosenbaum, A. (1986). Work stressors and wife abuse. *Journal of Applied Psychology, 71,* 346–348.

Bauer, H. M., Rodriguez, M. A., Quiroga, S., & Flores-Ortiz, Y. G. (2000). Barriers to healthcare for abused Latina and Asian immigrant women. *Journal of Healthcare for the Poor and Underserved, 11*(1), 33–44.

Bedrosian, R. C. (1982). Using cognitive and systems interventions in the treatment of marital violence. In L. R. Barnhill (Ed.), *Clinical approaches to family violence* (pp. 117–138). Rockville, MD: Aspen Systems Corp.

Belknap, R. A., & Sayeed, P. (2003). Te contaría mi vida: I would tell you my life, if only you would ask. *Health Care for Women International, 24,* 723–737.

The Belly News. (2002, Dec. 21). *Mexican women ban beer.* Retrieved February 14, 2007, from http://www.briansbelly.com/news/archive1202.shtml

Bem, S. L. (1981). Gender schema theory: A cognitive account of sex typing. *Psychological Review, 88,* 354–364.

Ben-David, A. (1995). Family functioning and migration: Considerations for practice. *Journal of Sociology and Social Welfare, 22*(3), 121–137.

Bensley, L., Macdonald, S., Van Eenwyk, J. Wynkoop Simmons K., & Ruggles, D. (2000). Prevalence of intimate partner violence and injuries—Washington, 1998. *Journal of the American Medical Association, 284,* 559–560.

Bernard, J. L., & Bernard, M. L. (1984). The abusive male seeking treatment: Jekyll and Hyde. *Family Relations, 33,* 543–547.

Berry, J. W., Poortinga, Y. H., Segall, M. H., & Dasen, P. R. (2002). *Cross-cultural psychology: Research and applications.* New York: Cambridge University Press.

Bordin, E. S. (1994). Theory and research on the therapeutic and working alliance: New directions. In A. O. Horvath & L. S. Greenberg (Eds.), *The working alliance* (pp. 13–37). New York: John Wiley.

Bornstein, R. (2006). The complex relationship between dependency and domestic violence. *American Psychologist, 61*(6), 595–606.

Brecklin, L. R., & Ullman, S. E. (2002). The roles of victim and offender alcohol use in sexual assaults: Results from the National Violence Against Women Survey. *Journal of Studies on Alcohol, 63,* 57–63.

Brislin, R. W., Lonner, W. J., & Thorndike, R. M. (1973). *Cross-cultural research methods.* New York: John Wiley.

Bronfenbrenner, U. (1979). *The ecology of human development.* Cambridge, MA: Harvard University Press.

Brown, J. (2004). Shame and domestic violence: Treatment perspectives for perpetrators from self psychology and affect theory. *Sexual and Relationship Therapy, 19*(1), 39–56.

Bruner, J. (1986). *Actual minds, possible worlds.* Cambridge, MA: Harvard.

Bureau of Justice Statistics. (2003). Crime Data Brief, *Intimate Partner Violence, 1993–2001* (NCJ 197838). Retrieved March 12, 2007, from http://www.ojp.usdoj.gov/bjs/abstract/ipv01.htm

Caesar, P. L. (1988). Exposure to violence in the families-of-origin among wife abusers and maritally non-violent men. *Violence and Victims, 3,* 49–63.

Caetano, R. (1988). Alcohol use among Hispanic groups in the United States. *American Journal of Drug Alcohol Abuse, 14,* 293–308.

Caetano, R., Clark, C. L., & Tam, T. (1998). Alcohol consumption among racial/ethnic minorities: Theory and research. *Alcohol Health and Research World, 22*(4), 233–241.

Caetano, R., Schafer, J., Clark, C. L., Cunradi, C. B., & Raspberry, K. (2000). Intimate partner violence, acculturation, and alcohol consumption among Hispanic couples in the United States. *Journal of Interpersonal Violence, 15*(1), 30–45.

Campbell, D., Sharps, P., Gary, F., Campbell, J., & Lopez, L. (2002). Intimate partner violence and African American women. *Online Journal of Issues in Nursing, 7*(1). Retrieved March 31, 2007, from http://www.nursingworld.org/pjin/topic17/tpc17_4.htm.

Campbell, J. C. (1992). Wife-*battering*: Cultural contexts versus Western social sciences. In D. A Counts, J. K. Brown, & J. C. Campbell (Eds.), *Sanctions and sanctuary: Cultural perspectives on the beating of wives* (pp 229–249). Boulder, CO: Westview.

Canadian Centre for Justice *Statistics*. (2005). *Family violence in Canada: A statistical profile 2005*. Retrieved February 21, 2007, from http://www.statcan.ca/english/freepub/85-224-XIE/85-224-XIE2005000.pdf

Cantos, A. L., Neidig, P. H., & O'Leary, K. D. (1994). Injuries of women and men in a treatment program for domestic violence. *Journal of Family Violence, 9,* 113–125.

Carrillo, C. (1982). Changing norms of Hispanic families. In E. E. Jones & S. J. Korchin (Eds.), *Minority mental health* (pp. 250–266). New York: Praeger.

Carrillo, R., & Tello, J. (Eds.) (1998). *Family violence and men of color.* New York: Springer.

Casas, J. M., Wagenheim, B. R., Banchero, R., Mendoza-Romero, J. (1994). Hispanic masculinity: Myth or psychological schema meriting clinical consideration. *Hispanic Journal of Behavioral Sciences, 16,* 315–331.

Centers for Disease Control and Prevention, National Center for Injury Prevention and Control. (2003). *Fact sheet, IPV overview*. Retrieved September 30, 2006, from www.cdc.gov/ncipc/factsheets/ipvoverview.htm.

Centers for Disease Control and Prevention, National Center for Injury Prevention and Control. (2006). *Risk factors for perpetration of IPV*. Retrieved December 14, 2006, from http://www.cdc.gov/ncipc/factsheets/ipvfacts.htm.

Central Intelligence Agency. (2007). *World factbook, Guatemala and Peru*. Retrieved April 26, 2007, from https://www.cia.gov/cia/publications/factbook/print/pe.html

Child Trends Data Bank. (2005). *Child maltreatment*. Retrieved May 10, 2007, from http:// http://www.childtrendsdatabank.org/indicators/40ChildMaltreatment.cfm

Coffin-Romig, N. (1997). The process of ending domestic violence among Latinas: Aguantando no más (University of San Diego, CA, 1997). *Dissertation Abstracts International, 58,* 3B.

Coker, A. L., Davis, K. E., Arias, I., Desai, S., Sanderson, M., Brandt, H. M., et al. (2002). Physical and mental health effects of IPV for men and women. *American Journal of Preventive Medicine, 23*(4), 260–268.

Coleman, D. H., & Straus, M. A. (1986). Marital power, conflict, and violence in a nationally representative sample of American couples. *Violence and Victims, 1,* 141–157.

Coleman, V. E. (2003). Treating the lesbian batterer: Theoretical and clinical considerations—A contemporary psychoanalytic perspective. In D. G. Dutton & D. J. Sonkin (Eds.), *Intimate violence: Contemporary treatment innovations* (pp. 159–205). New York: Haworth Maltreatment and Trauma Press.

Comas-Diaz, L., & Duncan, J. W. (1985). The cultural context: A factor in assertiveness training with mainland Puerto Rican women. *Psychology of Women Quarterly, 9,* 463–475.

Comisión Nacional para el Desarrollo de los Pueblos Indígenas. (2002, December). *Los números*. Nueva Época, *1*(3). Mexico City: Publicación trimestral del Instituto Nacional Indigenista. Retrieved April 23, 2007, from http://cdi.gob.mx/ini/mexicoin digena/diciembre2002/numeros.html

Corey, G. (1990). *Theory and practice of group counseling* (3rd ed.). Pacific Grove, CA: Brooks/Cole.

Corey, M. S., & Corey, G. (1993). *Becoming a helper.* Pacific Grove, CA: Brooks Cole.

Corsí, J. (Ed.). (1994). *Violencia familiar* [Family violence]. Buenos Aires: Paidos.

Cullen, K., & Travin, S. (1990). Assessment and treatment of Spanish-speaking sex offenders: Special considerations. *Psychiatric Journal, 61,* 223–236.

Deckenback, S., Smith-Resendez, J., & Wakamatsu, M. (1978). *Una examinación del niño maltratado en Tijuana* [A study of abused children in Tijuana]. Unpublished master's thesis, San Diego State University School of Social Work, San Diego, CA.

Dobash, R. E., & Dobash, R. P. (1979). *Violence against wives: A case against the patriarchy.* New York: Free Press.

Duarte, P. (Ed.). (1995). *Encuesta de opinión pública sobre la incidencia de violencia en la familia* [Public opinion survey on the incidence of violence in the family]. Mexico City, Mexico: COVAC.

Dunkas, N., & Nikelly, A. G. (1975). Group psychotherapy with Greek immigrants. *International Journal of Group Psychotherapy, 75,* 402–409.

Durst Palmer, K., Baker, R. C., & McGee, T. F. (1997). The effects of pretraining on group psychotherapy for incest-related issues. *International Group Psychotherapy, 47*(1), 71–89.

Dutton, D. G. (with Golant, S.). (1995). *The batterer: A psychological profile.* New York: Basic Books.

Dutton, D. G. (2000). Witnessing parental violence as a traumatic experience shaping the abusive personality. *Journal of Aggression, Maltreatment and Trauma, 3*(1), 59–67.

Dutton, D. G. (2003). Treatment of assaultiveness. In D. G. Dutton & D. J. Sonkin (Eds.), *Intimate violence: Contemporary treatment innovations* (pp. 7–23). New York: Haworth Maltreatment and Trauma Press.

Dutton, D. G. (2006a). *The abusive personality* (2nd ed.). New York: Guilford Press.

Dutton, D. G. (2006b). A briefer reply to Johnson. *The Journal of Child Custody, 3*(1), 28–30.

Dutton, D. G., Bodnarchuk, M., Kropp, R., Hart, S., & Ogloff, J. (1997). Client personality disorders affecting wife assault post treatment recidivism. *Violence and Victims, 12*(1), 37–50.

Dutton, D. G., & Holtzworth-Munroe, A. (1997). The role of early trauma in males who assault their wives. In D. Cicchetti & S. L. Toth (Eds.), *Rochester Symposium on Developmental Psychopathology* (pp. 379–401). Rochester, NY: University of Rochester Press.

Dutton, M., Orloff, L., & Aguilar Hass, G. (2000). Characteristics of help-seeking behaviors, resources, and services needs of battered immigrant Latinas: Legal and policy implications. *Georgetown Journal on Poverty Law and Policy, 7*(2), 245–305.

Dutton, D. G., & Strachan, C. E. (1987). Motivational needs for power and spouse-specific assertiveness in assaultive and non-assaultive men. *Violence and Victims, 2,* 145–156.

Edelson, J. L. (1999). The overlap between child maltreatment and women battering. *Violence Against Women 5*(2), 134–154.

Edgerton, R. B., & Karno, M. (1971). Mexican-American bilingualism and the perception of mental illness. *Archives of Geriatric Psychiatry, 24,* 286–290.

Ehrensaft, M. K., Cohen, P., Brown, J., Smailes, E., Chen, H., & Johnson, J. G. (2003). Intergenerational transmission of partner violence: A 20-year prospective study. *Journal of Consulting and Clinical Psychology, 71*(4), 741–753.

Ellis, A. (1977). *How to live with—and without—anger.* New York: Reader's Digest Press.

Ellison, C., Bartkowski, J., & Anderson, K. (1999). Are there religious variations in domestic violence? *Journal of Family Issues, 20*(1), 87–113.

Enright, R. D. (2001). *Forgiveness is a choice: A step-by-step process for resolving anger and restoring hope.* Washington, DC: American Psychological Association.

Eron, L. D., & Slaby, R. G. (1994). Introduction. In L. D. Eron, J. H. Gentry, & P. Schlege (Eds.), *Reason to hope: A psychosocial perspective on violence and youth* (pp. 1–22). Washington, DC: American Psychological Association.

Espín, O. (1994). Feminist approaches. In L. Comas-Díaz & B. Greene (Eds.), *Women of color: Integrating ethnic and gender identities in psychotherapy* (pp. 265–286). New York: Guilford Press.

Espinosa, G., Elizondo, V., & Miranda, J. (2003). *Hispanic churches in American public life: Summary of findings.* Institute for Latino Studies, University of Notre Dame. Retrieved April 23, 2007, from http://www.nd.edu/~latino/research/pubs/HispChurchesEnglishWEB.pdf

Fagan, J. (1990). Intoxication and aggression. In M. Tonry & J. Q. Wilson (Eds.), *Crime and Justice:* Vol. 13. *Drugs and Crime* (pp. 241–320). Chicago: University of Chicago Press.

Falicov, C. J. (1988). Learning to think culturally. In H. A. Liddle, D. C. Breulin, & R. C. Schwartz (Eds.), *Handbook of family therapy training and supervision* (pp. 335–357). Rockville, MD: Aspen.

Falicov, C. J. (1995). Training to think culturally: A multidimensional comparative framework. *Family Process, 34,* 373–388.

Falicov, C. J. (1996). Mexican families. In M. McGoldrick, J. Giordano, & J. K. Pearce (Eds.), *Ethnicity and family therapy* (pp. 169–182). New York: Guilford Press.

Fals-Stewart, W. (2003). The occurrence of partner physical aggression on days of alcohol consumption: A longitudinal diary study. *Journal of Consulting and Clinical Psychology, 71*(1), 41–52.

Family Violence Prevention Fund. (2007). *End abuse campaigns: Reaching African-Americans.* Retrieved March 31, 2007, from http://www.endabuse.org/programs/display.php3?DocID=9904

Fawcett, G., Heise, L., Isita-Espejel, L., & Pick, S. (1999). Changing community responses to wife abuse. *American Psychologist, 54*(1), 41–49.

Feldman, C. M., & Ridley, C. A. (1995). The etiology and treatment of domestic violence between adult partners. *Clinical Psychology: Science and Practice, 2,* 317–348.

Feldman, M. S. (1995). *Strategies for interpreting qualitative data.* Newbury Park: Sage Publications.

Fernández de Juan, T., Welland Akong, C., & Candelas Villagómez, J. A. (2007). Varones, migración y violencia conyugal: Un estudio comparativo sobre autoestima en mexicanos residentes en la frontera [Men, migration and conjugal violence: A comparative study of self-esteem in Mexican residents on the border]. *Psicología y Salud, 17*(1), 93–103.

Field, C. A., Caetano, R., & Nelson, S. (2004). Alcohol and violence related cognitive risk factors associated with the perpetration of intimate partner violence. *Journal of Family Violence, 19*(4), 249–253.

Finn, J. (1986). The relationship between sex role attitudes and attitudes supporting marital violence. *Sex Roles, 14,* 235–244.

Flaskerud, J. H. (1986). The effects of culture-compatible intervention on the utilization of mental health services by minority clients. *Community Mental Health Journal, 22*(2), 127–141.

Ford Foundation elibrary. (2007). *Domestic violence and Asian American women.* Retrieved March 31, 2007, from http://www.fordfound.org/elibrary/documents/5006/118.cfm

Fortune, M. *Faithtrust Institute.* (2005). Retrieved April 23, 2007, from http://www.faithtrustinstitute.org/index.php?p=Domestic_Violence&s=28

Fox, J. A., & Zawitz, M. W. (2004). *Homicide trends in the United States.* Washington, DC: U.S. Department of Justice. Retrieved February 26, 2007, from www.ojp.usdoj.gov/bjs/homicide/homtrnd.htm

Frankl, V. (1969). *The will to meaning: Foundations and applications of logotherapy.* New York: World Publications.

Fromm, E. (1973). *The anatomy of human destructiveness.* New York: Fawcett.

Fry, D. P. (1993). The intergenerational transmission of disciplinary practices and approaches to conflict. *Human Organization, 52,* 176–185.

Gazmararian, J. A., Petersen, R., Spitz, A. M., Goodwin, M. M., Saltzman, L. E., Marks, J. S. (2000). Violence and reproductive health: Current knowledge and future research directions. *Maternal and Child Health Journal, 4*(2), 79–84.

Geffner, R., Jaffe, P. G., & Sudermann, M. (2000). *Children exposed to domestic violence: Current research, interventions, prevention, and policy development.* New York: Haworth Maltreatment and Trauma Press.

Geffner, R., & Rosenbaum, A. (1990). Characteristics and treatment of batterers. *Behavioral Sciences and the Law, 8,* 131–140.

Gelles, R. (1974). *The violent home.* Beverly Hills, CA: Sage.

Gelles, R. (1998, October). Paper presented at the 4th International Conference on Children Exposed to Domestic Violence, San Diego, CA.

Genero, N. P., Baker Miller, J., Surrey, J., & Baldwin, L. M. (1992). Measuring perceived mutuality in close relationships: Validation of the Mutual Psychological Development Questionnaire. *Journal of Family Psychology, 6*(1), 36–48.

Gilbert, M. J., & Cervantes, R. C. (1986). Patterns and practices of alcohol use among Mexican Americans: A comprehensive review. *Hispanic Journal of Behavioral Sciences, 8,* 1–60.

Gilligan, C. (1982). *In a different voice: Psychological theory and women's development.* Cambridge, MA: Harvard University Press.

Glaser, B. G., & Straus, A. L. (1967). *The discovery of grounded theory.* Chicago: Aldine.

González, G., & Duarte, P. (1996). *La violencia de género en Mexico, un obstáculo para la democracia y el desarrollo.* [Gender violence in Mexico: An obstacle to democracy and development]. Mexico City: Universidad Autonoma Metropolitana-Azcapotzalco.

Gormley, B. (2005). An adult attachment theoretical perspective of gender symmetry in intimate partner violence. *Sex Roles, 52*(11/12), 785–795.

Gottman, J. (1994). *Why marriages succeed and fail.* New York: Simon and Schuster

Granados Shiroma, M. *Salud reproductiva y Violencia contra la mujer: Un análisis desde la perspectiva de género* [Reproductive health and violence against women: A gender perspective]. Nuevo León, México: Asociación Mexicana de Población, Consejo Estatal, México.

Greeley, A. T., García, V. L., Kessler, B. L., & Gilchrest, G. (1992). Training effective multicultural group counselors: Issues for a group training course. *Journal for Specialists in Group Work, 17*(4), 197–209.

Green, J. M., Trankina, F. J., & Chávez, N. (1976). Therapeutic interventions with Mexican American children. *Psychiatric Annals, 6,* 227–234.

Gutiérrez, L. M., & Ortega, R. (1991). Developing methods to empower Latinos: The importance of groups. *Social Work With Groups, 14,* 23–43.

Gutmann, M. C. (1996). *The meanings of macho: Being a man in Mexico City.* Berkeley: University of California Press.

Hage, S. M. (2000). The role of counseling psychology in preventing male violence against female intimates. *The Counseling Psychologist, 28*(6), 797–828.

Hamberger, L. K., & Hastings, J. E. (1986). Personality correlates of men who abuse their partners: A cross-validation study. *Journal of Family Violence, 1,* 323–341.

Hamberger, L. K., Hastings, J. E., & Lohr, J. M. (1991). Personality correlates of men who batter and nonviolent men: Some continuities and discontinuities. *Journal of Family Violence, 6,* 131–148.

Harway, M., & Evans, K. (1996). Working in groups with men who batter. In M. Andronico (Ed.), *Men in groups: Insights, interventions, and psychoeducational work* (pp. 357–375). Washington, DC: American Psychological Association.

Hastings, J. E., & Hamberger, L. K. (1988). Personality characteristics of spouse abusers: A controlled comparison. *Violence and Victims, 3,* 31–48.

Heise, L. L. (1998). Violence against women: An integrated ecological framework. *Violence Against Women, 4,* 262–290.

Helms, J. E. (1990). Black *and white racial identity: Theory, research, and practice.* Westport, CT: Greenwood Press.

Henry, W., Schacht, T., & Strupp, H. (1990). Patient and therapist introject, interpersonal process, and differential psychotherapy outcome. *Journal of Consulting and Clinical Psychology, 58,* 768–774.

Herrera, A. E., & Sánchez, V. C. (1976). Behaviorally oriented group therapy: A successful application in the treatment of low income Spanish-speaking clients. In M. R. Miranda, (Ed.), *Psychotherapy with the Spanish-speaking* (pp. 73–84). Los Angeles, CA: Spanish Speaking Mental Health Research Center.

Hill, H. M., Soriano, F. I., Chen, A., & LaFromboise, T. D. (1994). Sociocultural factors in the etiology and prevention of violence among ethnic minority youth (pp. 59–97). In L. D. Eron, J. H. Gentry, & P. Schlege (Eds.), *Reason to hope: A psychosocial perspective on violence and youth* (pp. 59–100). Washington, DC: American Psychological Association.

Hirschi, T., & Gottfredson, M. (1983). Age and the explanation of crime. *American Journal of Sociology, 89,* 552–584.

Hofstede, G. (1980). *Culture's consequences.* Beverly Hills, CA: Sage.

Holtzworth-Munroe, A., & Hutchinson, G. (1993). Attributing negative intent to wife behavior: The attributions of maritally violent versus nonviolent men. *Journal of Abnormal Psychology, 102*(2), 206–211.

Holtzworth-Munroe, A., & Meehan, J. C. (2004). Typologies of men who are maritally violent: Scientific and clinical implications. *Journal of Interpersonal Violence, 19*(12), 1369–1389.

Holtzworth-Munroe, A., Meehan, J. C., Herron, K., Rehman, U., & Stuart, G. L. (2000). Testing the Holtzworth-Munroe and Stuart (1994) batterer typology. *Journal of Consulting and Clinical Psychology, 68,* 1000–1019.

Holtzworth-Munroe, A., Meehan, J. C., Herron, K., Rehman, U., & Stuart, G. L. (2003). Do subtypes of maritally violent men continue to differ over time? *Journal of Consulting and Clinical Psychology, 7*(4), 728–740.

Holtzworth-Munroe, A., & Stuart, G. L. (1994). Typologies of male batterers: Three subtypes and the difference among them. *Psychological Bulletin, 116,* 476–497.

Holtzworth-Munroe, A., Stuart, G. L., Hutchinson, G. (1997). Violent versus nonviolent husbands: Differences in attachment patterns, dependency, and jealousy. *Journal of Family Psychology, 11*(33), 314–331.

Hotaling, G. T., & Sugarman, D. B. (1986). An analysis of risk markers in husband to wife violence: The current state of knowledge. *Violence and Victims, 1,* 101–124.

Immigration to the United States. (2007, August). In *Wikipedia, The Free Encyclopedia.* Retrieved February 12, 2007, from http://en.wikipedia.org/wiki/Immigration_to_the_United_States#Contemporary_immigration

INEGI (Instituto Nacional de Estadística, Geografía e Informática). (2007). *El INEGI, Inmujeres y Unifem dan a conocer los resultados de la encuesta nacional sobre la dinámica de las relaciones en los hogares, 2006 [INEGI, Inmujer, and Unifem announce the results of the national survey on relational dynamics in the home, 2006]*. Mexico City: Author. Retrieved June 6, 2007, from http://www.inegi.gob.mx/inegi/contenidos/espanol/prensa/Boletines//Boletin/Comunicados/Epeciales/2007/Junio/communica3

Inkeles, A. (1983). *Exploring individual modernity*. New York: Columbia University Press.

Inmujer. (2007). *Violencia contra la niñez [Violence against children]*. Mexico City: Instituto de las mujeres del distrito federal. Retrieved May 10, 2007, from http://www.inmujer.df.gob.mx/numeralia/violencia_genero/estadisticas_maltrato_infantil.html

Jacobson, N., & Gottman, J. (1998). *When men batter women*. New York: Simon & Schuster.

Jacobson, N. S., Gottman, J. M., & Wu Shortt, J. (1995). The distinction between Type 1 and Type 2 batterers—Further considerations: Reply to Ornduff et al. (1995), Margolin et al. (1995), and Walker (1995). *Journal of Family Psychology, 9*, 272–279.

Jaffe, P. (1998, October). Paper presented at the Fourth International Conference on Children Exposed to Domestic Violence, San Diego, CA.

Jang, D. L., & Morello-Rosch, R. (1991). Domestic violence in the immigrant and refugee community: Responding to the needs of immigrant women. *Response, 13*(4), 2–7.

Jasinski, J. L. (1998). The role of acculturation in wife assault. *Journal of Behavioral Sciences, 20*(2), 175–191.

Johnson, M. P. (1995). Patriarchal terrorism and common couple violence: Two forms of violence against women. *Journal of Marriage and the Family, 57*, 283–294.

Kaufman Kantor, G. & Asdigian, N. (1997). When women are under the influence: Does drinking or drug use by women provoke beatings by men. *Recent Developments in Alcoholism. Vol. XIII* (pp. 315–336). New York: Plenum Press.

Kaufman Kantor, G., & Straus, M. A. (1990). Response of victims and the police to assaults on wives. In M. A. Straus & R. E. Gelles (Eds.), *Physical violence in American families: Risk factors and adaptations to violence in 8,145 families* (pp. 473–487). New Brunswick, NJ: Transaction Press.

Kaufman Kantor, G., & Jasinski, J. (1998). Dynamics and risk factors in partner violence. In J. L. Jasinski & L. M. Williams (Eds.) (with D. Finkelhor, J. Giles-Sims, S. L. Hamby, G. Kaufman Kantor, P. Mahoney, C. M. West, & J. Wolak), *Partner violence: A comprehensive review of 20 years of research* (pp. 1–43). Thousand Oaks, CA: Sage Publications.

Kaufman Kantor, G., Jasinski, J. L., & Aldarondo, E. (1994). Sociocultural status and incidence of marital violence in Hispanic families. *Violence and Victims, 9*(3), 207–222.

Keen, B. (1992). *A history of Latin America*. Boston: Houghton Mifflin Company.

Kelly, P. F., & García, A. (1989). Power surrendered, power restored: The politics of home and work among Hispanic women in Southern California and Southern Florida. In L. Tilley & P. Guerin (Eds.), *Women and politics in America*. New York: Russell Sage Foundation.

Klevens, J., Restrepo, O., & Roca, J. (2000). Some factors for explaining resilience among young men in Colombia. *Revista de Salud Pública, 2*(2), 165–172.

Kolbo, J. R., Blakely, E. H., & Engleman, D. (1996). Children who witness domestic violence: A review of empirical literature. *Journal of Interpersonal Violence, 11*, 281–293.

Lara-Cantú, M. A. (1989). A sex role inventory with scales for "machismo" and "self-sacrificing woman." *Journal of Cross-Cultural Psychology, 20*, 386–398.

Leal, A. (1990). Hispanics and substance abuse: Implications for rehabilitation counselors. *Journal of Applied Rehabilitation Counseling, 21*, 52–54.

Leander, B. (1972). *In Xochitl In Cuicatl, Flor y Canto, La Poesía de los Aztecas*. Mexico: Secretaría de Educación Pública.

Leeming, D. A. (1990). *The world of myth*. Oxford, England: Oxford University Press.

Leong, F. T. L., Wagner, N. S., & Tata, S. P. (1995). Racial and ethnic variations in help-seeking attitudes. In J. G. Ponterotto, J. M. Casas, L. A. Suzuki, & C. M. Alexander (Eds.), *Handbook of multicultural counseling* (pp. 415–428). Thousand Oaks, CA: Sage Publications.

León-Portilla, M. (1963). *Aztec thought and culture*. Norman: University of Oklahoma Press.

Levenson, R., Carstensen, L., & Gottman, J. M. (1994). The influence of age and gender on affect, physiology, and their interrelations: A study of long-term marriages. *Journal of Personality and Social Psychology, 67*(1), 6–68.

Levinson, D. (1989). *Family violence in cross-cultural perspective*. Newbury Park, CA: Sage.

Ley para una Vida Libre de Violencia para las Mujeres [Law in favor of a Life Free of Violence for Women]. Retrieved May 5, 2007, from http://mexicousurpado.blogspot.com/2007/02/ley-para-una-vida-libre-de-violencia.html

Lie, G., Schilit, R., Bush, J., Montague, M., & Reyes, L. (1991). Lesbians in currently aggressive relationships: How frequently do they report aggressive past relationships? *Violence and Victims, 6*(2), 121–135.

Lightman, S., & Byrne, G. (2004, September). *Alcohol and domestic violence*. Paper presented at the International Conference on Family Violence, San Diego, CA.

Lincoln, Y. S., & Guba, E. G. (1985). *Naturalistic inquiry*. Beverley Hills, CA: Sage.

Lipsky, S., Caetano, R., Field, C. A., Bazargan, S. (2005). The role of alcohol use and depression in intimate partner violence. *American Journal of Drug and Alcohol Abuse, 31*(2), 225–242.

López, F. G., & Brennan, K. A. (2000). Dynamic processes underlying adult attachment organization: Toward an attachment theoretical perspective on the healthy and effective self. *Journal of Counseling Psychology, 47*(3), 283–300.

Maiuro, R. D., Cahn, T. S., Vitaliano, P. P., Wagner, B. C., & Zegree, J. B. (1988). Anger, hostility, and depression in domestically violent versus generally assaultive men and nonviolent control subjects. *Journal of Consulting and Clinical Psychology, 56*, 17–23.

Maramba, G. G., & Nagayama Hall, G. C. (2002). Meta-analyses of ethnic match as a predictor of dropout, utilization, and level of functioning. *Cultural Diversity and Ethnic Minority Psychology, 8*(3), 290–297.

Marin, G., & Triandis, H. C. (1985). Allocentrism as an important characteristic of the behavior of Latin Americans and Hispanics. In R. Diaz-Guerrero (Ed.), *Cross-cultural and national studies in social psychology* (pp. 85–104). Amsterdam: Elsevier Science Publishers.

Marín, B. V., Marín, G., Pérez-Stable, E., Otero-Sabogal, R., & Sabogal, P. (1990). Cultural differences in attitudes toward smoking: Developing messages using the theory of reasoned action. *Journal of Applied Social Psychology, 20*(6), 478–493.

Marín, G., & Marín, B. V. (1991). *Research with Hispanic populations*. Newbury Park, CA: Sage.

Markus, H. R., & Kitayama, S. (1991). Culture and the self: Implications for cognition, emotion, and motivation. *Psychological Review, 98*(2), 224–253.

Martinez, K. J. (1994). Cultural sensitivity in family therapy gone awry. *Hispanic Journal of Behavioral Sciences, 16*, 75–89.

Massachusetts School of Professional Psychology. (2005). *Annual report*. Retrieved August 27, 2007, from http://www.mspp.edu/images/files/mspp_2005_annual_report.pdf

Maxwell, J. A. (1996). *Qualitative research design: An interactive approach*. Thousand Oaks, CA: Sage.

Maykut, P., & Morehouse R. (1994). *Beginning qualitative research. A philosophic and practical guide*. Washington, DC: The Falmer Press.

McCracken, G. (1988). *The long interview.* Newbury Park, CA: Sage Publications.

McKinley, V. (1987). Group therapy as a treatment modality of special value for Hispanic patients. *International Journal of Group Psychotherapists, 37,* 255–268.

Meichenbaum, D. (1977). *Cognitive-behavior modification: An integrative approach.* New York: Plenum.

Mendoza, R. H. (1989). An empirical scale to measure type and degree of acculturation in Mexican American adolescents and adults. *Journal of Cross-Cultural Psychology, 20,* 372–385.

Merta, R. J. (1995). Group work: Multicultural perspectives. In J. G. Ponterotto, J. M. Casas, L. A. Suzuki, & C. M. Alexander (Eds.), *Handbook of multicultural counseling* (pp. 567–585). Thousand Oaks, CA: Sage Publications.

Mikawa, J. K., Morones, P. A., Gomez, A., Case, H. L., Olsen, D., & Gonzales-Huss, M. (1992). Cultural practices of Hispanics: Implications for the prevention of AIDS. *Hispanic Journal of Behavioral Sciences, 14,* 421–433.

Miller, W. R., & Rollnick, S. (1991). *Motivational interviewing: Preparing people to change addictive behavior.* New York: Guilford Press.

Mindel, C. H. (1980). Extended familism among urban Mexican Americans, Anglos, and Blacks. *Hispanic Journal of Behavioral Sciences, 2,* 21–34.

Minuchin, S. (1974). *Families and family therapy.* Cambridge, MA: Harvard University Press.

Miranda, L., Halperin, D., Limón, F., & Tunón, E. (1998). Características de la violencia doméstica y las respuestas de las mujeres en una comunidad rural de municipio de Las Margaritas, Chiapas [Characteristics of domestic violence and responses of women from the rural municipality of Las Margaritas, Chiapas]. *Salud Mental, 21*(6), 19–26.

Mirandé, A. (1997). *Hombres y machos: Masculinity and Latin culture.* Boulder, CO: Westview.

Molina, C., Zambrana, R., & Aguirre-Molina, M. (1994). The influence of culture, class and environment on health care. In C. Molina & M. Aguirre-Molina (Eds.), *Latino health in the United States: A growing challenge* (pp. 23–43). Washington, DC: American Public Health Association.

Murphy, C. M., & Baxter, V. A. (1997). Motivating batterers to change in the treatment context. *Journal of Interpersonal Violence, 12,* 607–619.

National Coalition against Domestic Violence. (2006). *Comparison of VAWA 1994, VAWA 2000 and VAWA 2005 Reauthorization Bill.* Retrieved April 2, 2007, from http://www.ncadv.org/files/VAWA_94_00_05.pdf

Neff, J. A., Holamon, B., & Schluter, T. D. (1995). Spousal violence among Anglos, Blacks, and Mexican Americans: The role of demographic variables, psychosocial predictors, and alcohol consumption. *Journal of Family Violence, 19,* 1–21.

Neff, J. A., Prihoda, T. J., & Hoppe, S. K. (1991). "Machismo," self-esteem, education and high maximum drinking among Anglo, black and Mexican-American male drinkers. *Journal of Studies on Alcohol, 52,* 458–463.

Novaco, R. W. (1979). The cognitive regulation of anger and stress. In P. C. Kendall & S. D. Hollon (Eds.), *Cognitive-behavioral interventions: Theory, research, and procedure* (pp. 203–206). New York: Academic Press.

O'Leary, K. D. (1993). Through a psychological lens: Personality traits, personality disorders, and levels of violence. In R. J. Gelles & D. R. Loseke (Eds.), *Current controversies on family violence* (pp. 7–30). Newbury Park, CA: Sage.

Olona, T. C. (1993). *An examination of predictors of domestic violence in Latino males.* Unpublished doctoral dissertation, California School of Professional Psychology, Los Angeles.

Orloff, L. E., Jang, D., and Klein, C. F. (1995). With no place to turn: Improving advocacy for battered immigrant women. *Family Law Quarterly, 29*(2), 313.

Orloff, L., & Little, R. (1999). *Somewhere to turn: Making domestic violence services accessible to battered immigrant women. A 'how to' manual for battered women's advocates and service providers.* Violence against Women Net. Retrieved January 21, 2007, from http://search.pcadv.net/phpdig/search.php

Padilla, A. M. (Ed.). (1995). *Hispanic psychology: Critical issues in theory and research.* Thousand Oaks, CA: Sage.

Pan American Health Organization. (2005). *Gender, health and development in the Americas: Basic indicators, 2005.* Retrieved February 12, 2007, from http://www.paho.org/English/AD/GE/GenderBrochure05.pdf

Pan, H. S., Neidig, P. H., & O'Leary, K. D. (1994). Predicting mild and severe husband-to-wife physical aggression. *Journal of Consulting and Clinical Psychology, 62,* 975–981.

Paniagua, F. A. (1994). *Assessing and treating culturally diverse clients.* Thousand Oaks, CA: Sage Publications.

Pence, E., & Paymar, M. (1993). *Education groups for men who batter.* New York: Springer.

Perilla, J. L. (1999). Domestic violence as a human rights issue: The case of immigrant Latinos. *Hispanic Journal of Behavioral Sciences, 21*(2), 107–133.

Perilla, J. L., Bakeman, R., & Norris, F. H. (1994). Culture and domestic violence: The ecology of abused Latinas. *Violence and Victims, 9,* 325–339.

Perilla, J. L., & Pérez, F. (2002). A program for immigrant Latino men who batter within the context of a comprehensive family intervention. In E. Aldarondo & F. Mederos (Eds.), *Programs for men who batter: Intervention and prevention strategies in a diverse society* (pp. 11–31). New York: Civic Research Institute.

Pew Hispanic Center (2006a), *Cubans in the United States.* Retrieved October 5, 2007, from http://pewhispanic.org/files/factsheets/23.pdf#search=%22pew%20hispanic%20center%20cubans%22

Pew Hispanic Center. (2006b). *A statistical portrait of Hispanics at mid-decade.* Retrieved April 19, 2007, from http://pewhispanic.org/files/other/middecade/Table-3.pdf

Pew Hispanic Center and Pew Forum on Religion & Public Life. (April, 2007). *Changing faiths: Latinos and the transformation of American religion.* Retrieved May 13, 2007, from http://pewhispanic.org/reports/report.php?ReportID=75

Polkinghorne, D. E. (1994). Narrative approaches in psychology: Theories, methods, and applications. *History and Philosophy of Psychology Bulletin, 6,* 12–18.

Pope John Paul II. (1981). *Familiaris consortio* [On the role of the Christian family in the modern world]. Vatican City: Librería Editrice Vaticana.

Prince, J. E., & Arias, I. (1994). The role of perceived control and the desirability of control among abusive and nonabusive husbands. *The American Journal of Family Therapy, 22,* 126–134.

Pyne, H. H., Claeson, M., Correia, M. (2002). Gender and alcohol consumption and alcohol-related problems in Latin America and the Caribbean. *Revista Panamericana de Salud Pública, 12*(1). Retrieved April 16, 2007, from http://www.scielosp.org/scielo.php?pid=s1020-49892002000700017&script=sci_arttext

Ramírez, M. (1991). *Psychotherapy and counseling with minorities.* New York: Pergamon.

Ramírez Hernández, F. A. (1999). *Violencia masculina en el hogar* [Male violence at home]. Mexico City: Editorial Pax.

Ramírez-Rodríguez, J. C., & Patino-Guerra, M. C. (1997). Algunos aspectos sobre la magnitud y trascendencia de la violencia doméstica contra la mujer: Un estudio piloto [Aspects of the magnitude and importance of domestic violence against women: A pilot study]. *Salud Mental, 20*(2), 5–16.

Rand, M. R., & Saltzman, L. E. (2003). The nature and extent of recurring IPV against women in the United States. *Journal of Comparative Family Studies, 34,* 137–149.

Reeves, K. (1986). Hispanic utilization of an ethnic mental health clinic. *Journal of Psychosocial Nursing, 24,* 23–26.

Renzetti, C. M. (1992). *Violent betrayal: Partner abuse in lesbian relationships.* Thousand Oaks, CA: Sage Publications.

Rodríguez, R. (1998). Clinical interventions with battered migrant farm worker women. In J. C. Campbell (Ed.), *Empowering survivors of abuse: Health care for battered women and their children* (pp. 271–279). Thousand Oaks, CA: Sage Publications.

Romero, G., Wyatt, G., Loeb, T., Carmona, J., & Solis, B. (1999). The prevalence and circumstances of child sexual abuse among Latina women. *Hispanic Journal of Behavioral Sciences, 21*(3), 351–365.

Rosenbaum, A., & O'Leary, K. D. (1981). Treatment of marital violence. In N. Jacobson & A. Gurman (Eds.), *Clinical handbook of marital therapy* (pp. 385–405). New York: Guilford Press.

Rotter, J. (1975). Some problems and misconceptions related to the construct of internal versus external control of reinforcement. *Journal of Consulting and Clinical Psychology, 43,* 56–67.

Rubin, H. J., & Rubin, I. S. (1995). What did you hear? Data analysis. In *Qualitative interviewing: The art of hearing data.* Thousand Oaks, CA: Sage.

Saltzman, L. E., Fanslow, J. L., McMahon, P. M., & Shelley, G. A. (2002). *Intimate partner violence surveillance: Uniform definitions and recommended data elements* (Version 1.0) [Data file]. Atlanta, GA: Centers for Disease Control and Prevention, National Center for Injury Prevention and Control.

San Diego Association of Governments. (2002). *Info: Mapping the census.* Retrieved October 12, 2006, from http://www.sandag.org/resources/demographics_and_other_data/demographics/census/data.asp

Saunders, D. G. (1991). *Men's group curriculum. Overview: Rationale, theory, and methods.* San Diego, CA: U.S. Navy.

Saunders, D. G. (1993). Husbands who assault. In N. Z. Hilton (Ed.), *Legal responses to wife assault.* Newbury Park, CA: Sage Publications, 9–34.

Saunders, D. G. (1995). Prediction of wife assault. In J. C. Campbell (Ed.), *Assessing dangerousness* (pp. 69–91). Thousand Oaks, CA: Sage Publications.

Schoen, C., Davis, K., Collins, K., Greenberg, L., Des Roches, C., & Abrams, M. (1997). *The Commonwealth Fund survey of the health of adolescent girls.* New York: The Commonwealth Fund.

Schreiner, M. (2006). *Un índice de pobreza para México [A poverty index for Mexico].* Center for Social Development, Washington University, Saint Louis, MO. Retrieved April 23, 2007, from http://www.microfinance.com/Castellano/Documentos/Scoring_Pobreza_Mexico.pdf

Seligman, M. (1991). *Learned optimism.* New York: Knopf.

Shapiro, S. (1995). *Talking with patients.* Northvale, NJ: Jason Aronson.

Share International Archives. (1994). *We must preserve our culture.* Retrieved April 26, 2007, from http://www.share-international.org/ARCHIVES/social-justice/sj_jswemust.htm

Shepard, M. F., & Campbell, J. A. (1992). The Abusive Behavior Inventory: A measure of psychological and physical abuse. *Journal of Interpersonal Violence, 7*(3), 291–305.

Shorris, E. (1992). *Latinos: A biography of the people.* New York: Norton.

Shupe, A., Stacey, W. A., & Hazlewood, L. R. (1987). *Violent men, violent couples.* Lexington, MA: Lexington Books.

Silverman, J., Raj, A., Decker, M., & Reed, E. (2006). Intimate partner violence victimization prior to and during pregnancy among women residing in 26 U.S. states: Associations with maternal and neonatal health. *American Journal of Obstetrics and Gynecology, 195*(1), 140–148.

Simon & Shuster's International Dictionary. English/Spanish. (1993). New York: Simon & Schuster.

Sluzki, C. E. (1989). Network disruption and network reconstruction in the process of migration/relocation. *The Bulletin: A Journal of the Berkshire Medical Center, 2,* 2–4.

Smith, M. D. (1990). Patriarchal ideology and wife beating: a test of a feminist hypothesis. *Violence and Victims, 5,* 257–274.

Sonkin, D. J., & Dutton, D. G. (2003). Treating assaultive men from an attachment perspective. In D. G. Dutton & D. J. Sonkin (Eds.), *Intimate violence: Contemporary treatment innovations* (pp. 105–133). San Diego, CA: Haworth Press.

Sorenson, S. B. (1996). Violence against women: Examining ethnic differences and commonalities. *Evaluation Review, 20,* 123–145.

Sorensen, S. B., & Telles, C. A. (1991). Self reports of spousal violence in a Mexican-American and non-Hispanic White Population. *Violence and Victims, 6,* 3–15.

Straus, M. A. & Gelles, R. J. (Eds.). (1990). *Physical violence in American families: Risk factors and adaptations to violence in 8,145 families.* New Brunswick, NJ: Transaction Publishers.

Straus, M. A., Gelles, R. J., & Steinmetz, S. K. (1980). *Behind closed doors.* Newbury Park, CA: Sage.

Straus, M. A., & Smith, C. (1990). Violence in Hispanic families in the United States: Incidence rates and structural interpretations. In M. A. Straus & R. J. Gelles (Eds.), *Physical violence in American families: Risk factors and adaptations to violence in 8,145 families* (pp. 341–367). New Brunswick, NJ: Transaction Publishers.

Straus, M. A., & Yodanis, C. L. (1996). Corporal punishment in adolescence and physical assaults on spouses in later life: What accounts for the link? *Journal of Marriage and the Family, 58,* Nov. 1996, 826–841.

Strauss, A., & Corbin, J. (1990). *Basics of qualitative research: Grounded theory procedure and techniques.* Newbury Park, CA: Sage.

Sue, D. W., & Sue, D. (2002). *Counseling the culturally diverse: Theory and practice.* New York: Wiley.

Sue, S. (1988). Psychotherapeutic services for ethnic minorities. *American Psychologist, 43,* 301–308.

Sue, S., Fujino, D. C., Hu, L., Takeuchi, D. T., & Zane, N. (1988). Community mental health services for ethnic minority groups: A test of the cultural responsiveness hypothesis. *Journal of Consulting and Clinical Psychology, 59,* 553–540.

Sue, S., & Zane, N. (1987). The role of culture and cultural techniques in psychotherapy. *American Psychologist, 42,* 37–45.

Sugarman, D. B., Aldarondo, E., & Boney-McCoy, S. (1996). Risk marker analysis of husband-to-wife violence: A continuum of aggression. *Journal of Applied Social Psychology, 26,* 313–337.

Taft, C. T., Murphy, C. M., Elliott, J. D., & Morrel, T. M. (2001). Attendance enhancing procedures in group counseling for domestic abusers. *Journal of Counseling Psychology, 48,* 51–60.

Taylor, B. A., Gambourg, M. B., Rivera, M., & Laureano, D. (2006). Constructing cultural competence: Perspectives of family therapists working with Latino families. *The American Journal of Family Therapy, 34,* 429–445.

Taylor, S. P., & Chermack, S. (1993). Alcohol, drugs, and human physical aggression. *Journal of Studies on Alcohol, 11,* 78–88.

Tello, J. (1998). El hombre noble buscando balance. [The noble man searching for balance.] In: Carrillo, R. & Tello, J. (Eds.) *Family violence and men of color.* (pp. 31–52).

Tjaden, P., & Thoennes, N. (2000). *Full report of the prevalence, incidence, and consequences of violence against women: Findings from the National Violence Against*

Women Survey (NCJ-181867). Washington, DC: U.S. Department of Justice. Retrieved February 21, 2007, from http://www.ojp.usdoj.gov/nij/pubs-sum/181867.htm

Tolman, R. M., & Bennett, L. W. (1990). A review of research on men who batter. *Journal of Interpersonal Violence, 5,* 87–118.

Townsend, R. F. (1992). *The Aztecs.* London: Thames and Hudson.

Triandis, H. C. (1989). The self and social behavior in differing cultural contexts. *Psychological Review, 96,* 506–520.

Triandis, H. C., Kashima, Y., Hui, H. C., Lisansky, J., & Marín, G. (1982). Acculturation and biculturation indices among relatively acculturated Hispanic young adults. *Interamerican Journal of Psychology, 16,* 140–149.

Triandis, H. C., Lisansky, J., Marín, G., & Betancourt, H. (1984). *Simpatía* as a cultural script of Hispanics. *Journal of Personality and Social Psychology, 47,* 1363–1375.

Triandis, H. C. (1994). *Culture and social behavior.* New York: McGraw-Hill.

Trujano Ruíz, P. (1991). Algunas consideraciones sobre la mujer víctima del delito de violación [Deliberations on female victims of the crime of rape]. *Sociología, 17,* 195–206.

Tseng, W.-S., & McDermott, J. F. (1981). *Culture, mind and therapy.* New York: Brunner/Mazel.

United Nations. (1948). *Universal Declaration of Human Rights.* Retrieved April 19, 2007, http://www.un.org/Overview/rights.html

United Nations. (2006). *Ending violence against women: From words to action.* Retrieved April 19, 2007, from http://www.un.org/womenwatch/daw/vaw/launch/english/v.a.w-fightE-use.pdf

United Nations Development Fund for Women (Unifem). (2007). *Working for women's empowerment and gender equality.* Retrieved April 19, 2007, from http://www.78y.net/nph-6.cgi/001000A/http/www.unifem.org/

U.S. Bureau of the Census. (2006a). *Fact sheet, income and poverty.* Retrieved October 16, 2006, from http://www.census.gov/Press

U.S. Bureau of the Census. (2006b). *Hispanic heritage month: Sept. 15–Oct. 15, 2006.* Retrieved October 16, 2006, from http://Release/www/releases/archives/income_wealth/007419.html

U.S. Conference of Catholic Bishops. (2002, November 12). *When I call for help: A pastoral response to domestic violence against women.* Retrieved February 15, 2007, from http://www.usccb.org/laity/help.shtml

U.S. Customs and Border Protection. (2005). *Border safety initiative.* Retrieved April 23, 2007, from http://www.cbp.gov/xp/cgov/border_security/border_patrol/safety_initiative.xml

Valdez, R., & Juárez, C. (1998). Impacto de la violencia doméstica en la salud mental de las mujeres: Análisis y perspectivas en México [Impact of domestic violence on women's mental health: Analysis and perspectives in Mexico]. *Salud Mental, 21*(6), 1–10.

Vandello, J. A., & Cohen, D. (2003). Male honor and female fidelity: Implicit cultural scripts that perpetuate domestic violence. *Journal of Personality and Social Psychology, 84*(5), 997–1010.

Vanderbilt-Adriance, E. (2006). *Protective factors and the development of resilience among boys from low-income families.* Retrieved February 14, 2007, from http://etd.library.pitt.edu/ETD/available/etd-06082006–154603/unrestricted/Vanderbilt-Adriance7.7.05.pdf

Vasquez, M. J. T. (1998). Latinos and violence: Mental health implications and strategies for clinicians. *Cultural Diversity and Mental Health, 4,* 319–334.

Vega, W. A. (1990). Hispanic families in the 1980s: A decade of research. *Journal of Marriage and the Family, 52,* 1015–1024.

Vega, W. A., & Kolody, B. (1985). The meaning of social support and the mediation of stress across cultures. In W. A. Vega & M. Miranda (Eds.), *Stress and Hispanic mental health* (DHHS Publication No. 85–1410). Rockville, MD: NIMH.

Walker, L.E.A. (1984). *The battered woman syndrome*. New York: Springer.

Walker, L.E.A. (1995). Current perspectives on men who batter women—Implications for intervention and treatment to stop violence against women: Comment on Gottman et al. (1995). *Journal of Family Psychology, 9,* 264–271.

Weaver, A. J., Larson, D. B., & Stapleton, C. L. (2001). Letter to the editor. Domestic abuse and religion. *American Journal of Psychiatry, 158,* 822–823. Retrieved April 23, 2007, from http://ajp.psychiatryonline.org/cgi/reprint/158/5/817.pdf

Welland, C. (1999). *A qualitative analysis of cultural treatment components for Mexican male perpetrators of partner abuse.* Unpublished doctoral dissertation, California School of Professional Psychology, San Diego, CA.

Welland, C., & Ribner, N. (2001). A demographic and risk factor survey of Mexican immigrants mandated to partner abuse treatment in San Diego County. *Family Violence and Sexual Assault Bulletin, 17*(1–2), 12–19.

Welland, C., & Ribner, N. (2005). What works in treatment for Latino men? Results of a qualitative analysis of cultural treatment components for partner abusive Latino men in the United States. *International Psychology Reporter, Division of International Psychology, American Psychological Association, 9*(1), 9–10.

Welland, C., Robinson, S., Elliott, E., & Arellano, C. (unpublished). Partner abuse among Latinos—Does risk factor research apply? Manuscript submitted for publication.

Welland, C., & Wexler, D. (2007a). *Sin golpes: Como transformar la respuesta violenta del hombre en la pareja y la familia [Without abuse: How to change violent men's behavior in the couple and the family].* Mexico City, Mexico: Editorial Pax.

Welland, C., & Wexler, D. (2007b). *Sin golpes. Cuaderno de trabajo [Without blows: Workbook].* Mexico City, Mexico: Editorial Pax.

Werner, E., & Smith, R. S. (1992). *Overcoming the odds: High risk children from birth to adulthood.* Ithaca, NY: Cornell University Press.

Wexler, D. B. (1999). The broken mirror: A self psychological treatment perspective for relationship violence. *Journal of Psychotherapy Practice and Research, 8*(2), 129–141.

Wexler, D. B. (2006). *STOP Domestic Violence.* New York: Norton.

Wexler, D. B., & Welland, C. (2003a). *Violencia doméstica 2000: Programa integrado de habilidades para hombres latinos con adaptaciones culturales. Manual para facilitadores.* San Diego, CA: Health Transformations.

Wexler, D. B., & Welland, C. (2003b). *Violencia doméstica 2000: Programa integrado de habilidades para hombres latinos con adaptaciones culturales. Recursos para hombres.* San Diego, CA: Health Transformations.

Wiist, W. H., & McFarlane, J. (1998). Utilization of police by abused pregnant Hispanic women. *Violence Against Women, 4,* 677–693.

Williams, O. J., & Becker, R. L. (1994). Domestic partner abuse treatment programs and cultural competence: The results of a national survey. *Violence and Victims, 9,* 287–296.

World Health Organization. (2002). *World report on violence and health.* Retrieved March 12, 2005, from www.who.int/violence_injury_prevention/violence/world_report/factsheets/en/ipvfacts.pdf

World Health Organization. (2005). *Multi-country study.* Retrieved August 20, 2006, from http://www.who.int/gender/violence/whomulticountry_study/summary_report_English2.pdf

World Health Organization. (2006). *Intimate partner violence and alcohol fact sheet.* Retrieved September 15, 2006, from http://www.who.int/violence_injury_prevention/violence/world_report/factsheets/ft_intimate.pdf

Wu, A. (2005). *Border apprehensions, 2005.* Department of Homeland Security. Retrieved April 23, 2007, from http://www.dhs.gov/xlibrary/assets/statistics/publications/ois_apprehensions_fs_2004.pdf

Yalom, I. D., & Lieberman, M. (1971). A study of encounter group casualties. *Archives of General Psychiatry, 25,* 16–29.

Yalom, I. D. (1985). *Theory and practice of group psychotherapy* (3rd ed.). Pacific Grove, CA: Brooks/Cole.

Ybarra, L. (1982). Marital decision making and the role of machismo in the Chicano family. *De Colores, 6,* 32–47.

Yllo, K. (1983). Sexual inequality and violence against wives in American states. *Journal of Comparative Family Studies, 14,* 67–86.

Yllo, K., & Straus, M. A. (1990). Patriarchy and violence against wives: The impact of structural and normative factors. In M. A. Straus & R. J. Gelles (Eds.), *Physical violence in American families: Risk factors and adaptations to violence in 8,145 families* (pp. 383–399). New Brunswick, NJ: Transaction Publishers.

Index